RACHAEL RAY 2
30-MINUTE MEALS

by Rachael Ray

Lake Isle Press

New York, New York

Published by:

Lake Isle Press, Inc.

16 West 32nd Street, Suite 10-B

New York, New York 10001

(212) 273-0796

E-mail: lakeisle@earthlink.net

Distributed to the trade by:

National Book Network (NBN), Inc.

4501 Forbes Boulevard, Suite 200

Lanham, MD 20706

1 (800) 462-6420

http://www.nbnbooks.com

Library of Congress Control Number: 2003106261

ISBN: 1-891105-10-8

Cover photos: Courtesy of The Food Network

Book and cover design: Ellen Swandiak

This book is available at special sales discounts for bulk purchases as premiums or special editions, including personalized covers. For more information, contact the publisher: (212) 273-0796 or by e-mail, lakeisle@earthlink.net.

DEDICATION

To 30-Minute Meal cooks everywhere—
First Timers, Every Nighters, Weekend Kitchen Warriors

To those who shake hands with their pans and
keep their pots hot!

Special Thanks

Huge hugs first, then many thanks to all of the fans of 30 Minute Meals, the TV show, and readers of the 30-Minute Meal cookbooks. You are more than fans to me: you are my partners and my bosses, too! I read your words and I pay attention to them. I love your ideas, recipes, guidance, and advice. You all rock! Thanks for taking such time and care to include me in your busy lives!

There are so many stories to share about all of you. To the kids who watch the show and use the books, you are wonderful beyond words! There's Rachel 2, who had her mom drive her two hours to a 30-Minute Meal cooking class and who writes me often with great new recipes. There's Chef Nick, just 12, who cooks my meals better than I can! Love those pictures, Nick—keep 'em coming! Alex, in the under-10 group, she started the first fan club and gave up karate to watch the show each night—she even defended me on the playground once! Wow!

Grown-ups have cool stories, too. There's the girl who got engaged with You-Won't-Be-Single-For-Long-Pasta—Congratulations! (He said it was the seconds!) There are firemen watching faithfully at firehouses from NYC to Hawaii—love you guys! There's Pat and all the fellas back in Green Bay, Wisconsin at the Heroes Bar who watch every night. Pat won't allow cussing in the bar during the show. (His rule, not mine.) There's the professor at MIT; Leroy and his daughter Heather from Georgia; Tamara Banks, bravest girl in the world, in Arizona. Coast to coast, to all of you, I shout out a mighty "Thank you!" Yes, I'm here and I hear you!

Oh, and thanks to the critics, too! All suggestions and complaints are duly noted, gang! I try with each book to improve on the format and content, as per your requests.

Thank You Credit for Rachael Ray the television cook and author actually goes to hundreds of people who, by contributing their ideas, recipes, and stories make possible my work as a cookbook author and TV cook. Rachael Ray everything else has many influences, but at it's core, there are three women: my mom, my publisher, and lastly ('cause I get to do the relatively easy stuff), me.

Mama Mia! Elsa Providenzia Scuderi is my mother. Job enough. But, beyond that she is: my business manager, my personal assistant, my researcher, my morale officer, my dog sitter, cat sitter and fish sitter, my caretaker, my groundskeeper and landscaper and Head Chef of the only cooking school I've ever attended—her 45 years working with food and creating dishes people love to eat, more than qualify her! Quite simply, she is the COO of Rachael Ray, the business.

Growing up, she cooked and cleaned for me, educated me and made me believe in The Golden Rule. She listened, even when I made no sense. She loved me unconditionally (and believe me, I tested this one!) She made sure I was well traveled and well fed, even when we were broke.

Today, she's still got it all: looks, brains, grace, and style—even under pressure—and the strength and energy of 10 men! Because of her, I have aspirations, self-esteem and I'll eat anything and go anywhere, at least once. I hope to become half of the amazing person she has always been. To say I owe her thanks is a gross understatement. She is too cool to be my mom, but she is. For that, I thank God.

One-Woman Show Hiroko Kiiffner is my publisher. Job enough. Her appearance is one of her strongest assets: beautiful, classy, urbane, and a little-bit-of-a-thing. And at 4' 9" (I'm guessing, but in the ballpark) she is hardly intimidating. Don' t be fooled! Hiroko is a tsunami in disguise. She has wheeled and dealed and quietly confounded some of the biggest wigs in town, to my benefit. I often think back to the day we met. NYC publisher of award-winning cookbooks meets country-bumpkin kid with armfuls of scribbles and poorly typed recipes on dog-eared paper. A few hours and a couple of cappuccinos later, she actually agrees to publish me. And that she did, in record time. Subsequently, we sold over 10,000 copies in upstate New York in the first two weeks of distribution. Five years later, that same cookbook made the NY Times Best Seller list and 30-Minute Meals, the show, is out there on Food Network coast to coast! Mind blowing! Hiroko, along with her talented team of editors and designers, continues to take my recipes, tidbits and table scraps, chatty gossip and all, and like Rumplestiltskin, weaves it all into books that I am proud of, books I want to buy, read, and share with friends and family. She is a wonderful friend and more, she's part of our family. She counsels, comforts, edits, and all too often, has to calm me. She is too cool to be my friend, but she is.

The Most-Honorable Mention Hiroko is married to Calvin Kiiffner, a wonderful NYC-and-beyond architect. To we three women, he's also: our voice of reason in a sea of panic, pressures, and deadlines; the provider of comic relief—albeit he cracks himself up before he shares the joke with the rest of us; a shoulder to cry on; the handsome man we can share at dinners out (thanks, Hiroko!); the one who gathers us at evening's end, collects our belongings and gets us around from place to place relatively on time; and in the leaner days, The Bank of New York, keeping us afloat. Calvin, you are one h-e-double-hockey-sticks of a fella! Thank you! And Isako, thanks for watching 30-Minute Meals almost as often as the Mets!

And the list goes on Thanks to Jon Rosen. The fifth Beatle. The newest member of the group. Jon is my too-cool-to-be-an-agent agent. He' s a great closer. A real Mariano Rivera. And thanks to Jason, Jon' s suave, Assistant Everything. Ja, you are the glue that holds this new branch of the family intact! Thanks for paving so many new roads, Guys!

Lois, Ria and Ginny: The Public Relations Team Thanks to Aunt Lois (no, I will not call you Louis!) who has e-mailed every person she knows in this world from Alaska to New York to personally "invite" them to watch her niece on The Food Network. Thanks to my sister, Maria, who works in a large company and lives in a large neighborhood. I feel certain Maria and her friend Linda have threatened peoples' jobs and their neighbors' small animals to make them all watch the show, loyally. Thanks to Ginny who's simply contagious! She gets so excited about my books and the TV stuff that she just constantly works it into every conversation and e-mail! Ladies, I am sure you are a large part of the reason I remain employed! Thank you.

The Family Thanks to Manny, my brother. Ladies, listen up! He's single, smart, and he's a great cook, too! Thanks to Dad, for all the time you've spent listening to these books over the phone, trying to give me literary advice and a second mention for getting every restaurant, bar and business in Saratoga to watch 30-Minute Meals rather than sports at 6 PM each night! Nanny, you remain an inspiration at any age! Cheech—love my mural!

That's an inspiration in paint! Vicky, you and Billy and the kids are a part of the family and I love you all. Thanks for making so many great meals and for welcoming me to your table—a few of those meals are in this book and all are in my heart! Anna Maria, you are a beauty, inside and out, and your food is delicious!

Food Network WOW! Is it cool to work here! Thank you one and all for making this country bumpkin cook feel welcome and adequate next to the top chefs on planet earth! Thank you for letting me be me. Thank you for all of your support, professional and personal. Thanks for setting the culinary bar higher and higher! I've learned so much and I am grateful for every opportunity given me. I am eager to continue cooking, eating, and growing with my Food Network family. Thank you: Judy, Eileen, Bob, Kathleen, Mark, Emily, New Guy Wes, Steve, Andrea, Ms. Jay, Cindy, Mike and The BEST cameramen and crew in the food TV biz (especially Jay!), Xav and Radu, Susan, Rob, and all the wonderful culinary artists in the Food TV production kitchens, Kate The Great, Miss Alli P., The Ladies of 1180, Adam and The Guys of 1180.

The Look I never had one. Thanks to Joanne Noel for giving the country girl as much of a city veneer as possible. You are The Ultimate Uptown Girl; a Bronx Bomber in high heels! Your hard work and heartfelt advice are much appreciated. Big hug!

The Other Show 30 Minute Meals, the television show, and the books get done only because I work on them constantly. This means that even when I'm away working on $40 A Day, which I LOVE, I still have recipes to write, 50 calls to return, book edits to read, and phone interviews to take. To everyone at Pie Town, thanks for being so supportive and understanding, even when I'm crazed, distracted, and juggling: Les, Toulani, Susan, Courtney, Mark, Nate Beta, Illana, Forrest, Fred, Nancy, too. Tara and Jen, you two have put together The A Team! Thanks! Wade, what can I say? You are my Mack Sugar Daddy of all time! Thank you so much for all of it—you know what I mean. You always do.

Old Friends To Cowan and Lobel and my girl Donna, thanks for letting me loose in the kitchen to make 30 Minute Meals for the very first time. To WRGB News, my thanks for letting me cook my 30 Minute Meals on air. Special thanks to Ed for the extra support and all the laughs! Thanks, Sony, for all the time, effort, and great care you gave to the work and projects we shared. You've always been so supportive and you made my mediocre, beginner's work look really great! Thanks to all the radio guys who have been so generous and encouraging: Don Weeks at WGY, Wendy, too; Joe Donahue at WAMC; Paul and Visher Ferry at WROW. Special thanks and a big wet kiss to Sean, World's Pickiest Eater at WGNA, who said all this would happen, over and over again! (I never believed you!) Hugs to Ritchie and Scott, too. Thanks to my local booksellers, such as The Open Door, who have supported the books for years. Thanks to Price Chopper, The Golub family, and The Golub Corporation for their continued support of me, my books and my food. Special thanks to The Girls: Maureen, Gail, Nancy, Cindy, Mel and JoAnne, so far away!

Thanks to my sweet dog Boo who continues to sample more meals than the vet would like. Boo is too wonderful and still loves me even though I have to be far away all too often. Big sloppy kisses to you, my old friend!

Special thanks to John Cusimano who amplifies my life in every way. Since I met you, food tastes even better! ERT! ERT! ERT!

TABLE OF CONTENTS

TOP-5 RECIPE LISTS 9

INTRODUCTION 12

RECIPES

MAKE YOUR OWN TAKE-OUT 15

MONDAY THRU FRIDAY DINNER SPECIALS 57

FAMILY-STYLE SUPPERS 91

DOUBLE-DUTY DINNERS 129

PASSPORT MEALS 145

BIG NIGHTS: VERY SPECIAL DINNERS 183

HEALTHY HUNGER BUSTERS 219

INDEX 244

TOP 5

RACHAEL'S FAVORITES

1

- Cooking with Wine: Sea Scallops with Vermouth
- Veal Scaloppini with Wine, Mushrooms, and Green Olives
- Ripe Peaches with Port
page 196

2

Passport to Florence:
- Prosciutto di Parma e Melone
- Ribollita-Bread Soup
- Rosemary Grilled Chicken with Wild Mushroom Sauce
page 160

3

- Pasta with Citrus Cream Sauce
- Veal Medallions with Lemon on a Bed of Spinach
- Champagne Freezes
page 188

4

- Shrimp Cocktail with Rach's Quick Rémoulade
- One Great Gumbo with Chicken and Andouille Sausage
- Tossed Salad with Snap Peas, Radishes and Sweet Red Pepper Relish Dressing
page 126

5

- John's Fish: Tilapia with Tomatillo Sauce
- Avocados with Creamy Maque Choux (Corn and Peppers)
- Margarita Granitas
page 206

TOP **5**

MEAT-FREE MEALS

1

• Roasted Garlic and Feta Walnut Dip with Toasted Flat Bread
• Green Risotto
• Grilled Radicchio Salad
page 98

2

• Green Minestrone
• Tomato Basil Panzanella
• Lemon Coconut Angel Food Cake
page 120

3

• Ravioli Vegetable "Lasagna"
• Romaine Hearts with Lemon Chive Vinaigrette
• Fresh Oranges with Lime Sorbet
page 96

4

• Portobello Burgers with Green Sauce and Smoked Mozzarella
• Spinach Artichoke Pasta Salad
page 20

5

• Winter Vegetable Stew
• Potato and Smoked Gouda Pancakes
• Ice Cream S'mores Cups
page 112

TOP 5

YES, THE KIDS WILL EAT IT

1

▪ Herb and Cheese Chicken Tenders Parmigiana with Spaghetti
▪ Antipasto Salad Toss
page 122

2

▪ Meatball and Macaroni Soup
▪ Grilled 4 Cheese Sandwiches
▪ Chocolate Dipped Bananas
page 100

3

<u>Back in the Day:</u>
▪ Super Sloppy Joes
▪ Deviled Potato Salad
▪ Root Beer Floats
page 26

4

▪ Philly Steak Sandwiches
▪ Supreme Pizza Pasta Salad
▪ Stuffed Hot or Sweet Cherry Peppers
page 28

5

▪ Pizza with Chicken, Sun-Dried Tomatoes, and Broccoli
▪ Cheesy POPcorn
▪ Ice Cream Sundae Sandwiches
page 32

I am the luckiest girl in the world!

This book is a scrapbook of my life over the last few years. When I go to work, I practice my favorite activity, cooking. I have no script, I'm simply there to talk about food and share my stories. I spend my days remembering everything and everyone I love, in a kitchen filled with the aromas of places and times familiar and pleasing to me. Some days, I get on and off airplanes, flying to places I've only day-dreamed about. When I get there, my job is to get to know the locals and find a few good places to eat on a budget. When I get home, my mom, my sweet girl-dog Boo, Lily, the cat and Jaws and Orca, the carp-sized gold fish are waiting for me with open hearts and open arms, paws, and fins. My cabin in the woods is warm and cozy and waiting. My pillow still remembers the shape of my big head. Life is good.

In this introduction I want to answer a few of the questions that I am most often asked these days. If we've met and you've heard it all before, you might want to skip ahead a few paragraphs.

Q: How did you get your shows on the Food NetworK?

A: By luck, really. A publicist representing Lake Isle Press, my publisher, got the attention of a producer at The Today Show with one of my books, *Comfort Foods*, which had perfect tie-in potential with the "Storm of the Century" that was threatening to arrive. The segment with Al Roker, featuring soups and one-pot meals, was a big success—the storm never hit NYC, but gave my cabin in the woods 4' of the white stuff, and it got me on The Today Show! At about the same time, I was booked to cook a 30-Minute Meal on a radio show for WAMC in Albany for my friend Joe Donahue, and was heard on-air by a guest lecturer at the Culinary Institute of America in Hyde Park who called his friend, a VP at the Food Network. The Food Network had already heard about me, thanks to the publicist, so we had a first meeting and I fell in love at first sight! I warned the Network executives that I was beer out of the bottle and that they were champagne, but they took me in anyway. I lived happily ever after and I hope they are all happy, too.

Q: What kind of knife do you use on television?

A: It's a Wustof Santoku with a double hollow edge and Grand Prix handle. The ultimate sports car of knives. I love it!

Q: What's the name, make and model of that retro stove on your show and where did it come from?

A: The fabulous set designers found this stove. It's a 1951 Chambers stove. Ask for help from a trusted antiques dealer.

Q: What's Emeril like? Is Bobby Flay really hot in person? Is Mario nice? Do you know The Iron Chef? I love that Sara Moulton! Don't you?

A: Yes! And Bobby Rivers, too! The chefs and great talents of the Food Network humble and amaze me! They have made me feel at home and appreciated. I am inspired by them and I pinch myself each time I see them up close and in person. To me, they are rock stars.

Q: Is it really a 30-Minute Meal?

A: Yup.

Q: Where do you get your ideas?

A: From everywhere. Many meals are 30-minute versions of family favorites or my "take" on traditionally elaborate dishes. Other menus are inspired by today's most popular take-out foods. These I simplify or adapt to today's diets. Passport 30-Minute Meals are 3-D postcards of places I've traveled to or long to visit. Still others and some of my favorite 30-Minute Meals are my versions of recipes given to me by friends, family, and fans alike.

Q: What was your most embarrassing moment, so far?

A: I love how many folks assume, correctly, that I must have many of these to choose from. Okay, here goes. There's a two-way tie: my first day at the Food Network I went in to do a pilot episode on Emeril's set. Someone preheated my pan for me, for like an hour. I added oil to the pan and set it on fire. All I could imagine was the headline the next morning in my local paper upstate: Local Woman Sets Emeril's Kitchen On Fire. BAM! Shortest Food Network Career in History Comes to Well-Done End. I kept going anyway. Then, on my first day taping my first show in my own kitchen, I cut my finger! I had my brand new knife, factory sharp. I started talking with my hands, while holding the new, very sharp santoku knife and I slice into the tip of my left index finger. "Do not stop tape, ever, but especially not on your first day!" I said to myself, in panic. I kept going and cooked the rest with one hand on my hip, while applying pressure. Once again, I proved to be one lucky, albeit accident-prone, girl.

How to make use of this book, beyond fixing a wobbly table

1 This 30-Minute Meal collection is written entirely as full menus. Read through all the recipes in a menu before you begin. You will see how each menu fits together more clearly. Begin the first recipe, then, as you create pockets of time, begin the next recipe. For instance, if a stew is simmering, go to work on your salad. If a sauce is reducing, stir the pasta and begin dessert.

2 These menus represent recipes that I've taught or will teach on air. Please feel free to mix and match the menus as you discover your own favorites.

3 The ingredients highlighted in green can be used as a quick scan to see what's in each recipe.

4 Use a garbage bowl. Whenever I cook, I keep a bowl handy on the counter near my cutting board and I use it to discard scraps, cans, wrapping, etc. This way, I save myself both time and steps running back and forth to the garbage can and recycling bins.

5 Pantry Building. Any ingredients I use in my recipes can be purchased in a large supermarket. You will not have to special order an ingredient or go to any specialty shops to make these meals. Ingredient lists will usually include many of the same spices, herbs, and oils. I try to write recipes using the same flavors in different combinations so that it becomes easier for you to build a useful pantry, one that is economical, too.

6 I still don't measure. I write every recipe in free-hand equivalents. A tablespoon is a palmful to me, or for liquids, once around the pan in a slow stream. I do give you my best guess for the measured equivalent, but the food will taste better if you let your own hands and taste buds be your guide. Recipes are suggestions, not written law. Trust yourself, too.

The promises I try to keep with my recipes:

• No fancy equipment or hard-to-find ingredients
• A high can-do factor that makes you feel like a rock star in your kitchen
• A kid-friendly factor. I started cooking on my own at twelve. Kids, you can cook, too!
• Beginners allowed! You can make any meal in here, even if you only make reservations!

The promise I keep to myself and my family, especially Mama, who always reminds me: Don't forget where you come from! I can't and I won't, Mama. I still live here!

MAKE
YOUR
OWN
TAKE-OUT

RACHAEL RAY
30-MINUTE MEALS 2

MAKE YOUR OWN TAKE-OUT

Why make your own take-out? Doesn't that defeat the purpose of eating take-out? Hear me out. We eat take-out, and by take-out I mean all of it—Chinese, Thai, Tex-Mex, wings, pizzas, burgers, etc.—because we like the taste and because we have no time. Who even knows how they make some of this stuff? We spread out the packaging in front of the TV. We belly up and chow down. But alas, take-out, too, can have a downside. Dinner ends and guilt is not far behind. As we lean back on the sofa, we contemplate what we just ate, while our stomachs regret the salt, the fat, the oil, the pants that won't fit tomorrow. We're often left with nothing more than indigestion.

What to do? In as much time as it takes to wait for the pizza guy or to drive to the local Chinese take-out, you can make your own, and be sure that the food is fresh and reasonably good for you by controlling the quality of ingredients, especially the salt and fat content.

So, take this chapter, devoted to fun foods and have fun with them! These are meals for casual, weeknight entertaining for friends and family. If you have kids: Yes! The kids will eat these meals and think you are way-cool for making them. Ladies, use these meals for a sexy date night or to have girls over to talk about the guys! Guys, this is food to watch sports with or to simply hang with your friends. Make your own take-out everybody! It's just more fun!

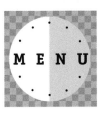

Thick-Cut O-Rings and Spicy Dipping Sauce

Refrigerate your onions and canned evaporated milk when you unpack from the grocery store. The colder the better for making onion rings!

MAKES 4 SERVINGS

Vegetable or canola oil, for frying
2 large sweet Vidalia onions
2 cans (5 ounces each) evaporated milk
1 cup all-purpose flour
1/2 teaspoon dry mustard
1/2 teaspoon cayenne pepper
1 teaspoon sweet paprika (1/3 palmful)
Coarse salt, to taste

DIPPING SAUCE
1 cup reduced-fat sour cream (eyeball the amount)
1/4 cup chili sauce (eyeball the amount)
1/2 teaspoon cayenne pepper
1/2 teaspoon ground cumin

Heat 1 inch of vegetable or canola oil in a large frying pan over medium-high heat.

Slice onions across into 1-inch rings and separate, discarding the outer layer of skin.

Pour evaporated milk into a small, deep bowl. Mix flour with seasonings in a pie plate or shallow dish. Dip individual rings in milk, then coat in flour. Fry in a single layer in hot oil until golden brown. Remove to brown paper bag or paper towel-lined surface to drain. Salt while hot, to taste.

For dipping sauce, combine all ingredients in a bowl and stir.

Drive Past The Drive Thru

1

Sirloin Burgers with Mushrooms, Swiss, and Balsamic Mayo
• • • • •

2

Thick-Cut O-Rings and Spicy Dipping Sauce
• • • • •

3

NY Egg Creams or Black and White Shakes
• • • • •

Sirloin Burgers with Mushrooms, Swiss, and Balsamic Mayo

MAKES 4 SERVINGS

Extra-virgin olive oil, for drizzling, plus 1 tablespoon (once around the pan)

3 tablespoons finely chopped yellow onion

1 & 1/3 pounds ground sirloin, 90% lean

1 tablespoon Worcestershire sauce (eyeball the amount)

Steak seasoning blend such as McCormick Montreal Steak Seasoning OR coarse salt and freshly ground black pepper

4 crusty rolls, split

12 baby portobello or crimini mushrooms, thinly sliced

Coarse salt and freshly ground black pepper, to taste

4 slices Swiss cheese

3 tablespoons aged balsamic vinegar (eyeball the amount)

1/2 cup mayonnaise or reduced-fat mayonnaise

Freshly ground coarse black pepper, to taste

4 leaves romaine lettuce

2 vine-ripe tomatoes, sliced

2 scallions, sliced

Preheat grill pan or large nonstick skillet for burgers over medium-high heat. In a small nonstick skillet over moderate heat, sauté chopped onion in a drizzle of olive oil for 2 or 3 minutes. Set pan aside.

In a medium bowl, combine meat with Worcestershire sauce, steak seasoning blend or salt and pepper. Mix in sautéed onion and form into 4 large patties. Drizzle patties with a touch of olive oil. Quick toast your split rolls on the hot grill pan or skillet and set aside. Then add burgers to hot pan or skillet and grill or pan-fry, 4 to 5 minutes on each side for medium to medium-well burgers.

Return small nonstick skillet to stove over medium-high heat. Add 1 tablespoon olive oil and sliced mushrooms. Season with salt and pepper, then sauté until just tender, about 3 to 5 minutes. Remove from the heat.

Pile mushrooms on top of burgers just before you are ready to take them off the grill or out of the pan. Fold each slice of Swiss cheese in half and rest on top of mushrooms. Place a loose tin foil tent over the burgers and turn heat off. Allow the cheese to melt down over the mushrooms and burgers, about 2 to 3 minutes.

Combine balsamic vinegar, mayonnaise and lots of coarsely ground or cracked black pepper in a small dish.

To assemble, place burgers topped with mushrooms and Swiss cheese on bun bottom. Slather tops of buns with balsamic, black pepper, mayo, and add romaine. Set burger tops in place and serve with sliced tomatoes, drizzled with oil, seasoned with salt and pepper and garnished with sliced scallions. Pile thick-cut onion rings and a dollop of dipping sauce alongside. For drinks, try NY Egg Creams or frozen Black and White Shakes — yum!

NY Egg Creams

MAKES 4 SERVINGS

1/2 cup chocolate syrup
1/2 cup half-and-half
2 quarts seltzer water, chilled

Combine 2 tablespoons chocolate syrup and 1 ounce half-and-half in the bottom of a soda glass. Stir with a parfait spoon to combine. Add cold seltzer to the top of the glass and serve with drinking straws.

Black and White Shakes

MAKES 4 SHAKES

1 cup chocolate syrup
2 pints vanilla ice cream
2 quarts skim milk
1 tray ice cubes

In a blender, for each shake, combine 3 squirts of chocolate syrup (about 1/4 cup), 1/2 pint vanilla ice cream (3 scoops), 2 cups skim milk and 4 ice cubes. Blend on high until smooth and icy. Serve with straws in a tall glass.

MENU

1

Portobello
Burgers with
Green Sauce
and Smoked
Mozzarella

• • • • •

2

Spinach
Artichoke
Pasta Salad

• • • • •

Portobello Burgers with Green Sauce and Smoked Mozzarella

Portobellos have a beefy taste once cooked. In this recipe, a balsamic vinegar reduction glazes the mushrooms, adding a sweet, slightly tangy flavor. Popular with meat-eaters and meat-free-ers alike.

MAKES 4 SERVINGS

2 tablespoons extra-virgin olive oil (twice around the pan)

4 large portobello mushroom caps

Steak seasoning blend such as Montreal Seasoning by McCormick OR salt and freshly ground black pepper to taste

1/4 cup balsamic vinegar

1/2 pound fresh smoked mozzarella cheese, sliced

GREEN SAUCE

1 cup loosely packed basil leaves

1/2 cup fresh flat-leaf parsley leaves

3 tablespoons capers

1/4 cup pignoli nuts (a handful)

1 clove garlic

The juice of 1/2 lemon

1/4 cup extra-virgin olive oil

Salt and freshly ground black pepper, to taste

1/2 cup grated Parmigiano Reggiano or Romano cheese

1/2 medium red onion, thinly sliced

4 leaves romaine or red leaf lettuce

Heat a nonstick skillet over medium-high heat. Add oil and mushroom caps. Season mushrooms with steak seasoning blend or salt and pepper, and sauté, 5 minutes on each side. Add vinegar and coat the mushrooms in it. When vinegar has evaporated, turn mushrooms cap side up and cover with sliced cheese. Turn off heat and cover pan with foil. Let stand 2 or 3 minutes for cheese to melt.

To make the sauce, combine basil, parsley, capers, pignoli, garlic, and lemon juice in the food processor. Pulse grind, until finely chopped and scrape into a bowl. Stir in oil, salt, pepper, and cheese.

Slather bun tops with green sauce. Pile portobellos on bun bottoms and top with red onion slices and lettuce.

**Make Your
Own Take-Out**

• • • • •

20

Spinach Artichoke Pasta Salad

MAKES 8 SIDE SERVINGS (leftovers make a nice light lunch)

1/3 cup extra-virgin olive oil (eyeball the amount)

3 tablespoons red wine vinegar (a couple splashes)

The juice of 1 small lemon

6 ounces (half a sack) baby spinach, chopped

1 can (15 ounces) artichoke hearts in water, drained and coarsely
  chopped

1/3 pound ricotta salata cheese, crumbled (available in specialty
  cheese cases)

1/2 cup pitted black olives, such as Kalamata, coarsely chopped

1/2 medium red onion, chopped

1/2 cup fresh flat-leaf Italian parsley (a couple handfuls), chopped

1 pound penne or other short pasta, cooked al dente,
  cooled, and well drained

Coarse salt and freshly ground black pepper

Combine the first three dressing ingredients in the bottom of a serving bowl.
Add remaining ingredients to the bowl and toss until well combined. Season
with salt and pepper, to taste and serve.

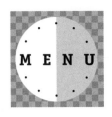

MENU

1

Cajun Pork
Burgers

· · · · ·

2

Red Bean
Salad

· · · · ·

Cajun Pork Burgers

I make this for my daddy, Jimmy Claude. He's Cajun-Creole and he loves this meal! I made it one Father's Day, and it became a family favorite. It's spicy, colorful, and classy enough for entertaining.

MAKES 5 BURGERS

3/4 pound andouille sausage, removed from casing

1 pound ground pork

1 rib celery, finely chopped

1/2 green bell pepper, finely chopped

1 small white onion, finely chopped

3 cloves garlic, minced

4 sprigs fresh thyme, chopped (about 1 tablespoon) OR 1 teaspoon dried thyme

1 teaspoon cayenne pepper sauce (several drops) such as Frank's Red Hot

Coarse salt and freshly ground black pepper, to taste

SPECIAL SAUCE

1/2 cup chili sauce (eyeball it)

1/4 cup mayo or reduced-fat mayonnaise (3 generous tablespoons)

1/4 cup prepared sweet red pepper relish (3 generous tablespoons)

TOPPINGS

Bibb lettuce or hearts of romaine

Sliced vine-ripe tomato

5 crusty rolls, split

Cut sausage into large chunks and place in a food processor. Grind sausage into crumbles, and combine in a bowl with pork, vegetables, thyme, hot sauce, and a little salt and pepper. Form mixture into patties and cook 7 minutes on each side on an indoor electric grill preheated to high. To cook in a skillet, heat a nonstick skillet over medium-high heat and cook burgers, 6 to 7 minutes, on each side. For outdoor grill, cook patties 6 inches from hot coals or over medium-high gas heat, 6 minutes on each side, covered.

Mix chili sauce, mayo, and sweet relish in a small bowl. Serve burgers on crusty rolls with special sauce, lettuce and tomato. Serve with Red Bean Salad, your favorite chips (Dad likes Firecracker Barbecue, Cape Cod brand), and/or buttered corn on the cob garnished with chopped chives and a sprinkle of chili powder.

P.S. Don't forget a cold beer for Pop!

Red Bean Salad

MAKES 6 SERVINGS

2 cans (15 ounces each) dark red kidney beans, rinsed and drained well

1 red bell pepper, seeded and chopped

3 scallions, whites and greens, chopped,

1 rib celery, chopped

1/4 cup chopped fresh flat-leaf parsley (a couple handfuls)

1 cup sweet red pepper relish (available on condiment aisle)

2 tablespoons light olive oil or vegetable oil (twice around the bowl in a thin stream)

1 tablespoon white distilled vinegar (2 splashes)

Coarse salt and freshly ground black pepper, to taste

Combine all ingredients in a medium bowl, toss well and adjust seasonings.

MENU

1
Jerky Turkey Burgers with Island Salsa
• • • • •

2
Chili Lime Avocados
• • • • •

3
Ripe Pineapple Wedges
• • • • •

Jerky Turkey Burgers with Island Salsa

MAKES 4 SERVINGS

1 & 1/3 pounds ground turkey breast (the average weight of 1 package)
2 scallions, thinly sliced
1 serrano or jalapeño pepper, seeded and minced
1 inch gingerroot, peeled and grated
2 teaspoons fresh thyme (a few sprigs), leaves stripped and chopped
1 teaspoon allspice (eyeball it)
1/2 teaspoon nutmeg, freshly grated or ground
Coarse salt, to taste
1 teaspoon freshly ground black pepper
Extra-virgin olive oil or vegetable oil, for drizzling
The juice of 1 lime
4 Bibb or green leaf lettuce leaves
4 crusty plain or corn-meal dusted Kaiser rolls, split

PAPAYA SALSA
1 large ripe papaya, seeded, peeled and diced
1/2 red bell pepper, seeded and diced
1/4 red onion, finely chopped
1 serrano or jalapeño pepper, seeded and finely chopped
2 tablespoons fresh cilantro (a palmful leafy tops), finely chopped
The juice of 1 navel orange
Coarse salt, to taste

Preheat a large nonstick skillet, indoor grill pan or tabletop grill to medium-high heat. Combine the turkey, scallions, pepper, ginger, thyme, allspice, nutmeg, salt and pepper in a medium bowl. Form mixture into 4 large patties no more than 1-inch thick. Drizzle with a touch of oil. Place patties oil side down in a hot pan or grill and cook 6 minutes on each side. Squeeze lime juice over the patties before removing them from the heat. Place on bun bottoms and top with lettuce leaves.

While burgers are grilling, make the salsa. Combine the papaya, red bell pepper, red onion, serrano or jalapeño, cilantro and orange juice in a bowl. Season with salt, to taste. Pile salsa on top of the lettuce and add bun tops to the burgers. Serve with Chili Lime Avocados and Ripe Pineapple Wedges.

Chili Lime Avocados

MAKES 4 SERVINGS

2 ripe Haas avocados
The juice of 2 limes
1 teaspoon sugar
1 teaspoon chili powder
1/2 teaspoon salt
3 tablespoons extra-virgin olive oil
Chopped chives or cilantro, for garnish (optional)

Halve the avocados and remove pits. Roll limes or heat in microwave for 10 seconds to get juices flowing. Halve the limes. Rub the avocado halves gently with 1/2 lime (cut side of lime) to prevent browning. Juice limes into small bowl and mix with sugar, chili powder and salt using a fork or small whisk. Add oil in a slow stream while mixing dressing. Pour dressing into the cavities of avocados, distributing it equally and serve, garnished with chives or cilantro if you wish.

Ripe Pineapple Wedges

MAKES 4 SERVINGS

1 whole ripe pineapple

Quarter the pineapple lengthwise leaving the top on. Following the skin of the pineapple, carefully pare the fruit away using your knife, keeping the green tops attached. Next, cut the pineapple into 1/2-inch wedges, arranged alternately to the left, then to the right. Each completed pineapple serving will look like a "boat" filled with the fruit slices.

TIDBIT

❝ A great tip! To select a sweet pineapple, look for one with large, uniform "eyes" (same size) from top to bottom. Color is not significant. ❞

M E N U

**Back in
the Day**

1

**Super Sloppy
Joes**
. . . . .

2

**Deviled Potato
Salad**
. . . . .

3

**Root Beer
Floats**
. . . . .

Super Sloppy Joes

"Kids" of any age love Sloppy Joes, a meal guaranteed to make you feel younger than you are. This menu is perfect for easy weeknight get-togethers, for movie night, or for watching the BIG Game.

MAKES 4 SUPER SLOPPY SANDWICHES

1 tablespoon extra-virgin olive oil (once around the pan)

1 & 1/4 pounds ground beef sirloin

1/4 cup brown sugar (a couple handfuls)

2 to 2 & 1/2 teaspoons steak seasoning blend such as McCormick Montreal Seasoning

1 medium onion, chopped

1 small red bell pepper, chopped

1 tablespoon red wine vinegar

1 tablespoon Worcestershire sauce

2 cups tomato sauce

2 tablespoons tomato paste

4 crusty rolls, split, toasted, and lightly buttered

Sliced ripe tomatoes, pickles, to garnish

Heat a large skillet over medium-high heat. Add oil and beef to the pan, spreading it around the pan to break it up. Combine brown sugar and steak seasoning, then add the mixture to the skillet and combine. When the meat has browned, add onion and red pepper. Reduce heat to medium and cook for 5 minutes. Add vinegar, stirring briefly to reduce, then add Worcestershire, tomato sauce and paste, stirring to combine. Reduce heat to simmer and cook Sloppy Joe mixture 5 minutes longer.

Using a large spoon or ice cream scoop, pile sloppy meat onto toasted, buttered bun bottoms and cover with bun tops. Serve with your favorite sides or sliced tomatoes seasoned with salt and pepper, dill pickles and Deviled Potato Salad. Have plenty of napkins on hand!

Deviled Potato Salad

MAKES 4 SERVINGS

2 & 1/2 pounds all-purpose potatoes (such as new or white round),
  peeled and diced

Coarse salt

1/4 medium onion

3 tablespoons prepared yellow mustard

1/2 cup mayonnaise (eyeball the amount)

1 teaspoon sweet paprika

1 teaspoon hot cayenne pepper sauce (such as Tabasco or Frank's
  Red Hot)

Salt and freshly ground black pepper, to taste

2 scallions, thinly sliced, for garnish

Boil potatoes in water seasoned with salt until they are tender, about 10
minutes. Drain and return cooked potatoes to the warm pot to dry them out.
Let the potatoes stand 2 minutes, then spread them out on a cookie sheet to
quick-cool them.

In the bottom of a medium mixing bowl, grate the onion using a hand grater.
Add mustard and mayonnaise, paprika and cayenne pepper sauce to the grated
onion and stir to combine. Add potatoes to the bowl and evenly distribute
dressing. Season with salt and pepper and adjust seasonings. Top with chopped
scallions.

TIDBIT

❝ Substitute plain low-fat yogurt or reduced-fat sour cream for the mayo and you'll get a tangy, trimmer potato salad. ❞

Root Beer Floats

MAKES 4 SERVINGS

1 pint vanilla bean ice cream
2 quarts root beer

Hang a large, well-packed scoop of vanilla ice cream on the edge of a fountain
glass or other tall drinking glass. Fill 3/4 full with root beer. Catch any overflow
on a small plate. Serve with straws and parfait spoons and don't forget to knock
the ice cream into the root beer and watch it fizz up as the ice cream floats.
Yummy! This is the simplest and my most favorite fountain drink!

M E N U

1

Philly Steak
Sandwiches

· · · · ·

2

Supreme Pizza
Pasta Salad

· · · · ·

3

Stuffed Hot or
Sweet Cherry
Peppers

· · · · ·

Okay, nothing compares to eating the real deal Philly steak sandwich in the streets of its host city. But, when you make this version at home, you can enjoy other virtues: the meat used in this recipe is leaner than what you'll find at Philly steak stands and it is more tender. Plus, you can control the oil and cheese content.

The pasta salad in this menu also makes a nice next day lunch entree. It is a crowd pleaser and an ideal picnic or tailgating contribution because it contains no mayonnaise, so refrigeration issues are of less concern. The stuffed cherry peppers are fun snacks for nights at home, hanging out with friends, or for snacking in front of the TV with any kind of hoagie.

Philly Steak Sandwiches

MAKES 4 SERVINGS

ONIONS

1 tablespoon extra-virgin olive oil (once around the pan)

2 large yellow onions, sliced very thin

Coarse salt and freshly ground black pepper or steak seasoning blend, to taste

MEAT

2 teaspoons extra-virgin olive oil, 2 drizzles

1 & 1/4 pounds lean beef tenderloin or sirloin, very thinly sliced, like carpaccio (ask butcher to do this)

1 teaspoon garlic salt

Coarsely ground fresh black pepper, to taste

8 slices provolone cheese (from the deli counter)

4 soft Italian sandwich hoagie rolls, each 6 to 8 inches long, split lengthwise

Heat a medium saucepan over medium-high heat. Add olive oil, onions and season with salt and pepper or steak seasoning blend. Cook, stirring occasionally, 10 minutes or until onions are soft and caramel in color.

Heat a heavy griddle pan over medium-high to high heat. Wipe griddle with a drizzle of oil using a paper towel. Sear and cook meat until brown but not crisp, about 2 minutes on each side. Cook in single layers in two batches and tenderize by cutting into meat with the side of your spatula while they cook. When browned, just before you remove them from heat, sprinkle with garlic salt and pepper. When all are cooked, line each of your split rolls with 2 slices of provolone cheese. Pile 1/4 of your meat and onions onto the griddle and mix together with your spatula. Remove and pile the meat and onions on top of the cheese. The heat from the meat and onions will melt the cheese. Repeat for remaining servings and serve.

Supreme Pizza Pasta Salad

MAKES 8 SERVINGS AS A SIDE (seconds for everyone!)

SALAD

2 plum tomatoes, seeded and chopped

1/2 medium red onion, chopped

8 fresh white button mushrooms, sliced

1 small green bell pepper, seeded and chopped

1 stick pepperoni, casing removed and cut into small dice

1 pound fresh mozzarella cheese or fresh smoked mozzarella cheese, diced

20 leaves fresh basil, torn or thinly sliced

1 pound wagon wheel pasta, cooked al dente, cooled under cold water, then drained

DRESSING

1 teaspoon garlic salt

1 teaspoon dried oregano leaves or Italian dried seasoning

1 rounded tablespoon tomato paste

2 tablespoons red wine vinegar (eyeball it)

1/3 cup extra-virgin olive oil (eyeball it)

Freshly ground black pepper, to taste

TIDBIT

❝ A neat way to thinly slice fresh basil leaves: stack them, roll into logs, slice with knife, forming confetti-like shavings. ❞

Combine tomatoes, onion, mushrooms, bell pepper, pepperoni, mozzarella, basil and pasta in a big bowl. Whisk garlic salt, oregano or Italian seasoning, tomato paste and vinegar together. Stream in olive oil while continuing to whisk. When oil is incorporated, pour dressing over pasta salad, add a few grinds of black pepper, then toss to coat evenly. Adjust your seasonings and serve. Leftovers make a great lunch or snack the next day!

Stuffed Hot or Sweet Cherry Peppers

MAKES 12 STUFFED PEPPERS, 4 servings of 3 peppers per person

FOR HOT STUFFED CHERRY PEPPERS:

12 hot cherry peppers, tops cut off and seeds removed

1/2 pound sharp Italian table cheese such as Asiago, pepato, provolone or red pepper flake sheep's milk cheese, cut in 1/2-inch cubes

6 slices capacolo (hot Italian ham), cut in half

FOR SWEET STUFFED CHERRY PEPPERS:

12 sweet peppers, tops removed and seeded

3 ounces herb and garlic spreadable cheese or goat cheese

2 ribs celery

4 slices prosciutto di Parma

For hot peppers, wrap each cheese cube in half a slice of hot ham, and stuff inside a cherry pepper. Repeat for all 12 peppers.

For sweet cherry peppers, spread each rib of celery with half of the cheese. Wrap each celery rib with prosciutto, using 2 slices per rib. Cut each rib into 6 pieces and stuff one piece into each of the sweet cherry peppers.

Harvest Turkey Burgers

MAKES 4 SERVINGS

1 pound ground turkey breast
2 tablespoons fresh thyme (4 or 5 sprigs), stripped and finely chopped
Coarse salt and freshly ground black pepper, to taste
2 scallions, finely chopped
1/2 red bell pepper, finely chopped
1 carrot shredded with box grater or 1/2 cup packaged shredded carrots
1/2 small zucchini, finely chopped or shredded
Extra-virgin olive oil, for drizzling
4 leaves green leaf or romaine lettuce
1 vine-ripe tomato, sliced
1 cup store-bought fresh refrigerated creamy ranch or herb dressing
4 crusty rolls, split

Combine first 7 ingredients in a bowl and form into 4 large patties. Brush or drizzle patties with olive oil and cook 7 minutes on each side over medium-high heat in a nonstick skillet. Serve on split crusty rolls with lettuce, tomato and creamy ranch or herb dressing.

Tarragon Pasta Salad

MAKES 4 ENTREES, 8 SIDE SERVINGS

4 scallions, whites and greens, chopped
1 small red bell pepper, seeded and finely chopped
1 cup frozen green peas (3 handfuls)
2/3 cup mayonnaise (just enough to bind salad), or to taste
6 sprigs fresh tarragon, about 3 tablespoons, chopped
1 pound medium size shell-shaped pasta, cooked al dente, cold shocked, well drained
Coarse salt and freshly ground black pepper, to taste
Chopped fresh parsley, for garnish

Pile salad ingredients in a serving bowl as you process them. Combine and taste to adjust seasoning. Serve.

1

Harvest Turkey
Burgers
• • • • •
2

Tarragon Pasta
Salad
• • • • •

MENU

1

Pizza with
Chicken,
Sun-Dried
Tomatoes, and
Broccoli

. . . . .

2

Cheesy
POPcorn

. . . . .

3

Ice Cream
Sundae
Sandwiches

. . . . .

Get ready to pig out and veg out all evening with a stream of munchies to get you from 7 to 11! In addition to pizza, there's cheesy popcorn, and killer ice cream sandwiches—all ready in 30 minutes, so you'll be ready for prime time! Caution: beware of food coma.

Pizza with Chicken, Sun-Dried Tomatoes, and Broccoli aka "The Only Pizza You'll Ever Want"

True story. I'm having a dinner-and-tv date. You know, stay in, make some fun foods, snuggle up on the sofa and tune in while you cool out. So, I make this complicated, fancy (and pricey) wild mushroom, smoked mozzarella, prosciutto and arugula pizza. My friend makes the following recipe. Long story short: his cost less, took less time to make and just tasted better than mine. I renamed his recipe. It became and remains: The Only Pizza You'll Ever Want.

MAKES 8 SLICES (4 servings)

CRUST

1 package (16 ounces) pizza dough, brought to room temperature

2 teaspoons extra-virgin olive oil

2 tablespoons grated Parmigiano Reggiano or Parmesan cheese

TOPPINGS

1/3 pound broccoli (from trimmed broccoli bin in produce section), about 1/3 head

1 tablespoon extra-virgin olive oil (once around the pan)

3 cloves garlic, cracked

1/3 pound chicken breast (cut for stir fry) or chicken tenders

Salt and freshly ground black pepper, to taste

1 cup part-skim ricotta cheese

10 sun-dried tomatoes in oil, drained and sliced

1 cup shredded mozzarella cheese (available on dairy aisle)

12 to 15 leaves fresh basil, torn or stacked and thinly sliced

Preheat oven to 500°F.

On a 12-inch nonstick pizza pan, stretch out your dough and form the pizza crust. Drizzle 2 teaspoons olive oil onto crust and spread it with a pastry brush to the edges. Sprinkle crust with grated Parmigiano Reggiano or Parmesan cheese.

In a small covered saucepan, bring 2 inches water to a boil. Separate broccoli tops into florets, discarding lower stalks or reserve for soup. Salt water and add broccoli florets. Cook covered, 3 to 5 minutes. Drain broccoli, set on cutting board and chop florets into small pieces.

Heat a small nonstick skillet over medium-high heat. Add oil, garlic and chicken.

Season with salt and pepper. Brown chicken until lightly golden, 5 minutes. Transfer sautéed chicken and garlic to a cutting board, and chop into small pieces.

To assemble pizza, dot crust with chopped broccoli bits, garlic and chicken. Add spoonfuls of ricotta throughout and spread ricotta gently with the back of your spoon. Add sliced sun-dried tomatoes, scattering them around the pizza to the edges. Complete the assembly with a thin layer of shredded mozzarella, about 1 cup. Place pizza in oven on middle rack and lower heat to 450°F. Bake 10 to 12 minutes, until cheese is deeply golden and crust is brown and crisp at the edges. Remove from the oven and let stand 5 minutes. Top with lots of torn or shredded basil. Cut pizza into 8 slices, using pizza wheel, and serve.

Cheesy POPcorn

MAKES 8 SERVINGS

2 tablespoons vegetable oil
1 cup popping corn kernels
3 tablespoons melted butter
1/2 cup grated Parmesan cheese

Heat oil in deep pot over medium-high heat. Add corn. Cover pot and pop the corn, shaking pan often. Remove from heat. Drizzle with melted butter. Sprinkle cheese evenly over hot corn and serve.

Ice Cream Sundae Sandwiches

MAKES 4 ICE CREAM SUNDAE SANDWICHES

1 cup shredded coconut
1 package (2 ounces) nut topping (available on baking aisle)
1 cup mini-chocolate chips
4 scoops vanilla or fudge swirl ice cream
8 large, chocolate chunk cookies or chocolate nut cookies,
  3 to 4 inches in diameter

Mix coconut, nuts, and mini chips in a shallow dish. Scoop large balls of ice cream onto 4 cookies. Top with a second cookie each and gently press down until ice cream comes to the edges of the cookies. Make sandwiches 1 & 1/2 to 2-inches thick. Roll ice cream in coconut, nut and chip topping and serve.

Smaller cookies may be substituted. The recipe will yield 8 small sandwiches, 2 inches in diameter, rather than 4 larger sandwiches. However, soft or thin cookies will break more easily using this method.

TIDBIT

❝ I am often asked where my recipes come from. Many come from my family. Others are versions of wonderful foods I've had during my travels. ❞

M E N U

Finger Foods Feast

1

Fried Mozzarella Bites

· · · · ·

2

Sausage and Spinach-Stuffed Mushrooms

· · · · ·

3

Rosemary Skewered Vegetables

· · · · ·

Just because it's finger food doesn't mean it has to be boring or predictable! These are classy munchies that you can use for a snacking supper when renting movies or for passing around at your next party. The mozzarella bites blow away any bar snack you've ever had! The skewers make a cool side with any chicken, fish or pork dinner as well. The mushrooms freeze well at the stuffed but not yet cooked stage, before they go in oven. They can be defrosted the day of a gathering and baked till hot and crispy at the edges.

Sausage and Spinach-Stuffed Mushrooms

MAKES 20 LARGE STUFFED MUSHROOMS

1 tablespoon extra-virgin olive oil (once around the pan)
12 large white gourmet stuffing mushroom caps, stems removed for stuffing, brushed with damp towel
Salt and freshly ground black pepper, to taste

STUFFING
1 & 1/2 teaspoons extra-virgin olive oil (half a turn around the pan)
3/4 pound sweet bulk Italian sausage
12 stems of mushrooms, finely chopped
2 cloves garlic, finely chopped
1 rib of celery and green, leafy top from the heart of the stalk, chopped
1/2 small onion, chopped
1/2 small red bell pepper, seeded and chopped
1 box (10 ounces) chopped frozen spinach, defrosted and squeezed dry
2 slices white toasting bread, toasted and buttered, chopped into small dice
1/4 cup grated Parmigiano Reggiano or Romano cheese (2 handfuls)

Preheat oven to 500°F.

Heat a large skillet over medium-high heat. Add oil and mushroom caps and season with salt and pepper. Sauté 5 to 7 minutes, until they are lightly browned and tender at edges. Turn caps topside up to let juices drain away. Transfer caps to a small nonstick baking sheet.

Wipe out skillet and return to heat. Add a touch of oil and the sausage to the hot skillet. Brown and crumble sausage for 3 minutes, then add chopped mushroom stems, garlic, celery, onion, and bell pepper. Sauté over medium-high heat, another 3 to 5 minutes. Add spinach and stir into stuffing. Add bread cubes and cheese and toss until bread is moist and stuffing is combined, 2 or 3 minutes.

Fill caps with stuffing using a small scoop or large spoon. Place in hot oven and reduce heat to 450°F. Bake 6 to 8 minutes to crisp edges of stuffing. Transfer to a serving plate.

Make Your Own Take-Out

· · · · ·

34

Rosemary Skewered Vegetables

MAKES 4 SERVINGS

1 medium zucchini, halved lengthwise, then cut into 1/2 inch slices

1 medium yellow squash, halved lengthwise, then cut into 1/2 inch slices

1 pint cherry tomatoes, washed and tops removed

The zest and juice of 1 lemon

1 & 1/2 tablespoons balsamic vinegar (eyeball it)

1/4 cup extra-virgin olive oil (eyeball it)

8 sturdy stems of fresh rosemary, 6 inches in length

Salt and freshly ground black pepper, to taste

Preheat grill pan over high heat.

Combine zucchini, yellow squash, and tomatoes in a bowl. To make the dressing, use a small bowl to combine the lemon zest and vinegar, then whisk in the olive oil.

Thread veggies on rosemary stems, threading from the bottom upwards. Place vegetable herb skewers on the hot grill pan. Baste liberally with dressing and season with salt and pepper. Cook 10 to 12 minutes, turning and basting occasionally. Transfer to a serving plate. Cut lemon in wedges and squeeze juice over skewers when served.

Fried Mozzarella Bites

MAKES 16 MOZZARELLA BITES

TIDBIT

❝ EVOO is too heavy to fry in. It will smoke. Buy light color olive oil to shallow fry these tasty mozzarella bites. ❞

Light in color olive oil, for frying

1-pound ball fresh mozzarella (buy a piece wrapped, not packed in water)

1 pound fresh smoked mozzarella (found in the specialty cheese case)

1 cup all-purpose flour

2 eggs

1/3 cup milk (eyeball it)

2 cups Italian-style bread crumbs

1/2 cup grated Parmigiano Reggiano or Romano cheese

2 tablespoons chopped fresh flat-leaf parsley

8 stems or large sprigs each fresh parsley, sage, thyme

Fine salt, to taste

2 cups pizza or spicy marinara sauce, for dipping

Heat 2 inches olive oil in a deep skillet over medium-high heat. Cut each pound of mozzarella and smoked mozzarella into 8 cubes. Set up a breading station: flour in one dish, eggs beaten with milk in a second, bread crumbs mixed with a couple of handfuls of grated cheese in the third. Reserve the chopped parsley. Roll fresh plain mozzarella in flour, dip in egg, then coat in bread crumbs. Bread all the plain mozzarella, then add chopped parsley to the bread crumbs. Coat the cubed smoked mozzarella in flour, egg mixture, then the bread crumbs mixed with parsley. The chopped parsley will allow you to distinguish between the plain and smoked cheese once fried.

Place herbs into hot oil and fry 30 seconds. Be careful not to stand over the pan; the oil will spatter a little because of the water content in the herbs. Remove with a slotted kitchen tool and transfer to a paper towel-lined plate to drain. Season immediately with fine salt.

Fry the mozzarella bites in batches in a single layer. Each batch will cook to an even, deep golden brown, 2 to 3 minutes. Drain and cool mozzarella bites on paper towel-lined surface. Let stand and cool a few minutes so that the cheese will not be too runny when bitten into.

For dipping sauce, heat a small sauce pan over medium heat. Warm pizza or marinara sauce and then transfer it to a serving dish.

To assemble your serving plate, pile mozzarella bites, alternating them with fried herbs. Set the dipping sauce in a bowl alongside the fried cheese and herbs.

MENU

Make-Your-
Own
Burrito Bar

1

Roasted Salsa
with Mint and
Cilantro
· · · · ·

2

Fillings:
Spicy Black
Beans and
Chicken, Red
Peppers, and
Chorizo
· · · · ·

3

Refried Beans
· · · · ·

Make-Your-Own Burrito Bar

Timing Note: First, set salsa ingredients in a pan to char. Next, make warm fillings and refried beans. Finally, arrange cold toppings and sides.

MAKES 12 BURRITOS, 6 of each filling

Roasted Salsa with Mint and Cilantro

4 plum tomatoes
1 jalapeño pepper, halved and seeded
1 small onion, peeled and cut into 3 thick slices across
3 or 4 sprigs fresh mint leaves
A handful cilantro leaves
Coarse salt, to taste

Add whole tomatoes and a seeded jalapeño, skin side down, and thick slices of onion to a dry pan over high heat. Allow them to char on all sides, then add to a food processor. Pulse grind with mint and cilantro leaves. Season with coarse salt. Pour salsa into a strainer, drain off liquid, and transfer to a serving dish.

Filling: Spicy Black Beans

1 tablespoon vegetable or olive oil (once around the pan)
1 jalapeño pepper, seeded and chopped
2 cloves garlic, chopped
1 medium onion, chopped
2 cans (15 ounces each) black beans, drained
2 tablespoons chopped cilantro (a palmful)
1 teaspoon ground cumin (eyeball it in your palm)
Coarse salt, to taste
1 teaspoon cayenne pepper sauce

Filling: Chicken, Red Peppers, and Chorizo

1 tablespoon vegetable or olive oil (once around the pan)
3/4 pound boneless chicken tenders, diced
1 teaspoon dark chili powder
Coarse salt, to taste
2 cloves garlic, chopped
1 red bell pepper, seeded and chopped
1/2 pound chorizo, casing removed and diced

12 burrito-size flour tortillas

Heat 2 nonstick skillets over medium-high heat.

In the first, add 1 tablespoon oil, chopped fresh jalapeño, garlic and onion. Sauté 2 or 3 minutes, add black beans, cilantro, cumin, salt, and cayenne pepper sauce. Reduce heat to low and simmer.

In the second skillet, add oil and, when hot, chicken. Season with chili powder and salt and lightly brown the meat, 2 to 3 minutes. Add garlic, red peppers and chorizo and sauté, 5 to 6 minutes, then reduce heat to low.

Char and soften tortillas by heating them over hot burner flame, 15 seconds on each side. If you do not have gas burners, heat your dry skillet used for salsa and cook tortillas one at a time, 15 seconds on each side.

Pile tortillas near stove and line up your toppings and sides. Serve fillings directly out of the pans.

Refried Beans

2 cans (15 ounces each) spicy vegetarian refried beans
  (as an accompaniment)
1 can (4 ounces) sliced jalapeño pepper
1 teaspoon garlic powder

Combine refried beans with jalapeños and garlic powder and heat in a bowl in the microwave. Loosely cover bowl with plastic wrap. Stop the timer and stir beans occasionally as you heat them. This should take 2 to 3 minutes.

Toppings and Sides

Sour cream
2 cups roasted salsa
1 & 1/2 cups grated Pepper Jack cheese
1 & 1/2 cups white smoked cheddar, shredded (such as Cabot brand)
4 to 6 scallions, chopped
1 heart romaine lettuce, chopped
Wedged ripe limes

TIDBIT

❝ Chicken tenders, the white meat tenderloins from chicken breasts, are perfect for 30-minute meals because they cook so quickly yet remain tender. Sliced or chopped chicken breast can always be substituted for tenders. ❞

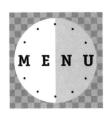

M E N U

1

**Grilled Halibut
Sandwiches**

· · · · ·

2

**Asparagus
Pasta Salad**

· · · · ·

3

**Fruit Salad
with Orange
Liqueur and
Sorbet**

· · · · ·

Grilled Halibut Sandwiches

MAKES 4 SERVINGS

1 & 1/4 to 1 & 1/2 pounds fresh halibut, cut into 4 servings
   (4 to 6 ounces each, 1-inch thick)

Vegetable or olive oil, for drizzling

2 teaspoons Old Bay Seasoning (found near seafood counter in most
   markets)

Salt and freshly ground black pepper, to taste

2 tablespoons butter, melted

The juice of 1/2 lemon

ZESTY TARTAR SAUCE

1 cup mayonnaise or reduced-fat mayonnaise

2 tablespoons sweet pickle relish

1 dill or half-sour pickle, finely chopped

2 tablespoons onion finely chopped

2 tablespoons fresh dill chopped

10 blades fresh chives, chopped or 2 thin scallions thinly sliced

The juice of 1/2 lemon

A few drops cayenne pepper sauce (such as Tabasco brand)

1 large ripe tomato, sliced

4 leaves green leaf or Boston lettuce

4 crusty rolls, split

1 bag gourmet chips (such as Terra Chips in Yukon Gold Onion and
   Garlic flavor)

Preheat a nonstick skillet or well-seasoned cast iron grill pan over medium-high
heat. Drizzle halibut with oil, season with Old Bay, salt and pepper, and grill on a
hot pan, 4 or 5 minutes on each side.

Place melted butter in a small dish and add juice of 1/2 lemon.

Combine all ingredients for the tartar sauce in a small bowl: mayonnaise, sweet
relish, chopped dill or half-sour pickle, onion, dill, chives, lemon, and pepper
sauce. Stir to combine.

Lightly toast buns on grill pan when you remove fish from heat.

To assemble, brush bun bottoms and fish with lemon butter. Top fish with tomato and lettuce and slather the bun tops with tartar sauce, then serve. Asparagus
Pasta Salad (recipe follows) and fancy chips complete your meal. Then dessert!

Asparagus Pasta Salad

MAKES 4 SERVINGS

1/2 pound bow tie pasta (farfalle) cooked al dente and cooled

1 small shallot or 1/2 large shallot, finely chopped
1/3 cup extra-virgin olive oil (eyeball it)
1 pound asparagus, thin spears
2 endive, cored and thinly sliced
1/2 small red bell pepper, chopped
1/2 cup frozen green peas
1/4 cup chopped fresh flat-leaf parsley (a couple handfuls)
3 tablespoons white wine vinegar
Salt and freshly ground black pepper

Heat the shallots and oil in a microwave-safe covered dish for 30 seconds or in a small pan on the stovetop over medium-low heat for 5 minutes. Let oil cool.

Parboil the trimmed asparagus tops in 1 inch simmering water, covered, 3 to 5 minutes. Cool under cold running water and drain. Cut into 1-inch pieces on an angle and add to a bowl. Combine with endive, red bell pepper, cooked pasta, green peas and chopped parsley. The peas will defrost as you toss salad. Pour vinegar into a small bowl and whisk in cooled shallot oil. Pour dressing over salad and toss. Season with salt and pepper, to taste and toss again.

TIDBIT

❛❛ To trim asparagus, hold a spear at each end and snap it. The spear will break where the tender top meets the tough bottom. Line the broken spear up with the bundle of cleaned asparagus. Cut using the guideline of the snapped spear. ❜❜

Fruit Salad with Orange Liqueur and Sorbet

MAKES 4 SERVINGS

2 fresh ripe peaches, pitted and diced OR 1 can (15 ounces) whole peaches, drained and diced
1 ripe Bartlett or Anjou pear, diced
1 pint ripe strawberries, halved
2 kiwis, peeled and sliced
2 ounces orange liqueur, such as Grand Marnier
1 pint orange or strawberry sorbet

Combine fruit in a bowl and douse with liqueur. Let stand a few minutes for flavors to combine. To serve, spoon fruit into dessert cups and top with scoops of sorbet.

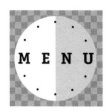

M E N U

1

Pecan-Crusted Chicken Tenders and Salad with Tangy Maple Barbecue Dressing
• • • • •

2

Cheddar and Chive Bread
• • • • •

3

My Sister Maria's Easy Apple and Cinnamon Cake and Ice Cream
• • • • •

My Sister Maria's Easy Apple and Cinnamon Cake and Ice Cream

MAKES 6 SERVINGS

1 box yellow cake mix for a single layer cake, such as Jiffy brand, prepared to package directions
2 tablespoons softened butter
1 McIntosh apple, diced
1 teaspoon ground cinnamon
1/4 cup sugar
1 pint butter pecan or rum raisin ice cream

Preheat oven to directions on box.

Mix cake mix to directions on box. Butter a 9" x 9" square cake pan. Arrange diced apple on top of the cake and sprinkle liberally with cinnamon and sugar. Bake 20 to 25 minutes. Serve warm cake squares with small scoops of butter pecan or rum raisin ice cream.

Cheddar and Chive Bread

MAKES 4 TO 6 SERVINGS

1 loaf baguette or French bread, split lengthwise, then cut in half
2 cups shredded sharp cheddar cheese
10 blades fresh chives, chopped

Heat broiler. Lightly toast bread under hot broiler, then remove and cover with shredded cheddar cheese. Sprinkle cheese liberally with chopped chives and set aside. When you are ready to serve your meal, return bread to broiler to melt cheese. When cheese is bubbly and lightly browned, remove from broiler and cut into 2-inch slices or large cubes. They can also serve as an alternative to croutons, when needed.

Pecan-Crusted Chicken Tenders and Salad with Tangy Maple Barbecue Dressing

MAKES 4 TO 6 SERVINGS

Vegetable oil, for frying
1 & 1/3 to 2 pounds chicken tenders
Salt and freshly ground black pepper, to taste
1 cup all-purpose flour
2 eggs, beaten with a splash of milk or water
1 cup plain bread crumbs
1 cup pecans, finely chopped in a food processor
1/2 teaspoon nutmeg, freshly grated or ground
The zest of 1 orange

DRESSING
1/4 cup maple syrup
1/4 cup tangy barbecue sauce
The juice of 1 navel orange
1/4 cup extra-virgin olive oil
3 hearts of romaine lettuce, shredded
6 radishes, thinly sliced
6 scallions, trimmed and chopped on an angle
Salt and freshly ground black pepper, to taste

Heat 1 & 1/2 to 2 inches oil over medium-high heat in a skillet.

Season chicken tenders with salt and pepper. Set out 3 shallow dishes. Place flour in one, eggs beaten with water or milk in a second. In the third dish, combine bread crumbs with ground pecans, nutmeg, and orange zest. Coat tenders in batches in flour, then egg, then bread crumbs and pecans. Fry tenders in small batches, 6 to 7 minutes, and drain them on paper towels.

For dressing, combine maple syrup, barbecue sauce and orange juice in a bowl. Whisk in oil, and set aside while cooking the chicken tenders.

Combine romaine, radishes, and scallions in a large salad bowl or on a serving platter. Toss with 3/4 of the dressing. Season with salt and pepper, to taste. Top with pecan-crusted chicken tenders and drizzle remaining dressing over top.

TIDBIT

❝ My friend Wade entertains with this great main-dish salad. His secret? A salad tossed with barbecue sauce and chopped chocolate biscotti. Really! I'll have to try it sometime. Keep cookin', man!❞

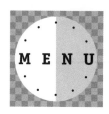

M E N U

1

Special Fried
Rice
.....

2

Sesame
Chicken Salad
.....

Special Fried Rice

MAKES 4 SERVINGS

2 to 3 cups cold, leftover rice OR

2 cups water

1 cup white rice

3 tablespoons vegetable or wok oil

2 eggs, beaten

2 cloves garlic, chopped

2 inches fresh gingerroot, minced or grated

1/2 cup shredded carrots (available in pouches in produce section)

1/2 red bell pepper, diced

4 scallions, thinly sliced on an angle

1/2 cup frozen peas

1/4 to 1/3 cup Tamari, dark soy sauce (found on Asian foods aisle)

Bring water to a boil. Add rice, reduce heat, cover and cook over medium-low heat until tender, 15 to 18 minutes. Spread rice on a cookie sheet to quick cool it.

Heat a wok or large nonstick skillet over high heat. Add 1 tablespoon oil to the pan. Add eggs and scramble, then move them off to the side of the pan and add a little more oil to the center. Add garlic and ginger, then carrots, pepper, and scallions and quick-fry veggies, 2 minutes. Add rice and combine with veggies. Incorporate the scrambled eggs and continue to cook another 2 or 3 minutes. Add peas and soy sauce and stir-fry 1 minute more, then serve.

Sesame Chicken Salad

The Asian sesame-crusted chicken salad is a favorite of mine at Eatery, a funky, Hell's Kitchen not-a-diner. My friend Joanne and I often share an order. This lighter, make-at-home version of the salad, is still interesting enough to stand on its own come dinnertime.

MAKES 4 SERVINGS

1/4 cup pure dark maple syrup (eyeball the amount)

2 to 3 tablespoons Tamari, dark soy sauce (eyeball the amount)

1/4 cup sweet hot mustard (eyeball the amount)

1 & 1/3 pounds chicken tenders

Salt and freshly ground black pepper, to taste

1/2 cup sesame seeds, a mix of black and white or all white

1/4 cup vegetable oil (3 or 4 times around the pan)

DRESSING

1-inch fresh gingerroot, grated or minced

2 tablespoons rice vinegar (2 generous splashes)

1/4 cup Chinese duck sauce or apricot all-fruit spread

1/4 cup vegetable oil (eyeball the amount)

SALAD

1 bag (10 ounces) mixed baby greens

1/4 English or seedless cucumber, halved lengthwise, thinly sliced on an angle

1/2 cup shredded carrots (a couple handfuls)

4 scallions, thinly sliced on an angle

1/4 pound snow peas, trimmed, sliced on an angle

Fried Chinese noodles of any size, for garnish

Combine syrup, soy sauce, and sweet hot mustard in a large bowl. Season chicken tenders with salt and pepper on both sides. Add chicken tenders to the bowl and coat. Set aside.

Preheat a large nonstick skillet over medium-high heat. Spread sesame seeds on a sheet of wax paper or into a shallow dish. Coat the pan with a thin layer of oil Coat chicken in sesame seeds and cook chicken in small batches, 3 minutes on each side and remove to plate.

Whisk ginger, vinegar, and the duck sauce or apricot all-fruit spread together in a medium bowl, then stream in the oil while continuing to whisk the dressing.

Combine all of the salad ingredients in a bowl. Toss with dressing and serve, topping with sesame chicken tenders. Toss some crunch into your salad with fried noodles, if you have any leftover packets from ordering Chinese take out, for the last time!

MENU

1

Super Stuffed
Potatoes with
The Works

· · · · ·

2

Hot Buffalo
Chicken
Sandwiches

· · · · ·

3

Orange
Sherbet
Freezes

· · · · ·

I often take restaurant food, even bar food, and try and come up with more healthful and/or quicker versions to make at home. This more adult "take" on Buffalo Hot Wings and Stuffed Potatoes will hit the right flavor bells in your mouth and kids will love it as well! My version calls for boneless, skinless white meat chicken as opposed to deep-fried dark meat with skin, and the blue cheese topping is made with reduced-fat sour cream. The orange freezes, using sherbet, are a not-too-sweet alternative to a milk shake.

Super Stuffed Potatoes with The Works

MAKES 4 SERVINGS, 1/2 stuffed potato each

4 slices center-cut bacon, chopped
2 all-purpose potatoes, such as russet
1/2 cup sour cream or reduced-fat sour cream
2 scallions, finely chopped
Salt and freshly ground black pepper, to taste
1 cup shredded cheddar, Colby or smoked cheddar cheese

In a small nonstick skillet over medium-high heat, brown bacon pieces, then drain on paper towel.

Pierce potatoes a few times each with a fork. Microwave on high for 12 minutes. Let potatoes cool for a few minutes before handling.

Preheat broiler.

Carefully split potatoes and scoop out flesh into a small bowl. Combine with sour cream, scallions, salt, pepper and cheese. Scoop back into the potato skins, and place under broiler to lightly brown the tops and serve.

Hot Buffalo Chicken Sandwiches

MAKES 4 SERVINGS

4 pieces boneless, skinless chicken breast (about 6 ounces each)
Salt and freshly ground black pepper, to taste
1 teaspoon sweet paprika (1/3 palmful)
1 teaspoon chili powder (1/3 palmful)
A drizzle extra-virgin olive oil

SAUCE

2 tablespoons butter

1/2 cup (4 ounces) cayenne pepper sauce such as Frank's Red Hot

4 crusty rolls, split

Bibb or leaf lettuce leaves

2 cups reduced-fat sour cream

4 scallions, thinly sliced

1/2 pound blue cheese, crumbled

8 ribs celery, cut into sticks

2 large carrots, peeled, and cut into sticks

Heat a large nonstick skillet over medium-high heat. Season chicken with salt, pepper, paprika, and chili powder, and drizzle with a little olive oil to coat. Pan grill, 5 minutes on each side.

Heat a metal or oven-safe glass bowl over low heat to melt the butter. Add hot sauce to the butter and combine. When the chicken breasts are done, remove from pan and add to the bowl and coat evenly with the hot sauce mixture.

Place chicken breasts on bun bottoms and top with crisp lettuce.

Combine sour cream, scallions, and blue cheese and slather on bun tops. Top sandwiches and serve, using remaining sauce for dipping your veggies. Arrange on dinner plates with Super Stuffed Potatoes and celery and carrot sticks.

Orange Sherbet Freezes

MAKES 4 FREEZES

2 pints or 1/2 gallon tub orange sherbet

1 pint vanilla ice cream or frozen yogurt

1 liter lemon lime soda, diet soda or lemon lime seltzer

1 lime, for garnish (optional)

Ice cubes

For each freeze, in a blender combine 3 scoops orange sherbet and 1 scoop vanilla ice cream or frozen yogurt. Add 1/4 liter lemon lime soda or lemon lime seltzer. Add ice cubes to the blender to fill. Cover and blend on high until frothy and smooth. Pour into fountain or tall glass and garnish glass rim with a round of lime and a straw. Repeat with remaining ingredients.

1

Five-Spice
Beef and
Pepper Stir-Fry
and
Rice with
Smoked
Almonds

.....

2

Mixed Baby
Greens with
Mandarin
Orange
and Cucumber
in Sesame
Dressing

.....

Five-Spice Beef and Pepper Stir-Fry and Rice with Smoked Almonds

MAKES 4 SERVINGS

Jasmine rice or short grain white rice, 1 to 1 & 1/2 cups, prepared to package directions

2 cups beef broth or stock, paper container or canned

2 tablespoons wok or clear oil (twice around the pan)

1 & 1/2 pounds beef sirloin or beef tenderloin tips, trimmed, sliced and cut into bite-size pieces

2 green bell peppers, seeded and diced (1-inch pieces)

1 medium onion, coarsely diced

1/2 cup dry cooking sherry

2 tablespoons Tamari dark soy sauce (eyeball the amount)

2 tablespoons corn starch

1 teaspoon Chinese five-spice powder (1/2 palmful, found on Asian foods aisle of market)

Cracked freshly ground black pepper, to taste

3 scallions, thinly sliced on an angle, for garnish

1/2 cup smoked whole almonds (available on snack aisle), for garnish

Boil water for rice and prepare to package directions.

Place beef broth in a small pot over low heat to warm the broth.

Heat a wok-shaped skillet or pan over high heat. Add oil (it will smoke) and beef bits, stir-fry for 3 minutes then remove meat from pan or move off to the side. Return pan to heat and add peppers and onions. Stir-fry, 2 minutes, and stir the meat back in. Add sherry and stir-fry until liquid almost evaporates, about 1 minute. Add soy sauce. Dissolve cornstarch with a ladle of warm beef broth. Add beef broth to the pan, then the cornstarch combined with broth, the five-spice powder and black pepper. Stir until it thickens enough to coat the back of a spoon. Adjust seasonings. Add more soy or salt if necessary. Remove from heat.

Fill dinner bowls with beef stir-fry and with an ice cream scoop, place a nicely rounded scoop of rice on top of beef. Garnish with chopped scallions and smoked almonds.

Mixed Baby Greens with Mandarin Orange and Cucumber in Sesame Dressing

MAKES 4 SERVINGS

1 bag (10 ounces) mixed baby greens
1 can (10 ounces) mandarin oranges, drained
1/4 English or European seedless cucumber, thinly sliced
2 tablespoons rice wine or white vinegar (eyeball it)
2 teaspoons sugar
3 tablespoons vegetable oil (eyeball it)
1 teaspoon toasted sesame oil (a drizzle)
Sesame seeds, for garnish (2 tablespoons)
Salt and freshly ground black pepper, to taste

Combine greens, oranges, and cucumber in a salad bowl. In a small bowl, combine vinegar and sugar. Whisk in vegetable and sesame oils. Pour dressing over salad. Add sesame seeds, salt and pepper and toss.

MENU

1

Chicken Tikka
with Charred
Tomato
Chutney
and Warm
Flat Bread

· · · · ·

2

Potatoes with
Cumin

· · · · ·

3

Banana Raita

· · · · ·

Chicken Tikka with Charred Tomato Chutney and Warm Flat Bread

MAKES 4 SERVINGS

1 cup plain yogurt
1 rounded tablespoon mild curry paste (found in Asian section of
   international foods aisle)
The juice of 1 lemon
A handful cilantro leaves, finely chopped (3 tablespoons)
1 & 1/2 pounds chicken tenders
3 plum tomatoes
1/2 cup tomato sauce or tomato puree
1 teaspoon mustard seeds
1 teaspoon coriander seeds
1/2 to 1 teaspoon crushed red pepper flakes
Coarse salt
Packaged flat breads (sold near packaged pita bread in market)
1 heart romaine lettuce, shredded

Preheat grill pan or indoor electric grill to high.

Combine yogurt, curry paste, lemon juice and cilantro in a shallow dish. Add chicken tenders and coat evenly. When you are about 10 minutes away from eating, place chicken on hot grill and cook 5 minutes on each side, until chicken is firm.

Place a small heavy skillet on stovetop over high heat. When very hot, add whole tomatoes. Pan roast the tomatoes until charred on all sides, then place in a food processor with the tomato sauce. Return skillet to heat and toast mustard and coriander seeds and crushed red pepper until they pop. Add seeds and flakes to food processor with a few pinches coarse salt. Pulse grind into a chunky chutney and transfer to a small bowl.

After removing chicken from grill, blister and warm the flat bread quickly. Set chicken onto a serving dish with a bowl of tomato chutney and serving spoon alongside. Pile chicken onto flat bread, topping with tomato chutney and shredded romaine. Potatoes with Cumin are a perfect side dish to this meal.

Potatoes with Cumin

MAKES 4 SERVINGS

2 pounds white potatoes, peeled and diced into small cubes
1 teaspoon cumin seeds
2 tablespoons peanut or vegetable oil (twice around the pan)
1 small sweet onion, chopped
1/2 cup frozen green peas
Coarse salt, to taste

Boil potatoes in salted water to cover for 7 minutes, until tender. Drain, return to hot pot to dry them out.

Heat skillet over medium-high to high heat. Add cumin seeds. When seeds pop and crackle, add oil, then onion, sauté 2 minutes, stirring constantly. Add potatoes to the pan and toss to coat and lightly brown, about 3 minutes. Remove pan from heat and toss potatoes with peas, season with salt, and serve.

Banana Raita

MAKES 4 SERVINGS

1/2 cup shredded coconut
3 bananas, cut into 2-inch pieces
A wedge of lemon
1 cup plain or vanilla yogurt

Toast coconut in a small pan or in toaster oven.

Slice bananas into a serving dish and squeeze a little lemon juice over bananas to keep them from browning. Coat bananas with yogurt and top with lightly toasted coconut. Serve.

M E N U

Lost in Spice

1

Sweet 'n Spicy
Chicken Curry
In a Hurry
with
Fragrant
Basmati Rice

• • • • •

2

Indian Spiced
Fruit

• • • • •

In this menu, you can control the heat and spice by adjusting the garlic, ginger and curry paste in varying amounts. The addition of mincemeat and the mix of chutney and peanuts as toppings create unusual textures.

This meal is fun for entertaining. Try it out at the next block or tailgate party, or covered-dish gathering. My mom came up with the use of mincemeat. She wanted to sweeten her curry without adding coconut milk. A cup of mango chutney may be substituted if you wish.

Sweet 'n Spicy Chicken Curry In a Hurry with Fragrant Basmati Rice

MAKES 4 SERVINGS

2 cups basmati rice, prepared to package directions
1 teaspoon each coriander seeds, cumin seeds, mustard seeds

2 tablespoons vegetable or canola oil (twice around the pan)
1 & 1/3 to 1 & 1/2 pounds chicken tenders, diced
2 to 4 cloves garlic, minced (mild to extra spicy, to taste)
1 to 2 inches fresh gingerroot, minced or grated (mild to extra spicy, to taste)
1 large yellow onion, chopped
1 can chicken broth (about 2 cups)
2 tablespoons curry paste, mild or hot
1 cup mincemeat (found on the baking aisle of most markets)
Coarse salt, to taste

TOPPINGS AND GARNISHES (MIX AND MATCH)
4 scallions, chopped
1 cup toasted coconut
1/2 cup sliced almonds or Spanish peanuts
1 cup prepared mango chutney
1/4 cup cilantro finely chopped

For spicy rice, toast coriander, cumin, and mustard seeds in the bottom of a medium saucepan. When seeds pop and become fragrant, add water, bring to a boil, and prepare rice as directed. For plain rice, prepare as usual.

Heat oil in a large, deep, nonstick skillet over medium-high heat. Add chicken and lightly brown. Add garlic, ginger, and onion, and sauté together another 5 minutes. Add chicken broth and bring to a bubble. Stir in curry paste and mincemeat and reduce heat to medium low. Add salt, to taste. Simmer, 5 to 10 minutes.

Assemble toppings in small dishes. Serve chicken curry in shallow bowls with scoops of plain or spiced basmati rice. Garnish with any or all of your toppings.

Indian Spiced Fruit

MAKES 4 TO 6 SERVINGS

2 green apples, cored and chopped
1 red pear, cored and chopped
1 banana, sliced
1 can (15 ounces) apricots in syrup, drained
1 can (15 ounces) pitted black cherries, drained
1-inch gingerroot, grated or minced
The juice of 1 lemon
2 teaspoons sugar
1 teaspoon salt
1/2 teaspoon each ground nutmeg, cinnamon, and cloves

Combine all ingredients in a bowl and serve or chill.

TIDBIT

ff The spiced fruit salad can be made with any combination of fresh and/or canned fruits. **JJ**

Make Your
Own Take-Out
. . . . .
53

M E N U

Snacks as
Supper

1

Stuffed
Potatoes with
Ham, Thyme,
and Gruyère
· · · · ·

2

Spinach
Artichoke
Calzones
· · · · ·

3

Sausage
Calzones
· · · · ·

**Snacks as supper: Match any of the following recipes with a tossed salad
and you've got supper!**

Stuffed Potatoes with Ham, Thyme, and Gruyère

MAKES 4 SERVINGS

4 medium to large russet potatoes, washed
A drizzle extra-virgin olive oil

FILLING
1 tablespoon extra-virgin olive oil (once around the pan)
2 shallots, chopped
1/2 pound baked ham from deli, 1/8-inch thick slices, cut into 1/4-inch
    strips
1/2 pound Gruyère cheese, shredded
2 tablespoons butter, in small pieces
1/2 cup milk or half-and-half
6 sprigs fresh thyme, leaves stripped and chopped (about 2 tablespoons)
Salt and freshly ground black pepper, to taste

Rub potatoes with a drizzle of oil and pierce with a fork. Microwave on high,
12 minutes or until tender. Cool potatoes 5 minutes, then split down the center
and scrape potato flesh into a bowl. Set skins aside on a nonstick baking sheet.
Preheat broiler to high with oven rack 6 inches from heat source.

While potatoes cook in microwave, heat a small skillet over medium heat. Add
1 tablespoon of olive oil and sauté shallots, 2 to 3 minutes or until bits are just
tender.

To the cooked potato in the mixing bowl, add shallots, ham strips, cheese,
butter, milk or half-and-half, thyme, and salt and pepper. Mash with a potato
masher or fork until mixture is combined, but not entirely lump-free. Scoop
mixture in even amounts into skins and broil, 2 or 3 minutes, to lightly brown on
top. Serve 2 halves with salad, dark bread and butter.

Spinach Artichoke Calzones

MAKES 4 CALZONES

2 cups low-moisture part-skim ricotta cheese

1/4 teaspoon freshly grated nutmeg, or a few pinches ground

A few grinds freshly ground black pepper

1/2 cup grated Parmigiano Reggiano cheese (a couple handfuls)

1 package (10 ounces) frozen chopped spinach, defrosted, and squeezed dry

1 can (15 ounces) quartered artichoke hearts in water, drained and coarsely chopped

2 cloves garlic, finely chopped

2 tubes prepared, refrigerated pizza dough (10 ounces each)

2 cups shredded mozzarella cheese (available in pouches on dairy aisle)

2 cups tomato, marinara or pizza sauce, warmed, for dipping

TIDBIT

❝ Freeze any remaining filling in a small plastic container and use it to stuff a chicken breast on another day. ❞

Preheat oven to 425°F.

Combine first 7 ingredients in a bowl to make the filling. Roll both tubes of pizza dough out on 2 separate nonstick cookie sheets and cut each dough in half across. Spread 1/2 cup mozzarella and up to 1/4 of filling on each rectangle. Work on just half of the surface of each rectangle of dough, then fold dough over top of filling and pinch edges firmly to seal. For a half-moon "pizza parlor" look to your calzones, mound filling into a half-moon shape, fold dough over top, and trim edges following the rounded shape, then seal by pinching with fingers.

If your dough tears, remove a little of your filling and repair. Repeat process, spacing calzones evenly on baking sheet, and bake 12 to 15 minutes or until golden brown. Serve with warm tomato, marinara, or pizza sauce for dunking.

Sausage Calzones

MAKES 4 CALZONES

1 & 1/3 pounds Italian bulk sweet sausage
A drizzle extra-virgin olive oil
2 cups ricotta cheese
A handful fresh flat-leaf parsley, chopped
2 cloves garlic, chopped
A handful grated Parmigiano Reggiano cheese
1/4 teaspoon nutmeg, freshly grated or a couple pinches ground
A few grinds freshly ground black pepper
2 tablespoons chopped pimiento
2 tubes of prepared, refrigerated pizza dough (10 ounces each)
2 cups shredded mozzarella cheese
2 cups tomato, marinara or pizza sauce, warmed, for dipping

Preheat oven to 425°F.

Brown sausage in a small skillet in a drizzle of olive oil. Transfer crumbles to a paper towel-lined plate to drain.

Combine sausage with ricotta cheese, parsley, garlic, grated Parmigiano, nutmeg, pepper, and pimiento. Roll both tubes of pizza dough out on 2 separate nonstick cookie sheets and cut each dough in half across. Spread 1/2 cup mozzarella and up to 1/4 of filling on each rectangle. Work on just half of the surface of each rectangle of dough, then fold dough over top of filling and pinch edges firmly to seal. For a half-moon "pizza parlor" look to your calzones, mound filling into a half-moon shape, fold dough over top, and trim edges following the rounded shape, then seal by pinching with fingers.

If your dough tears, remove a little of your filling and repair. Repeat process, spacing calzones evenly on baking sheet, and bake 12 to 15 minutes or until golden brown. Serve with warm tomato, marinara, or pizza sauce for dunking.

MONDAY THRU FRIDAY DINNER SPECIALS

RACHAEL RAY
30-MINUTE MEALS 2

I write 30-Minute Meals for two groups of people. First, for those who don't often cook and feel intimidated by the thought. For them, I try to make every meal a can-do cooking experience, so I work very hard at making recipes accessible and achievable. Then, there are those who, like myself, simply have no time to spare. I work at least two jobs every day, and my friends and family seem to do the same. Like many of you, my best friend Vicky and my sister Maria, both married with families, manage to work full-time, and are active in their communities, too. My Mama, bless her, worked for more than 40 years, often putting in up to 100 hours a week, and still raised the three of us. How did she do it?

Just getting meals on the table every night is a challenge, but you do it, anyway you can. It's an even greater challenge to keep meals simple and appealing, day after day. Am I right? Let these Monday thru Friday Dinner Specials help you break the routine. Smokey Orange Barbecued Chicken Sandwiches with Crispy-Topped Baked Beans with Bacon, for example, may just get you out of that cooking rut. With their broad appeal—even kids will love 'em—these recipes will make your weekday meals seem like special occasions. I've written them just for you!

Braciole with Mushroom Tomato Gravy

MAKES 4 SERVINGS

8 slices beef braciole, very thinly sliced from top round
Coarse salt and freshly ground black pepper
8 slices prosciutto di Parma
1 & 1/2 cups plain bread crumbs (eyeball it)
1/2 cup milk (eyeball it)
2/3 cup grated Parmigiano Reggiano cheese (3 handfuls)
1 small onion, finely chopped
1/2 cup chopped fresh flat-leaf parsley (a couple handfuls)
1 cup chopped arugula
Plain round toothpicks
2 tablespoon extra-virgin olive oil (twice around the pan)
2 cloves garlic, cracked away from skin
2 tablespoons butter
12 crimini mushrooms, finely chopped
2 tablespoons flour
1 cup dry white wine
1 cup beef broth
1 rounded tablespoon tomato paste

Season meat with salt and pepper. Top each slice of meat with a slice of pro-sciutto. In a medium bowl, moisten bread crumbs with milk. Add grated cheese, onion, parsley, arugula, salt and pepper to the crumbs and combine well. Spread a thin layer of stuffing down the center of each beef and prosciutto slice and roll tightly. Fasten rolls with plain toothpicks.

Heat a large nonstick skillet over medium-high heat. When hot, add oil along with garlic. Set meat rolls into pan and brown on all sides, 6 minutes. Remove the meat to a platter and add butter to the pan. Add mushrooms and sauté, 5 minutes. Add flour to the pan and cook, 2 minutes. Whisk wine into the flour and mushrooms and scrape up pan drippings. Reduce wine, 1 minute, then whisk in beef broth and tomato paste. Set meat back into sauce and reduce heat to medium low. Partially cover pan leaving about an inch for steam to escape. Simmer, 10 to 15 minutes. Transfer beef rolls to a platter. Remove toothpicks, and pour pan gravy down over the rolls and serve.

MENU

1
Braciole with Mushroom Tomato Gravy
. . . . .

2
The Best Basic Risotto
. . . . .

3
Wilted Spinach with Garlic and Oil
. . . . .

4
Neapolitan Ice Cream with Cherry Sauce
. . . . .

The Best Basic Risotto

MAKES 4 SERVINGS

4 cups chicken or vegetable broth
2 tablespoons butter
1 tablespoon extra-virgin olive oil (once around the pan)
1 small to medium onion, chopped
1 & 1/2 cups arborio rice
1/2 cup dry white wine
1/2 cup grated Parmigiano Reggiano cheese
Salt and freshly ground black pepper

Place chicken or vegetable broth in a saucepan and simmer.

In a deep skillet, melt butter into olive oil over medium to medium-high heat. Add onions and sauté, 3 minutes. Then add arborio and sauté, 2 minutes more. Add wine and let it cook away, 1 or 2 minutes. Add broth a few ladles at a time over the next 18 minutes, stirring it into the rice each time the liquid has been fully absorbed. Stir in the cheese and season with salt and pepper, to taste.

Wilted Spinach with Garlic and Oil

MAKES 4 SERVINGS

2 tablespoons extra-virgin olive oil (twice around the pan)
4 cloves garlic, minced
1 pound triple-washed spinach, stems removed
Salt and freshly ground black pepper, to taste
1/2 teaspoon ground or freshly grated nutmeg

Heat a skillet over medium heat. Add oil and garlic, and sauté 2 or 3 minutes. Add spinach to the pan, a handful at a time, turning the leaves in warm oil until wilted. Repeat the process until all of the spinach is incorporated. Season with salt and pepper and nutmeg, then serve.

Neapolitan Ice Cream with Cherry Sauce

MAKES 4 SERVINGS

1 can (15 ounces) black pitted cherries, drained, juice reserved
1 tablespoon each sugar and cornstarch, combined
1 teaspoon lemon juice
1 half-gallon container of Neapolitan ice cream (chocolate, vanilla and
  strawberry)
Slivered almonds (optional)
Italian amaretti cookies, 2 per person (optional)

In a small saucepan, stir 1 cup of the reserved cherry juice into sugar and corn-starch mixture over moderate heat. Continue to stir until thickened, 1 to 2 minutes, then add cherries, and lemon juice. Stir 1 minute longer and remove from heat.

Open the top and one end of a half gallon of Neapolitan ice cream. Using a bread knife, cut 1-inch slices of the brick, giving each slice a stripe of each flavor.

Ladle cherries in their sauce on dessert plates and top with slices of ice cream. Pass extra sauce at table. Slivered almonds and amaretti cookies make a nice finishing touch to this dessert.

**Menu for
Picky Eaters**

1

**No Mystery:
Marinated
Beef, Chicken,
Pork or
Portobello
Mushrooms**

• • • • •

2

Cheezy Orzo

• • • • •

3

**Balsamic
(or Honey)
Glazed
Vegetables**

• • • • •

Yes! They can have it their way! Mix and match, swap and switch ingredients in this menu to please any fussy eaters' palate. Meat eaters and vegetarians under the same roof? This menu is the answer.

No-Mystery: Marinated Beef, Chicken, Pork or Portobello Mushrooms

MAKES 4 SERVINGS

BASIC MARINADE

3 tablespoons red wine vinegar

1/3 cup extra-virgin olive oil

2 cloves garlic, chopped

1/4 to 1/2 teaspoon crushed red pepper flakes

1 tablespoon chopped fresh thyme, a few sprigs

1 tablespoon chopped fresh parsley (half a palmful)

MARINADE AND GRAVY RECIPES WILL BE ENOUGH FOR ONE OF THE
FOLLOWING:
  • 4 beef tournedos (fillet mignon steaks, 6 ounces each, 1-inch thick)
  • 4 strip steaks (12 ounces each)
  • 4 pieces boneless skinless chicken breast (6 to 8 ounces each)
  • 4 center-cut pork loin chops (8 ounces each, 1-inch thick)
  • 4 portobello mushroom caps

Salt and freshly black pepper

BASIC PAN GRAVY

2 tablespoons butter

2 tablespoons chopped shallots or onion

4 mushrooms, crimini or button, finely chopped (optional)

2 tablespoons flour (a palmful)

1 cup beef, chicken or vegetable stock

Combine marinade ingredients in the bottom of a shallow dish. Season meat of
choice with salt and pepper and set into marinade and turn to coat. Allow meat
to hang out 10 minutes, turning occasionally.

Heat a nonstick skillet over medium-high heat. Add marinated meat and cook,
5 or 6 minutes on each side. Remove to a warm platter. Add butter to the skillet,
then chopped shallots or onion and mushroom bits (optional), and sauté 3
minutes over moderate heat. Add flour to the pan and cook 2 minutes, stirring
constantly. Whisk in stock and reduce for another minute. Pour over meat and
serve.

Cheesy Orzo

MAKES 4 SERVINGS

2 tablespoons extra-virgin olive oil (twice around the pan)
1/2 small onion, chopped
2 cloves garlic, chopped
2 cans (14 ounces each) chicken or vegetable broth or stock
2 cups orzo pasta (enriched rice may be substituted)
1/2 cup grated Parmigiano Reggiano or Romano cheese
Salt and freshly ground black pepper, to taste

Preheat an 8-inch pot with a tight-fitting cover over moderate heat. Add oil, onion and garlic and sauté, 2 or 3 minutes. Add broth and bring to a boil. Stir in orzo and return to a boil. Cover and reduce heat to simmer. Cook 15 minutes, stirring occasionally, or until liquid is absorbed and pasta tender. Then stir in cheese, and season with salt and pepper to taste. To add even more flavor, stir in your favorite fresh herbs, finely chopped.

Balsamic (or Honey) Glazed Vegetables

MAKES 4 SERVINGS

1 & 1/2 to 2 pounds total, your choice of the following, or any combination:
  • "baby" packaged fresh carrots
  • brussel sprouts
  • broccoli
  • cauliflower
  • zucchini
  • yellow squash
1/2 cup water
1/2 cup balsamic vinegar
1 tablespoon butter
Salt and freshly ground black pepper, to taste

Place veggies in a pan with water and vinegar. Bring to a boil and cover. Reduce heat to medium and cook 10 minutes. Remove lid and increase heat, to allow water and vinegar to reduce and glaze the veggies, about 5 to 7 minutes. When glazed to a sweet, rich brown color, add butter to coat veggies lightly. Season with salt and pepper, and serve.

HONEY GLAZED VEGETABLES: For an optional glaze for carrots and/or sugar snap peas, substitute 1/4 cup melted butter and 1/4 cup honey for 1/2 cup balsamic vinegar. Follow above method.

MENU

1
Lamb Chops
with Mint and
Mustard
Dipping Sauce
· · · · ·

2
Tabouleh-
Stuffed
Tomatoes
· · · · ·

3
Warm White
Beans with
Thyme
· · · · ·

4
Limoncello
Dessert
· · · · ·

Lamb Chops with Mint and Mustard Dipping Sauce

Try this Mother's Day favorite from my own sweet Mom.

MAKES 4 SERVINGS

2 cloves garlic, smashed
2/3 cup extra-virgin olive oil (eyeball it)
12 loin lamb chops, 1/2 to 3/4 inch-thick each
Salt and freshly ground black pepper, to taste
3 rounded tablespoons grainy mustard
2 tablespoons white wine vinegar (2 splashes)
1 tablespoon honey (a good drizzle)
1/4 cup mint leaves (a couple handfuls), reserve 4 leaves, for garnish
4 leaves radicchio lettuce

Preheat broiler to high.

Place garlic in a small saucepan, add olive oil to cover and heat over low heat for 5 minutes, then remove. Arrange lamb chops on broiler pan. Drizzle 3 teaspoonfuls of the garlic oil over the lamb, brushing to coat evenly. Season chops with salt and pepper and set aside.

To make the dipping sauce, add mustard, vinegar, and honey to a food processor or blender and while processing or blending, stream in remaining garlic and oil. Turn the processor or blender off and add mint to the container. Pulse grind to incorporate the mint leaves.

Broil lamb chops, 3 minutes on each side, then let them rest up to 10 minutes, allowing the juices to redistribute. The lamb will be cooked to medium. Serve 3 chops per person with portions of dipping sauce and radicchio leaves set alongside the chops. Garnish with sprigs of mint. Tabouleh-Stuffed Tomatoes and White Beans with Thyme make wonderful side dishes. See recipes below.

Tabouleh-Stuffed Tomatoes

MAKES 4 SERVINGS

3/4 cup bulgur wheat (available in rice section of your market)
1 cup boiling water
The juice of 2 lemons
1 cup chopped fresh flat-leaf parsley (1 bunch)
1/2 cup chopped mint leaves (1/2 bunch)
4 scallions, thinly sliced

Monday Thru
Friday Dinner
Specials
· · · · ·
64

1 plum tomato, seeded and diced
2 tablespoons extra-virgin olive oil (twice around the bowl)
Salt and freshly ground black pepper
4 large vine-ripe tomatoes or beefsteak tomatoes

In a medium bowl, cover bulgur wheat (tabouleh) with boiling water and stir.
Cover the bowl, place it in the refrigerator, and let stand, 20 minutes to soften.
Then add lemon juice, parsley, mint, scallions, plum tomato to the tabouleh and
toss to combine. Dress the salad with olive oil, salt and pepper, to taste.

To serve, cut a large, ripe tomato into quarters, leaving the skin intact on the
bottom so that the tomato resembles an open flower. Season with salt and pepper and pile a generous amount of tabouleh salad on top of the tomato, allowing the salad to spill down and over the wedges of tomato onto the plate.

Warm White Beans with Thyme

MAKES 4 SERVINGS

3 tablespoons extra-virgin olive oil
2 large cloves garlic, chopped
2 tablespoons fresh thyme leaves, chopped, plus 4 extra sprigs for garnish
1/2 cup chopped radicchio lettuce, half a head, shredded
1 large can (1 pound, 13 ounces) white cannellini beans, drained well
Salt and freshly ground black pepper to taste

In a medium skillet, heat olive oil and garlic over medium heat, 2 minutes. Add
thyme and radicchio and cook 1 minute longer. Add beans, and toss with radicchio and garlic to combine. Season with salt and pepper. Warm beans through,
2 minutes, then serve. Garnish with extra sprigs of fresh thyme.

Limoncello Dessert

MAKES 4 SERVINGS

1 pint each lemon sorbet and vanilla ice cream
4 shots limoncello or any lemon liqueur
The zest of 1 lemon, grated
Wafer cookies, for garnish

Place one scoop of lemon sorbet alongside a scoop of vanilla ice cream in each
dessert cup or stemmed cocktail glass. Top each serving with 1 shot lemon
liqueur and grated lemon zest. Garnish with wafer cookies placed directly into
the ice cream and sorbet scoops, then serve.

TIDBIT

**❝ Limoncello
is an Italian
lemon liqueur
available at any
large liquor
store. ❞**

**Monday Thru
Friday Dinner
Specials**
• • • • •

MENU

1

Roquefort,
Pear and
Walnut Toasts

. . . . .

2

Chicken
Paillard on
Baby Greens

. . . . .

3

Citrus White
Wine Spritzer

. . . . .

TIDBIT

❝ Either buy
walnuts already
packaged in bits
or put halves in
a baggie and
give them a
good whack! ❞

Monday Thru
Friday Dinner
Specials

. . . . .

66

This meal can serve many or few, whether you are home alone or have a small crowd to feed. It is healthful and the ingredients for the chicken paillard are items that you can always have on hand: prewashed mixed baby salad greens in a sack, individually portioned chicken cutlets stored in the freezer and quickly defrosted, flour and chicken broth to make the pan gravy.

Roquefort, Pear and Walnut Toasts

MAKES 4 SERVINGS

1 baguette, thinly sliced on an angle
A wedge of lemon
1 pear, quartered lengthwise and thinly sliced
3/4 pound Roquefort cheese, crumbled
1 cup walnut pieces

Preheat your broiler to high. Arrange 12 slices of baguette on your broiler pan in a single layer. Toast lightly on each side. Squeeze lemon juice over the pear slices to keep them from browning. Place a slice of pear on each toast and top with Roquefort crumbles and walnut pieces. Return pan to broiler 6 inches from heat source and broil toasts 2 or 3 minutes to melt cheese and toast walnuts. Transfer to a plate and start snacking!

Chicken Paillard on Baby Greens

The paillard is my version of a favorite dish at Balthazar and Pastis restaurants in New York City where I often enjoy brunch. While not quite the same thing as being there, you'll find it is just as delicious and much more economical to prepare in your own kitchen.

MAKES 4 SERVINGS

8 chicken breast cutlets
Extra-virgin olive oil, for drizzling
4 sprigs fresh thyme, stripped and finely chopped (2 tablespoons)
2 tablespoons chopped fresh flat-leaf parsley (a handful)
The zest of 1 lemon
Coarse salt and freshly ground black pepper, to taste
2 tablespoons butter
2 tablespoons flour
2 cups chicken stock or broth
1 sack (5 ounces) mixed baby salad greens
The juice of 1 lemon
2 tablespoons extra-virgin olive oil (twice around the bowl)

Preheat a large nonstick skillet over medium-high heat. Arrange the chicken in a shallow dish and drizzle with olive oil to just coat the chicken, about 1 & 1/2 tablespoons total. Combine chopped herbs and lemon zest and sprinkle over the chicken. Season with salt and pepper. Using your hands, rub the chicken to coat evenly with the herbs and seasonings.* Using tongs, transfer chicken in a single layer to hot skillet and cook 3 or 4 minutes on each side. Remove cooked chicken to a warm serving dish and cover loosely with foil and repeat with remaining cutlets.

Return pan to heat and add butter. When the butter melts, add flour to the butter and cook, stirring with whisk, 1 or 2 minutes to make a light roux. Whisk in chicken broth and when it thickens to just coat the back of a spoon, remove pan from heat and turn off burner.

Toss salad greens with lemon juice and coarse salt. Drizzle 2 tablespoons olive oil around the bowl and retoss greens.

To serve, cover the bottom of a dinner plate with the warm sauce. Top with a small pile of salad greens and 2 grilled chicken cutlets.

* Wash hands with hot water and soap.

TIDBIT

❝ Store chicken breast cutlets, 1 portion, in small plastic food storage bags and keep on hand in the freezer. To quickly defrost, run warm water over the bags for 10 minutes. Remove chicken and continue per recipe directions. ❞

Citrus White Wine Spritzer

White grape juice may be substituted for the wine for a nonalcoholic or kid-friendly spritzer "mocktail."

MAKES 1 SERVING

Ice
2 thin slices lemon
2 thin slices lime
4 ounces (1/2 cup) Pinot Grigio or other dry crisp white wine
2 ounces (1/4 cup) lemon-lime seltzer water

In a large stem glass, arrange slices of lemon and lime among ice cubes to fill the glass. Pour the white wine and lemon-lime seltzer down over fruit and ice. Stir with straw and serve.

MENU

1

Elsa's Jumbo
Shrimp
with Sage and
Pancetta
• • • • •

2

Mom's Wasabi
and
Watercress
Potato Salad
• • • • •

3

Green Bean
Salad with Red
Onion and
Tomato
• • • • •

Elsa's Jumbo Shrimp with Sage and Pancetta

MAKES 4 SERVINGS

These are a few of my mom Elsa's favorite things (She's biased—these are her recipes.) My mom is very low maintenance, so is this recipe. If not dinner, try this recipe out at your next party. It's a crowd pleaser!

12 jumbo shrimp, peeled and deveined
A drizzle extra-virgin olive oil
12 large sage leaves
12 very thin slices of pancetta (available at deli counter of market)
12 wooden 4-inch party picks (big toothpicks, no frills)

Place shrimp on a dish and drizzle with a touch of olive oil and toss to coat lightly. Press sage leaves down the backs of the shrimp where deveined, and wrap each shrimp with 1 slice of pancetta held in place with a toothpick placed lengthwise through shrimp. Set aside until ready to grill.

Heat an indoor electric grill to highest setting. Grill shrimps, 3 minutes on each side or until pink and just firm, and pancetta is crisp. To pan-fry shrimp, heat a nonstick skillet over medium-high to high heat and sear shrimp 3 minutes per side. Serve 3 shrimp per person with Potato Watercress Salad and Green Bean Salad.

Mom's Wasabi and Watercress Potato Salad

MAKES 4 SERVINGS

1 & 1/2 pounds small, white baby or red potatoes
A drizzle extra-virgin olive oil

DRESSING
1/2 cup plain yogurt
1/4 cup extra-virgin olive oil
1 teaspoon wasabi paste

1 bunch watercress, washed and stems removed
Coarse salt, to taste

**Monday Thru
Friday Dinner
Specials**
• • • • •

Quarter potatoes and place in a medium saucepan, cover with water and bring to a boil over high heat. Boil until just tender, about 10 minutes. Drain and return to warm saucepan. Drizzle potatoes with a touch of oil and let stand 5 minutes in warm pot to dry them out.

Transfer cooked potatoes to a bowl. Combine yogurt, oil and wasabi paste and pour over potatoes. Coarsely chop the leafy tops of watercress and add to the mixing bowl with potatoes. Sprinkle with a little coarse salt and toss to coat evenly. Adjust salt to taste and serve.

Green Bean Salad with Red Onion and Tomato

MAKES 4 SERVINGS

1 pound fresh green beans, washed and trimmed
1/4 medium red onion, sliced thin
1/4 European cucumber, cut into thin sticks (green-bean size)
1/2 pint grape tomatoes, halved
Extra-virgin olive oil, for drizzling
The juice of 1/2 lemon
Coarse salt and freshly ground black pepper

Steam green beans in 1/2-inch boiling water, covered, for 3 or 4 minutes. Cold shock beans by running under cold water and drain well. Place beans in a bowl and combine with onions, cucumber, and tomato. Dress with a generous drizzle of olive oil and lemon juice. Season with coarse salt and pepper to taste.

MENU

1

Smoky Orange
Barbecued
Chicken
Sandwiches

· · · · ·

2

Red Cabbage
and Beet Slaw
Salad
with Currant
Dressing

· · · · ·

3

Crispy-Topped
Baked Beans
with Bacon

· · · · ·

Smoky Orange Barbecued Chicken Sandwiches

MAKES 4 SERVINGS

1 tablespoon olive or vegetable oil (once around the pan), plus some for drizzling

1 small onion, chopped

2 chipotle peppers (smoky hot peppers) in adobo sauce (found in cans in Mexican foods section)

1/2 cup ketchup (eyeball it)

1/4 cup orange juice concentrate

The zest of 1 orange, wedge the orange (after peeling), for garnish

1 cup chicken broth

4 pieces boneless, skinless chicken breasts (6 to 8 ounces each)

Vegetable oil, for drizzling

Steak seasoning blend such as Montreal Seasoning by McCormick OR salt and pepper to taste

TOPPINGS

Romaine lettuce

Thinly sliced red onions

4 crusty rolls, split, toasted and buttered

Preheat a grill pan over medium-high heat.

Heat a small saucepan over moderate heat. Add oil and sauté onion 3 to 5 minutes or until soft. Combine chipotle peppers in adobo, ketchup, orange juice concentrate, orange zest and chicken broth in a blender. Blend on high until sauce is smooth. Pour sauce into saucepan with the onion and heat to a bubble. Reduce heat to simmer.

Coat chicken lightly with a drizzle of oil and season with grill seasoning blend or salt and pepper. Grill 5 to 6 minutes on the first side, turn. Remove half of the barbecue sauce to a small bowl and baste chicken liberally with it. Turn chicken after 4 minutes, coat with sauce again and cook another 2 to 3 minutes.

To serve sandwiches, slice grilled chicken on an angle and fan out 1 breast on each bun bottom. Spoon remaining sauce from saucepan over the sliced chicken. Serve open faced with the lettuce and red onions setting on bun tops to the side. Garnish with orange wedges.

Red Cabbage and Beet Slaw Salad with Currant Dressing

MAKES 4 SERVINGS

1 pound red cabbage, trimmed of core, then shredded with knife
1 can sliced beets, drained and sliced into sticks (julienned)
1 cup walnut pieces
1/4 cup dried currants (a couple handfuls)
1/2 cup water
The juice of 1 lemon
1/4 cup apple cider or white vinegar
3 tablespoons brown sugar
1/2 cup prepared red currant jelly
1/2 cup extra-virgin olive oil or vegetable oil
Salt and freshly ground black pepper, to taste

Combine cabbage and beets in a salad bowl, and sprinkle with walnuts. Bring the following ingredients to a simmer in a small pot: currants, water, lemon juice, vinegar and brown sugar. Simmer 5 minutes, stirring to dissolve sugar and transfer mixture to a bowl. Whisk in currant jelly and oil. Pour dressing over your slaw salad. Add salt and pepper and toss to coat evenly with dressing. Adjust seasonings and serve, or chill and store up to 3 days.

Crispy-Topped Baked Beans with Bacon

MAKES UP TO 6 SERVINGS

6 slices bacon, chopped
1 cup plain bread crumbs
4 scallions, thinly sliced
Coarse freshly ground black pepper, to taste
2 cans (15 ounces each) barbecued baked beans

Preheat oven to 425°F.

In a medium skillet over medium-high heat, brown bacon but do not fully crisp. Remove the skillet from heat and toss bread crumbs in with the bacon and drippings. Add scallions and season with cracked black pepper.

Add barbecued beans or extra spicy beans to a shallow casserole dish. Top with bread crumb mixture and, bake 15 minutes or until top is crispy and beans are bubbly.

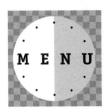

1

**Grilled Honey
Lime Chicken
Sandwiches
with
Flavored
Tortilla Chips**

· · · · ·

2

**Mexican
Chunk
Vegetable
Salad**

· · · · ·

Mexican Chunk Vegetable Salad

MAKES 4 SERVINGS

2 vine-ripe tomatoes, seeded and chopped

1/3 European seedless cucumber, cut into bite-sized chunks

1/2 medium red onion, chopped

1 medium bell pepper, red or green, cut into bite-sized chunks

2 ribs celery, chopped

1 jalapeño, seeded and finely chopped

2 tablespoons cilantro or fresh flat-leaf parsley, chopped

2 teaspoons hot sauce, such as Tabasco (several drops)

The juice of 2 limes

2 tablespoons extra-virgin olive oil (eyeball it)

Salt and freshly ground black pepper, to taste

Combine vegetables in a bowl. Sprinkle with chopped cilantro or parsley. Dress salad with hot sauce, lime juice, and olive oil. Season with salt and pepper. Toss salad and adjust seasonings, to taste.

Grilled Honey Lime Chicken Sandwiches with Flavored Tortilla Chips

MAKES 4 SERVINGS

The juice of 1 lime

2 tablespoons honey (a healthy drizzle)

1 rounded teaspoon cumin (1/3 palmful)

A handful cilantro, finely chopped (about 1 & 1/2 tablespoons)

2 tablespoons extra-virgin olive oil, canola or corn oil (a glug)

4 pieces boneless skinless chicken breasts (6 to 8 ounces each)

1 teaspoon steak seasoning blend such as Montreal Seasoning by McCormick OR salt and pepper, to taste

TOPPINGS

Lettuce, sliced tomato, red onion and avocado

1 cup prepared salsa verde

4 crusty rolls, split

Assorted flavored tortilla chips, such as black bean, red corn, blue corn or chili lime chips

Combine first 5 ingredients in a small bowl to make dressing. Sprinkle chicken with seasoning blend or salt and pepper. Coat chicken in dressing and set aside for 10 minutes.

Grill chicken on an indoor electric grill, 6 to 7 minutes on each side or pan-fry over medium-high heat in a large nonstick skillet, uncovered, 6 minutes per side.

Slice grilled chicken on an angle and pile on roll bottoms. Top with lettuce, tomato, red onion and sliced avocado. Spread salsa on roll tops. Serve with Mexican Chunk Vegetable Salad, and assorted tortilla chips.

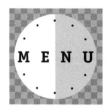

1

Herb and
Goat Cheese
Toasts
· · · · ·

2

Grilled
Balsamic
Chicken Cutlets
over
Spinach Salad
with Warm
Shallot
Vinaigrette
· · · · ·

Herb and Goat Cheese Toasts

MAKES 4 SERVINGS

1 baguette, sliced
Fresh flat-leaf parsley (2 handfuls of leaves)
12 blades fresh chives
2 sprigs fresh rosemary, leaves stripped from stem
Coarse freshly ground black pepper
8 ounces fresh goat cheese

Arrange baguette slices on a cookie sheet or broiler pan. Toast under broiler until lightly golden on each side. Remove and arrange on a serving plate. Chop and combine fresh chives, rosemary and parsley. Add coarse black pepper to the herb mixture, then roll goat cheese in the herbs to coat evenly. Set alongside toasts to serve, using a butter knife to spread herbed cheese on warm toasts.

Grilled Balsamic Chicken Cutlets over Spinach Salad with Warm Shallot Vinaigrette

MAKES 4 SERVINGS

1 & 1/2 pounds (8 pieces) chicken breast cutlets (sometimes marked "thin cut")
2 tablespoons balsamic vinegar, enough to just coat the breast slices
3 tablespoons extra-virgin olive oil (eyeball it)
Steak seasoning blend such as Montreal Seasoning by McCormick OR salt and pepper to taste
4 sprigs fresh rosemary, stripped and finely chopped (about 2 tablespoons)

SPINACH SALAD
1 pound center-cut bacon, chopped into 1-inch pieces
1 pound fresh spinach leaves, trimmed and cleaned
8 gourmet white stuffing mushrooms, thinly sliced
8 radishes, thinly sliced
4 scallions, thinly sliced on an angle
Salt and freshly ground black pepper, to taste

DRESSING
2/3 cup extra-virgin olive oil (eyeball the amount)
1 large shallot, minced
3 rounded teaspoonfuls Dijon mustard
3 tablespoons balsamic vinegar

Coat chicken with vinegar, oil, seasonings, and rosemary and set aside.

In a skillet, add chopped bacon (work in two batches if preparing salad for four). Brown over medium-high heat, then transfer the bits to a paper towel-lined plate to drain. (Using center-cut bacon will cut down on the pan drippings that spatter.)

Coarsely chop spinach leaves and add to salad bowl. Top with mushrooms, radishes, and scallions. Season with salt and pepper.

Preheat another large nonstick skillet over medium-high heat for the chicken.

For your dressing, wipe out the bacon pan and return to stove over medium-low heat. Add oil and shallots and sauté, 3 minutes. Remove from heat.

In a bowl, combine mustard and balsamic vinegar. Stream in shallot oil slowly while whisking the dressing to emulsify it. Pour warm dressing over spinach salad and toss to coat evenly. Add cooked bacon and toss again.

Cook chicken cutlets, 4 minutes on each side, in a single layer in the preheated nonstick skillet. Before serving, slice breasts on an angle. Then, pile spinach salad onto dinner plates and top each salad with 2 sliced cutlets.

Turkey Cutlets with Rosemary and Corn-Meal-Dusted Ravioli

MAKES 4 SERVINGS

RAVIOLI

1 package (12 to 14 ounces) fresh ravioli, either filled with cheese, spinach and cheese, or mushroom and cheese (found on dairy aisle of most markets)

Salt, to taste

1 cup corn meal (eyeball it)

1/4 cup Parmigiano Reggiano or Romano grated cheese (a couple handfuls)

1/2 teaspoon nutmeg, freshly grated or ground

1/2 teaspoon freshly ground black pepper

2 tablespoons extra-virgin olive oil (twice around the pan)

1 tablespoon butter

TURKEY CUTLETS

1 & 1/3 pounds turkey cutlets (available pre-wrapped in poultry case)

2 tablespoons fresh rosemary, chopped, the yield of a few sprigs, stripped

Salt and coarse freshly ground black pepper

A few sprigs of fresh bay leaves, 1 for each cutlet, (available in produce herb section), or, small dried bay leaves

2 to 3 tablespoons extra-virgin olive oil (twice around the pan)

The zest and juice of 2 lemons

1 cup dry white wine or dry vermouth

1 tablespoon butter

Place a large pot of water to boil over high heat and cover. When it comes to a boil, add a healthy dose of salt and cook ravioli to package directions for al dente.

Pour corn meal onto a plate and combine with grated cheese, then mix in nutmeg and black pepper.

Heat a medium nonstick skillet over moderate heat and add oil and butter. Drain ravioli. Dust hot ravioli in corn meal on the plate, then add to the skillet and brown on both sides, 3 or 4 minutes total. Set aside.

While pasta is cooking, preheat a large skillet for turkey cutlets over medium to medium-high heat.

Season cutlets with chopped rosemary, salt and pepper. Choose small fresh or dried bay leaves or halve large leaves with kitchen scissors. Press a small bay leaf or half leaf into each turkey cutlet. Add olive oil to the pan, then the cutlets, bay leaf side down. Sauté in a single layer, working in 2 batches if necessary, 4 or 5 minutes on each side. Transfer to a warm plate. Add the lemon zest and juice to the pan and deglaze with wine or vermouth, pulling up any pan drippings with a whisk. Add a pat of butter, whisk it in and pour the sauce down over the cutlets. Serve alongside the fried ravioli with cooked broccoli rabe or a green tossed salad.

Broccoli Rabe with Golden Raisins

MAKES 4 SERVINGS

2 tablespoons extra-virgin olive oil (twice around the pan)
1 small onion, chopped
1/4 cup golden raisins (a couple handfuls)
1 & 1/2 pounds fresh broccoli rabe, trimmed and coarsely chopped
Salt, to taste
1 can (14 ounces) chicken broth or 2 cups water

Heat a deep skillet over medium heat. Add oil and onions and cook 3 minutes. Add raisins and broccoli rabe, and season with salt. Add broth or water, and bring to a bubble, then reduce heat to simmer. Cover the pan and cook broccoli rabe 12 minutes or until tender and no longer bitter. Remove lid and allow liquid to reduce by half, 2 or 3 minutes. Transfer cooked broccoli rabe and plumped raisins to a serving dish.

Warm Cherry, Orange, and Cranberry Compote with Vanilla Ice Cream

MAKES 4 SERVINGS

1 can (15 ounces) pitted cherries
The zest and juice of 1 orange
1/4 cup dried, sweetened cranberries
1 pint vanilla ice cream
Ginger snaps, vanilla wafers or cinnamon sugar cookies, to garnish

In a microwave-safe bowl, combine cherries and their juice, orange zest and juice and the dried, sweetened cranberries. Loosely cover dish with plastic wrap and microwave on high, 1 minute.

Stir fruit, and microwave 1 minute longer. Let fruit stand 5 minutes, then spoon over scoops of vanilla ice cream. Garnish with ginger snaps, vanilla wafers or cinnamon sugar cookies.

TIDBIT

❝ The compote may also be prepared on a conventional stove top. Combine ingredients in a small saucepan and simmer over low heat, 7 or 8 minutes or until cranberries plump. ❞

MENU

1

Rio Grande
Spice Rub
Strip Steaks
• • • • •

2

Cracked Corn
and Cheese
Squares
• • • • •

3

Mexican Fiesta
Salad
• • • • •

Rio Grande Spice Rub Strip Steaks

MAKES 4 SERVINGS

4 sirloin strip steaks, 1-inch thick (8 to 10 ounces each)
1 & 1/2 tablespoons ground ancho chili or dark chili powder (a palmful)
1 & 1/2 tablespoons ground cumin (a palmful)
1 teaspoon ground coriander
1/2 teaspoon ground cayenne pepper
1 large red onion, cut into 4 thick slices
Extra-virgin olive or vegetable oil, to coat onion
Salt and freshly ground black pepper

Remove steaks from refrigerator and let them rest for a few minutes to take the chill off.

Preheat grill pan or indoor electric grill to high heat. Combine spice rub ingredients: ground ancho chili, cumin, coriander, and cayenne, and rub well into steaks.

Coat red onion slices in a drizzle of oil. Season with salt and pepper.

Grill steaks and onion slices, 5 minutes on each side. Remove from heat. Let meat stand 5 minutes for juices to redistribute. Season with salt. Top with separated rings of grilled onions. Serve with hot Cracked Corn and Cheese Squares and Mexican Fiesta Salad.

TIDBIT

❝ Make 4X the rub recipe and store the extra in your pantry (airtight container) for up to 6 months. Try the rub on chicken and jumbo shrimp, too! ❞

**Monday Thru
Friday Dinner
Specials**
• • • • •
78

Cracked Corn and Cheese Squares

MAKES 6 SQUARES

1 package (8 & 1/2 ounces) corn muffin mix, mixed to package directions
Softened butter, to grease baking dish
1/3 pound Monterey Jack cheese or Pepper Jack cheese, cut into
   1/4-inch dice
1/2 cup frozen corn kernels
1 scallion, thinly sliced

Preheat oven to 400°F. Grease an 8" square baking dish with butter. In a mixing
bowl, stir cheese, corn, and scallions into corn muffin batter. Pour batter into
baking dish and bake until golden, 15 to 18 minutes.

Mexican Fiesta Salad

MAKES 4 SERVINGS

2 ripe avocados
3 vine-ripe tomatoes
1/2 sweet onion, sliced
Chopped cilantro (about 2 tablespoons)
2 limes, halved
Coarse salt
Extra-virgin olive oil, for drizzling

Cut avocados in half, working around the pit. Separate the 2 halves. Remove pit
and carefully scoop out avocado halves with a spoon. Cut avocados into
wedges and pile in the center of a large platter. Seed and wedge tomatoes and
arrange around the avocados. Arrange sliced onion over platter and sprinkle all
with cilantro. Squeeze the juice of 2 limes evenly over vegetables. Season with
coarse salt, drizzle with oil and serve.

MENU

1

**Tuscan-Style
Grilled Tuna
Steaks**

• • • • •

2

**Grilled Stuffed
Portobellos
with
Tomatoes,
Rosemary,
and Smoked
Mozzarella**

• • • • •

Tuscan-Style Grilled Tuna Steaks

MAKES 4 SERVINGS

4 fresh tuna steaks (8 ounces each) 1-inch thick
The zest of 1 lemon
3 sprigs fresh rosemary, leaves stripped from stem (about 2 tablespoons)
A handful fresh flat-leaf parsley leaves
3 cloves garlic, crushed
Steak seasoning blend such as Montreal Seasoning by McCormick OR
    coarse salt and freshly ground black pepper, to taste
Extra-virgin olive oil, a generous drizzle

Rinse and pat tuna steaks dry. Zest the lemon using the finest side of a hand or box grater over a cutting board. Pile rosemary and parsley leaves on top of zest. Pile garlic and some grill seasoning or coarse salt and black pepper on top of herbs. Mill the garlic, herbs, and spices with your knife into a finely chopped mixture. Drizzle olive oil over the tuna steaks, just enough to coat each side. Rub herb and garlic mixture into fish, coating pieces evenly on each side. Let stand 10 minutes.

Grill tuna steaks 2 to 3 minutes on each side if you prefer your tuna pink at the center, 5 minutes per side for well done. Cook steaks over high setting on indoor electric grill, medium-high heat on outdoor gas grill, or 6 inches from hot, prepared charcoal. Serve with grilled stuffed portobello caps, and mixed green salad dressed with oil and vinegar.

Grilled Stuffed Portobellos with Tomatoes, Rosemary, and Smoked Mozzarella

MAKES 4 SERVINGS

2 tablespoons balsamic vinegar (eyeball it)

The juice of 1 large lemon

2 teaspoons Worcestershire sauce (several drops)

2 tablespoons extra-virgin olive oil (a couple of glugs)

4 medium to large portobello mushroom caps

Steak seasoning blend such as Montreal Seasoning by McCormick OR coarse salt and freshly ground black pepper, to taste

3 large, firm plum tomatoes, seeded and diced

2 sprigs fresh rosemary, stripped from stem and finely chopped (about 2 tablespoons)

A drizzle of extra-virgin olive oil

Salt and freshly ground black pepper

1/2 pound fresh smoked mozzarella, thinly sliced

Combine first 4 ingredients in a bowl or large food storage plastic bag. Coat mushroom caps evenly in marinade.

Place mushroom caps on the grill cap-side-up and season with grill seasoning blend or salt and pepper. For an indoor tabletop electric grill, preheat to 400°F or "high" setting. If you are using an outdoor gas grill, preheat to medium-high; for a charcoal grill, prepare coals and cook mushrooms 6 inches from hot coals. Cook mushrooms covered or under foil tent and turn occasionally. They will need 4 to 6 minutes on each side.

Combine tomatoes and rosemary. Drizzle with oil, season with salt and pepper, and toss.

Uncover mushrooms and turn capside-down, then fill caps with tomato mixture and top with sliced smoked mozzarella. The mushrooms will look like small pizzas. Close grill lid or replace foil tent over mushrooms to melt cheese, about 1 to 3 minutes. Serve as is, or place stuffed caps on garlic toast or sliced crusty bread to catch the juices.

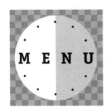

M E N U

1

**Spinach and
Mushroom
Lasagna
Roll-ups with
Gorgonzola
Cream Sauce**

· · · · ·

2

**Steamed
Asparagus Tips**

· · · · ·

3

**Broiled
Tomatoes**

· · · · ·

Spinach and Mushroom Lasagna Roll-ups with Gorgonzola Cream Sauce

MAKES 4 SERVINGS

2 tablespoons extra-virgin olive oil (twice around the pan), plus extra for drizzling

16 crimini mushroom caps, cleaned with a damp towel and finely chopped in food processor

1 small yellow onion, finely chopped

2 cloves garlic, minced

Salt and freshly ground black pepper, to taste

1 package (10-ounce) frozen chopped spinach, defrosted and squeezed dry

1/4 teaspoon freshly grated or ground nutmeg (eyeball the amount)

2 cups part-skim ricotta cheese

8 curly-edge lasagna noodles, cooked al dente (12 to 14 minutes)*

1 cup fat-free chicken broth

8 ounces gorgonzola cheese, crumbled

1/2 cup heavy cream (3 times around the pan)

1 to 1 & 1/2 cups shredded mozzarella cheese

Steamed Asparagus Tips

1 & 1/2 pounds asparagus, trimmed

*TIMING NOTE: While you boil your lasagna noodles, place fresh asparagus tips in a small colander over the boiling water in the pasta pot. Place a lid on the colander and steam asparagus, while you are cooking your pasta, for 4 minutes or until tips are just tender. Set aside and keep warm while rolling up the lasagna.

In a medium skillet over moderate heat, sauté mushrooms bits, chopped onion and garlic in oil until mushrooms give off their juices and darken, and onions are tender, about 7 or 8 minutes. Season with salt and pepper; the salt will help draw water out of veggies as they cook. Add dry chopped spinach to the pan and heat through for 1 minute. Adjust salt and pepper and season mixture with a little nutmeg. Add ricotta and stir 1 minute longer. Remove pan from heat but leave veggies and cheese in the warm skillet while you are rolling the lasagna.

Heat broth in a small pan over moderate heat. Melt gorgonzola cheese into broth and bring to a bubble. Add cream and stir to thicken sauce, 2 minutes.

Place cooked lasagna noodles on a large work surface. Spread each noodle with a layer of spinach mushroom filling. Roll up and arrange the 8 lasagna bundles in a shallow casserole dish. Pour warm sauce over roll-ups and top with mozzarella. Place casserole under broiler to melt cheese alongside the dish with the Broiled Tomatoes.

Broiled Tomatoes

4 vine-ripe tomatoes
Fresh herbs, **basil, thyme or rosemary**

Split tomatoes across the center and drizzle with olive oil, salt, and pepper. Broil tomatoes alongside your lasagna casserole. Top with any fresh herb available.

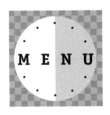

1

Spaghetti alla
Carbonara:
Bacon and Egg
"Coal Miner's"
Pasta

· · · · ·

2

Sugared Stone
Fruits with
Cookies and
Cream

· · · · ·

Spaghetti alla Carbonara:
Bacon and Egg "Coal Miner's" Pasta

MAKES 4 GENEROUS SERVINGS

1 pound spaghetti
Salt

A drizzle, plus 2 tablespoons extra-virgin olive oil (twice around the pan)
1/3 pound pancetta, chopped (Italian meat, available at deli counter)
4 or 5 cloves garlic, finely chopped
1/4 to 1/2 teaspoon crushed red pepper flakes, a few pinches, crushed
   in palm of hand
1/2 cup dry white wine or chicken stock
2 large egg yolks OR 1/2 pint container pasteurized egg product
1/4 cup boiling pasta water
1/4 cup grated Parmigiano Reggiano cheese (2 handfuls) plus extra, for
   passing at the table
A handful fresh parsley leaves, finely chopped
Coarse salt, to taste
Several grinds of black pepper

Place a large pot of water on the stove, and when it comes to a rolling boil, add
salt and pasta and cook to al dente, about 7 to 8 minutes.

Meanwhile, heat a large skillet over moderate heat. Sauté pancetta in a drizzle of
oil until it browns, 3 to 5 minutes. Add 2 tablespoons olive oil, garlic and crushed
pepper flakes and sauté, 2 minutes. Add wine or stock to the pan and reduce liquid by half, about 1 minute.

Beat together egg yolks or egg product, and while whisking vigorously stir in a
ladle of the boiling pasta water.

Drain pasta, and add pasta to pan with pancetta and garlic and remove from
heat. Add egg mixture, cheese, parsley, salt, black pepper and toss 2 minutes
until sauce is absorbed and thickly coating the pasta. Adjust seasonings and
serve immediately with extra cheese.

Sugared Stone Fruits with Cookies and Cream

MAKES 4 SERVINGS

3 **ripe** apricots
2 **ripe** plums
2 **ripe** peaches
2 **tablespoons** sugar
1 **cup** heavy cream
12 sugar cookies, **Nilla Wafers or ginger snaps, crumbled**

To prepare fruits, section into wedges slicing down to the pits. Pull wedges away from pits, combine in a bowl and toss with 2 tablespoons sugar. Set aside or cover and chill until ready to serve.

To serve, spoon fruits into dessert bowls, pour 1/4 cup heavy cream over each serving, and top with crumbled sugar cookies, Nilla Wafers or ginger snaps.

M E N U

**Backyard
Picnic**

1

**Honey
Mustard
Barbecued
Chicken**
• • • • •

2

**Butter Bean
Salad**
• • • • •

3

**Corn on the
Cob with Chili
and Lime**
• • • • •

4

**Fluffernutter
Brownies**
• • • • •

Honey Mustard Barbecued Chicken

MAKES 4 SERVINGS

SAUCE
2 tablespoons vegetable oil (eyeball it)
1/2 red onion, chopped
1/4 cup apple cider vinegar
1/4 cup brown sugar (a couple handfuls)
1 cup chicken stock
1/2 cup prepared honey mustard, such as Honey Cup brand
1/2 teaspoon allspice (eyeball it)
1/2 teaspoon curry powder (eyeball it)

CHICKEN
4 pieces boneless, skinless chicken breast (6 to 8 ounces each)
4 boneless, skinless chicken thighs
Vegetable oil, for drizzling
Salt and freshly ground black pepper

Preheat grill pan or griddle over medium-high heat.

Add vegetable oil to a small saucepan over moderate heat. Add red onions and sauté, 3 to 5 minutes. Add vinegar and reduce by half, 1 minute or 2. Add brown sugar and cook 1 minute to incorporate. Whisk in stock and honey mustard, allspice, and curry powder. Bring sauce to a bubble and reduce heat to lowest setting.

Coat chicken with a drizzle of oil and salt and pepper, to taste. Place chicken on hot grill and cook 4 to 5 minutes, then turn. Baste chicken liberally with sauce and grill another 5 minutes. Turn once again and baste. Cook 2 or 3 minutes more, then transfer chicken to a platter and serve.

Butter Bean Salad

MAKES 4 SERVINGS

2 cans (15 ounces each) butter beans, rinsed and drained
1/2 red bell pepper, diced
1/2 green bell pepper, diced
1/4 red onion, chopped
2 cloves garlic, peeled and minced
1 teaspoon ground cumin (1/3 palmful)
2 tablespoons extra-virgin olive oil (a glug)
The juice of 1 large lemon
Coarse salt and freshly ground black pepper, to taste

Combine all ingredients in a medium bowl. Toss to coat beans and vegetables evenly in dressing.

Corn on the Cob with Chili and Lime

MAKES 4 SERVINGS

4 ears sweet corn, shucked and cleaned
1 lime, cut into wedges
1/3 stick butter, cut into pats
Chili powder, for sprinkling
Salt, to taste

In a medium pot, bring water to a boil, and simmer corn, 3 to 5 minutes. Drain and arrange the ears on a shallow plate in a single row. Squeeze lime juice liberally over all the ears. Nest pats of butter into paper towels and rub lime-doused hot corn with butter. Season with a sprinkle of chili powder and salt, and serve immediately.

Fluffernutter Brownies

MAKES 12 BROWNIES

1 package chocolate brownie mix, prepared to package directions
1 cup peanut butter chips
Softened butter, for greasing your baking dish
1 package (2 ounces) chopped nuts (available on baking aisle)
1 cup mini-marshmallows

Preheat oven to 425°F.

To mixed brownie batter, stir in peanut butter chips. Grease an 8 x 8 baking dish with softened butter and spread the brownies into an even layer. Sprinkle with chopped nuts and bake, 20 to 22 minutes total, removing the dish momentarily to scatter marshmallows on top for the last 3 to 5 minutes of baking time. Remove from oven and cut into 12 brownies.

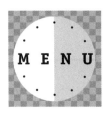

MENU

1

**Maple Mustard
Pork Chops
with Grilled
Apples**

· · · · ·

2

**Mom's Oil and
Vinegar Potato
Salad and
3 Bean Salad**

· · · · ·

3

**Fruit and
Cheese Board**

· · · · ·

Maple Mustard Pork Chops with Grilled Apples

MAKES 4 SERVINGS

1/2 cup dark amber maple syrup

4 tablespoons spicy brown mustard (1/4 cup)

1/4 cup apple cider

1/4 medium onion, finely chopped

1/2 teaspoon allspice (eyeball it in your hand)

1 teaspoon ground cumin (1/3 palmful)

8 center-cut boneless pork loin chops, 1/2 to 3/4-inch thick

Extra-virgin olive oil, for drizzling

Grill seasoning blend such as Montreal Seasoning by McCormick OR
  salt and pepper to taste

3 Golden Delicious apples, sliced across into 1/2-inch rounds, with core
  and peel intact

The juice of 1/2 lemon

1/2 teaspoon freshly grated or ground nutmeg

Preheat grill or nonstick griddle pan over medium-high heat, or preheat electric table top grill to high. Also preheat oven to 350°F.

Combine maple syrup, mustard, cider, onion, allspice and cumin in a small saucepan and cook over moderate heat, 7 to 10 minutes, until sauce begins to thicken a bit.

Coat chops lightly in oil, season with grill seasoning blend or salt and pepper, and cook on the grill pan of your choice, 3 minutes on each side. Baste chops liberally with sauce and cook, 2 or 3 minutes more, then transfer to a baking sheet. Baste again with sauce and place in a hot oven to finish cooking them. Bake 10 to 12 minutes, until your apples are ready to come off the grill pan.

Coat apple rounds with lemon juice and a drizzle of oil. Season with grill season-ing or salt and pepper and a little nutmeg. Cover grill pan surface with as many pieces of apple as possible. As the apples get tender, remove and replace with remaining slices. Apples should cook 3 minutes on each side, as you don't want them too soft, just tender.

Serve chops with apples alongside.

Mom's Oil and Vinegar Potato Salad and 3 Bean Salad

MAKES 6 SERVINGS of each salad

POTATO SALAD
16 new red potatoes
Coarse salt
1 red bell pepper, seeded and chopped
1/2 medium red onion, chopped.
1/4 cup chopped fresh mint (a couple handfuls)
1/4 cup chopped fresh flat-leaf parsley (a couple handfuls)
3 tablespoons red wine vinegar (eyeball the amount)
1/3 cup extra-virgin olive oil (eyeball the amount)
Salt and freshly ground black pepper

3 BEAN SALAD
1/2 pound fresh green beans, cut into thirds
2 rounded teaspoons Dijon mustard
2 tablespoons sugar
1/4 cup red wine vinegar (eyeball the amount)
1/2 cup extra-virgin olive oil (eyeball the amount)
1 can (15 ounces) red kidney beans, drained
1 can (15 ounces) garbanzo beans, drained
1/4 cup chopped fresh flat-leaf parsley
Salt and freshly ground black pepper, to taste

Put red potatoes in a pot, cover with water, replace lid, and bring to a boil over medium-high heat. Then add a liberal amount of coarse salt. Place a colander over boiling pot. Take your first ingredient from the bean salad, the fresh green beans, and place them in the colander. Cover with pot lid and steam beans, 5 minutes, while potatoes boil below. Remove beans and cold shock under running water, drain well and set aside.

When the potatoes are just tender, about 12 minutes, remove from heat, drain and cold shock them until just cool enough to handle. Coarsely chop and return them to the warm pot. Add bell pepper, onion, mint, parsley, and vinegar to the pot and toss to allow the potatoes to absorb the vinegar. Add oil and stir the potatoes until they mash up a bit and salad has a spoonable consistency. Season with salt and pepper, to taste and transfer to a serving bowl.

In another serving bowl, combine mustard, sugar and vinegar. Whisk in oil. Add kidney beans, garbanzo beans, steamed green beans and parsley and toss to coat Season with salt and pepper and serve.

TIDBIT

❝ Leftovers of either salad only get tastier. ❞

Monday Thru Friday Dinner Specials
•••••

Fruit and Cheese Board

MAKES 6 SERVINGS

1/2 pound Havarti cheese with dill
1/2 pound sharp cheddar cheese
1/2 pound spiced cheese, such as Leyden (gouda with cumin)
1 pound red seedless grapes
1 pound green seedless grapes
2 ripe pears, any variety
1 box water crackers, plain or your favorite flavor

Arrange cheese and fruits on a cutting board with a cheese knife. Cut a few slices of each cheese from bricks and fan out.

FAMILY-STYLE SUPPERS

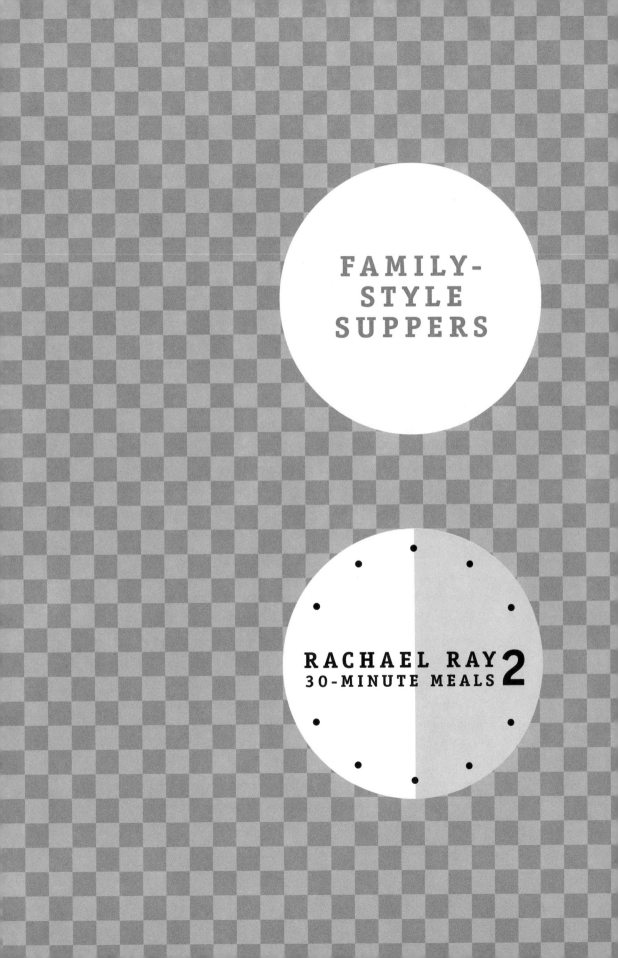

RACHAEL RAY
30-MINUTE MEALS 2

My family taught me about life through food. I remember working with my mother in the kitchen from the time I was very small. Elsa, my Mama, the eldest of 10, cooked like her Daddy. Today, I cook as she did for me. Now I make recipes that tie together three generations, and when I smell familiar foods simmering on my stove top, I am not alone.

One of my oldest and certainly dearest friends, Vicky, was helping me prepare materials for a 30-Minute Mediterranean meal cooking class that I was going to teach. My first class, ever. I had a recipe for caponata, an eggplant dish. My recipe was Mama's who learned how to make caponata from her dad, my Grandpa Emmanuel. My recipe had: eggplant, garlic, peppers, onions, olives, capers, a little tomato, parsley, hot pepper flakes, golden raisins for sweetness and toasted pine nuts. Vicky's mom, Gilda, put in sugar and vinegar, as many families do. Just not my family. When Vicky saw that I had "forgotten" the sugar and vinegar, she came right up to me and pointed it out, firmly. I explained, extra-firmly, that in my family, we do not, nor will I be the first, to add sugar and vinegar to our caponata. She pointed out that I could be wrong, and I was. No! She was wrong! We can make it any way we want! And ours is good! No, GREAT! As is! We both started to cry: big, puffy-eyed crying with exaggerated breathing. Drama! It was in that moment that we recognized something very familiar in one another. We hugged out of respect for the fact that we were both so passionate about food and family. We went out to share a drink that night and we've been family to each other ever since. I love you, Vick.

Food can be a scrapbook of your life and times. Recipes can tie you to your past and help you take root in the present, if you take at least 30 minutes to cook!

Emmanuel's Baked Artichoke Hearts

My Grandpa made so many wonderful dishes but an all-time favorite were his stuffed artichokes; they look like huge Christmas stars, fitting for the time of year we usually ate them. My brother, his namesake, makes them for the family. Mom does too, on occasion, but they take a while; you have to trim and remove the chokes from HUGE artichokes, boil them with lemons, drain them, then make the stuffing, stuff each and every leaf, then bake them—WHOA! I can't find the time to do all that! In this menu, I take the same stuffing, make a small amount and top artichoke hearts with it, then bake the dish just long enough to brown the topping. DONE! I think Grandpa would approve.

MAKES 4 SERVINGS

2 cans (15 ounces each) artichoke hearts in water, 6 to 8 count, drained
1 tablespoon extra-virgin olive oil (twice around the pan), plus a drizzle
   to coat baking dish
1/4 lemon
1 tablespoon butter
3 cloves garlic, chopped
6 anchovy fillets
1 cup Italian-style bread crumbs (3 handfuls)
1/4 cup chopped fresh flat-leaf parsley
1/4 cup grated Parmigiano Reggiano (a couple handfuls)
Coarse freshly ground black pepper

Preheat oven to 400°F.

Turn drained artichokes upside down to get all the liquid out, and cut them in half lengthwise. Drizzle a small casserole dish with a little olive oil and spread it around the dish with a pastry brush. Arrange the halved artichoke hearts with tops up, bottoms down, in a layered pattern in the dish. Squeeze the juice of 1/4 lemon over them.

Preheat a small nonstick skillet over medium heat. Add oil and butter to the skillet. When the butter melts into the oil, add garlic and anchovies. Using the back of a wooden spoon, work the anchovies into the oil as they break up. When anchovies have dissolved, add bread crumbs and lightly toast, about 2 to 3 minutes. Add parsley, cheese, and black pepper, stir to combine and remove from heat. Top artichokes with an even layer of bread topping and set in the middle of oven. Bake 10 minutes or until artichokes are warm and topping is deep golden brown.

MENU

1
Emmanuel's
Baked
Artichoke
Hearts
· · · · ·

2
Chicken
Piccata Pasta
Toss
· · · · ·

3
Quick Italian
Rum Cake
Cups
· · · · ·

TIDBIT

❝ Cooked anchovies have a wonderful nutty taste, not at all fishy, just yummy! ❞

Family-Style
Suppers
· · · · ·

Chicken Piccata Pasta Toss

Piccata is a meal with a quick cooking time, but there are times I don't feel like going through the stages of preparation: pounding out the chicken or veal cutlets, dredging and sautéing, then making the sauce, yadda, yadda, ya. This Piccata Pasta Toss offers the same flavors, but it's made like a stir-fry. Also, its not as rich as regular piccata because the sauce is based in chicken stock, not butter.

MAKES 4 SERVINGS

1 pound penne rigate pasta, cooked al dente to package directions
2 tablespoons extra-virgin olive oil (twice around the pan)
1 & 1/4 pounds chicken tenders, cut into 1-inch pieces
Salt and freshly ground black pepper, to taste
2 tablespoons butter
4 cloves garlic, chopped
2 medium shallots, chopped
2 tablespoons flour
1/2 cup white wine
The juice of 1 lemon
1 cup chicken broth or stock
3 tablespoons capers, drained
1/2 cup chopped fresh flat-leaf parsley
Chopped or snipped chives, for garnish

Heat a deep nonstick skillet over medium-high heat. Add 1 tablespoon of olive oil and the chicken to the pan. Season with salt and pepper, and brown until lightly golden all over, about 5 to 6 minutes. Remove chicken from pan and set it in your serving dish while you complete the sauce. Return the skillet to the heat, reduced to medium. To the skillet, add another tablespoon olive oil, 1 tablespoon butter, the garlic and the shallots and sauté, 3 minutes. Stir in flour and cook 2 minutes. Whisk in wine and reduce liquid, 1 minute. Whisk lemon juice and broth into sauce. Stir in capers and parsley. When sauce comes to a bubble, add remaining tablespoon butter to give it a little shine. Put chicken back in the pan and heat through a minute or two. Toss hot pasta with chicken and sauce. Adjust salt and pepper to taste. Top with fresh snipped chives and serve.

Quick Italian Rum Cake Cups

This dessert is a great example of calculated cooking. I wanted to find a no-bake way of enjoying Italian rum cake. Rum cake is always my birthday cake. I love it! My family drives more than an hour each way to my favorite Italian bakery, Villa Italia, to get me a golden cake soaked in rum and layered with custard, covered with buttercream frosting and almonds. Since I cannot bake, it would be silly to attempt a project like a rum cake. But this knockoff, done in minutes, rings all of the flavor bells in my mouth and gets me through many a weeknight the rest of the year, until I can enjoy the real thing again.

MAKES 4 SERVINGS

1 package ladyfingers or 4 individual servings store-bought sponge cakes

3 ounces rum

2 cups vanilla instant pudding, prepared to package directions OR
  4 servings store-bought prepared vanilla pudding

8 large ripe strawberries, sliced

1 teaspoon sugar

1 package (2 ounces) sliced almonds (available on baking aisle of market)

Separate 8 ladyfingers or spread out 4 individual sponge cakes on a work surface. Using a pastry brush, liberally paint the cake with rum. Line small glass dessert cups or cocktail glasses with cake. Top with heaping spoonfuls of prepared vanilla instant pudding, about 1/2 cup per serving dish. Sprinkle sliced strawberries with sugar and toss to coat. Top dessert cups with sliced berries and sliced almonds and serve or refrigerate until dessert time.

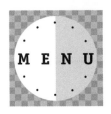

M E N U

1

Ravioli
Vegetable
"Lasagna"
· · · · ·

2

Romaine
Hearts with
Lemon Chive
Vinaigrette
· · · · ·

3

Fresh Oranges
with Lime
Sorbet
· · · · ·

Ravioli Vegetable "Lasagna"

I met a real working mom on a set for a TV commercial who shared a cooking secret. She told me that when she runs short of time, she layers red meat sauce with ravioli, like a lasagna, and adds lots of cheese on top. I thought, GREAT idea for a fast even-more-time-consuming vegetable lasagna, too!

MAKES 4 TO 6 SERVINGS

2 packages (12 ounces each) chopped frozen spinach, defrosted in microwave

2 tablespoons extra-virgin olive oil (twice around the pan)

4 to 6 cloves garlic, finely chopped

2 cans (15 ounces each) quartered artichokes in water, drained well

Salt and freshly ground black pepper, to taste

WHITE SAUCE

2 tablespoons butter

2 tablespoons flour

2 cups vegetable or chicken stock

1/2 cup cream or half-and-half

1/2 cup grated Parmigiano Reggiano cheese (a couple handfuls)

1/4 teaspoon nutmeg, freshly grated

Salt and freshly ground black pepper, to taste

1 large package (24 to 28 ounces) fresh ravioli, such as Contadina brand, in your favorite filling, such as wild mushroom or 4 cheese.

1 pound thin asparagus spears, trimmed of tough ends, cut on an angle into 2-inch pieces

2 cups shredded provolone or Italian 4-Cheese-Blend

Bring a pot of water to boil for the ravioli.

While water comes to a boil, drain defrosted frozen chopped spinach by wringing it dry in a kitchen towel, working over a garbage bowl or your sink. Heat a medium skillet over medium heat. Add the olive oil and the garlic and sauté 1 minute, then sprinkle spinach into the garlic oil. Add artichokes and turn to combine and heat through. Season with salt and pepper and remove from heat to a bowl. Place skillet back on the heat and melt butter. Whisk in flour and cook 1 minute or 2. Whisk in stock and let it bubble. Whisk in cream and Parmigiano cheese, season with nutmeg, salt and pepper and thicken 1 minute or 2.

Preheat broiler to high. Set rack about 8 inches from heat.

When water boils, add salt, then ravioli and cook, 4 to 5 minutes. (Ravioli should be less than al dente, still a bit chewy; it will continue cooking when combined with sauce and vegetables.) Place a colander over ravioli as it cooks, add asparagus and cover. Steam the chopped asparagus while pasta cooks, 2 to 3 minutes, until just fork-tender, but still green. Remove asparagus and add to bowl with spinach and artichokes. Place colander in your sink and drain ravioli.

Drizzle a touch of olive oil onto the bottom of a medium-sized oval casserole or a rectangular baking dish and brush to coat evenly. Arrange a layer of cooked ravioli, about 1/3 of the amount, in the dish. Layer half of the cooked vegetables over the ravioli. Next, add a few ladles of sauce, another layer of ravioli, then vegetables, then top casserole with the last of the ravioli. Dot top of "lasagna" with any remaining sauce and cover liberally with shredded provolone or 4-cheese blend. Brown in broiler, about 5 minutes, until cheese is golden and "lasagna" is heated through.

Romaine Hearts with Lemon Chive Vinaigrette

MAKES 4 SERVINGS

1/4 cup lemon curd
2 tablespoons white vinegar
10 blades chives, chopped or snipped
1/3 to 1/2 cup extra-virgin olive oil
Salt and freshly ground pepper, to taste
2 hearts romaine lettuce
1/2 pint grape tomatoes

In a small bowl, heat lemon curd 15 seconds in microwave. Remove from microwave and whisk in vinegar. Allow mixture to cool 2 minutes, add chives, and whisk in olive oil in a slow stream. Season with salt and pepper.

Quarter each heart of romaine lengthwise. Trim core at ends. Place 2 quarters on each salad plate. Halve a few grape tomatoes and place at plates' edges for garnish. Drizzle liberally with vinaigrette and serve.

Fresh Oranges with Lime Sorbet

MAKES 4 SERVINGS

2 large naval oranges
1 pint lime, lemon or other fruit sorbet

Trim a piece of skin off the top and bottom of each orange, then cut in half, across. Section each half as you would a grapefruit. Set oranges upright and top each half orange with sorbet. The halved, sectioned oranges double as the dessert bowls for sorbet.

1

**Roasted Garlic
and Feta
Walnut Dip
with Toasted
Flat Bread**

· · · · ·

2

Green Risotto

· · · · ·

3

**Grilled
Radicchio
Salad**

· · · · ·

Roasted Garlic and Feta Walnut Dip with Toasted Flat Bread

MAKES 4 SERVINGS

1 medium bulb garlic, end cut off, 1 large clove reserved
1 tablespoon extra-virgin olive oil, plus some for drizzling
1 cup walnut halves, toasted
1 & 1/2 cups feta cheese, crumbled
1/2 cup milk
1 teaspoon dried oregano
1/4 cup fresh flat-leaf parsley (a handful leaves)
Freshly ground black pepper
1/2 teaspoon crushed red pepper flakes
1 large clove garlic (reserved from above) cracked away from skin
4 flat breads or pitas, cut into wedges and toasted

Preheat oven or toaster oven to highest setting. Pour oil over cut side of garlic bulb and rub into skin. Double-wrap garlic in foil and roast, 25 minutes.

Combine walnuts, feta, milk, oregano, parsley, black pepper, red pepper flakes and garlic clove in food processor and pulse until smooth. Scrape into serving dish with spatula, drizzle with olive oil.

Remove garlic from the oven, and turn heat off. Arrange triangles of cut pita or flat bread on a small, heat-resistant tray or cookie sheet. Place bread into the hot oven. The bread will be warmed through and lightly toasted in 5 minutes.

Serve with feta walnut dip and soft, sweet roasted garlic for spreading.

Green Risotto

MAKES 4 SERVINGS

2 cups water
1 quart vegetable stock
2 tablespoons extra-virgin olive oil (twice around the pan)
1 tablespoon butter
1 medium onion, finely chopped
2 cups arborio rice
1/2 cup dry white wine or dry sherry
1 pound triple-washed spinach, chopped

1 cup loosely packed basil leaves, chopped or torn
1/2 cup fresh chopped flat-leaf parsley (a couple handfuls)
1/4 teaspoon nutmeg, freshly grated or ground
Coarse salt and freshly ground black pepper, to taste
1/2 to 2/3 cup grated Parmigiano Reggiano cheese (2 or 3 handfuls)

Bring 2 cups water and all of the stock to a boil, then reduce heat to low.

In a large skillet, heat oil and butter over medium to medium-high heat. Add onions and sauté, 3 minutes. Add Arborio rice and sauté, 2 or 3 minutes more. Add wine or sherry and allow liquid to absorb for 1 minute. Add half the stock or broth and reduce heat slightly. Simmer, stirring frequently, until liquid is absorbed, then add more liquid a few ladles at a time. As liquid cooks out, ladle in a bit more.

When risotto has cooked almost to al dente, about 18 minutes, fold in spinach, basil, and parsley. Season with nutmeg, salt and pepper and stir in any remaining broth. Risotto will cook for a total of 22 minutes. Stir in cheese and serve immediately.

Grilled Radicchio Salad

MAKES 4 SERVINGS

2 tablespoons extra-virgin olive oil, plus additional for drizzling
2 medium-to-large heads raddichio
Salt and freshly ground black pepper, to taste
1 can (15 ounces) sliced beets, drained
1/4 red onion, very thinly sliced
Balsamic vinegar, for drizzling (about 1 & 1/2 tablespoons)

Preheat a grill pan over high heat. Pour a couple of tablespoons of olive oil into a small dish. Slice radicchio heads into quarters and remove core. Brush each quarter with oil and grill 3 minutes or so on each side. Season with salt and pepper. Arrange grilled radicchio on a platter. Top with sliced beets, sprinkle with red onion, and drizzle with balsamic vinegar and oil. Adjust salt and pepper and serve.

MENU

1
Meatball and Macaroni Soup
·····

2
Grilled 4 Cheese Sandwiches
·····

3
Chocolate Dipped Bananas
·····

Chocolate Dipped Bananas

MAKES 8 CHOCOLATE-DIPPED BANANAS

4 bananas, cut in half across

8 popsicle sticks

4 bars good quality bittersweet chocolate (3 & 1/2 ounces each), such as Ghirardelli

TOPPINGS: USE ANY OR ALL

Chopped nuts

Toasted coconut

Cookie crumbles

Colored sprinkles or chocolate jimmies

Mini chocolate candies or mini semi-sweet chips, for chocoholics

Granola

Place banana halves on sticks. Line a cookie sheet with parchment or wax paper. Bring 2 inches of water to a boil in a saucepan. Place a metal bowl over the simmering water to melt chocolate, stirring with a rubber spatula. Dip bananas in the melted chocolate and roll in your favorite topping. Cool to room temperature on the lined cookie sheet, or chill or freeze until ready to serve.

Meatball and Macaroni Soup

MAKES 4 BIG SERVINGS

TIDBIT

❝ This is a fast version of Italian Wedding Soup, a favorite at many receptions. Broken dried pasta bits never tasted so good! ❞

2 tablespoons extra-virgin olive oil (twice around the pan)

2 carrots, peeled and chopped

2 ribs celery, chopped

1 medium onion, chopped

2 bay leaves, fresh or dried

Salt and freshly ground black pepper, to taste

1 pound ground beef, pork, and veal combined

1 egg beaten

2 cloves garlic, minced

1/2 cup grated Parmigiano Reggiano or Romano cheese (a couple handfuls)

1/2 cup plain bread crumbs (a couple handfuls)

1/2 teaspoon freshly grated or ground nutmeg

6 cups chicken stock or broth

2 cups water

1 & 1/2 cups dried pasta: rings, broken fettuccini or ditalini

1 pound triple-washed fresh spinach, coarsely chopped

Family-Style Suppers
·····

In a deep pot over medium heat, add oil, chopped carrots, celery, onions, and bay leaves. Season with salt and pepper. Cover pot and cook veggies, 5 or 6 minutes, stirring occasionally.

While the veggies cook, combine ground meats, egg, garlic, grated cheese, bread crumbs, salt, pepper, and nutmeg.

Add broth and water to the pot of veggies. Increase heat to high and bring soup to a boil, then reduce heat a bit and start to roll meat mixture into small balls, dropping them straight into the pot. When you are done rolling the meat, add pasta to the soup and stir. Cover and simmer soup, 10 minutes. When pasta is tender, stir in chopped spinach in batches. When spinach has wilted, the soup is done and ready to serve. Adjust your seasonings, and serve with crusty bread or grilled 4 cheese sandwiches.

Grilled 4 Cheese Sandwiches

MAKES 4 SANDWICHES

2 tablespoons extra-virgin olive oil (twice around the pan)
3 tablespoons butter
1 clove garlic, cracked away from the skin
8 slices crusty Italian semolina bread
1 cup shredded provolone cheese
1 cup shredded mozzarella cheese
1/2 cup grated Parmigiano Reggiano or Romano cheese
1 cup shredded Asiago cheese

TIDBIT
❝ All of these cheeses are available in specialty cheese case and dairy aisle already shredded. ❞

In a small skillet over medium-low heat combine oil, butter, and garlic, and cook gently for 2 or 3 minutes, then remove from heat.

Place a large nonstick skillet on the stove over medium-high heat. Using a pastry brush, brush one side of 4 slices of bread with garlic and butter oil and place buttered side down in skillet. Top each slice with equal amounts of the 4 cheeses, distributing them equally over the 4 slices. Top each sandwich with another slice of bread, and brush top with garlic butter. Flip the sandwiches a few times until cheeses are melted and gooey and bread is toasty and golden. Cut sandwiches from corner to corner and serve.

MENU

1

Boeuf
Bourguignon
with Butter
and Parsley
Egg Noodles
• • • • •

2

Baby Spinach
Salad with
Swiss Cheese
Crisps
• • • • •

Boeuf Bourguignon with Butter and Parsley Egg Noodles

MAKES 4 SERVINGS

This slow-cooking dish has been reinvented as a 30-minute meal by using a tender cut of meat. It is warm and comforting on a chilly day and tastes even better the next day. Those cooking for 1 or 2 should make a full recipe for leftovers.

3 slices bacon, chopped

3 tablespoons butter, divided

16 medium-sized white mushrooms, cleaned gently with damp cloth, thinly sliced

Salt and freshly ground black pepper, to taste

1 cup frozen pearl onions, defrosted and drained

2 pounds lean sirloin, 1-inch thick, trimmed and cubed

3 tablespoons flour

1 cup Burgundy wine

1 & 1/2 cups store-bought beef stock

1 bay leaf, fresh or dried

Bouquet of 3 or 4 sprigs each of fresh sage and thyme, tied with kitchen string

BUTTER AND PARSLEY EGG NOODLES

12 ounces wide egg noodles, cooked to package directions

2 tablespoons butter, cut into small pieces

1/4 cup chopped fresh parsley (2 handfuls)

12 blades of fresh chives, snipped or finely chopped

Heat a large deep skillet with a heavy bottom and a lid over medium-high heat. Add bacon to the pan and brown. When crisp, remove with slotted spoon. Add 1 & 1/2 tablespoons butter to the pan and melt into bacon drippings. Add mushrooms and turn to coat evenly with butter and bacon drippings. Season with salt and pepper and sauté mushrooms, 2 to 3 minutes. Add onions to the pan, and continue cooking, 2 to 3 minutes longer, then transfer to a plate and return pan to the heat. Add remaining butter to the pan and when it's sizzling add meat and brown evenly on all sides, keeping the meat moving. When the meat is all browned, add flour and cook about 2 minutes. Stir wine slowly into the pan and when it comes up to a bubble and you have scraped up the pan drippings, add the stock along with bay leaf and bouquet of fresh sage and thyme. Cover the pan. When the liquids boil, reduce heat to medium, and cook, covered, 5 minutes. Remove lid and add mushrooms, onions and bacon back to the pan. Simmer with the cover off until sauce thickens a bit. Adjust seasoning and remove bay and herb bouquet.

Toss hot egg noodles with butter, parsley and chives. Place a bed of noodles in a shallow bowl and pour beef and burgundy over noodles and serve.

Baby Spinach Salad with Swiss Cheese Crisps

The cheese crisps remind me of Swiss cheese bows my mom made when I was little. She would fry a slice of Swiss, scrunch it up with a spatula and pinch it in the middle to make a bow tie. She would give us these as a snack. I remember trying to make her one in our restaurant kitchen when I was 3 or 4 and she was on the telephone, distracted. Not tall enough to reach the grill, I ended up cooking my thumb instead of the cheese crisp. This is one of my first bittersweet memories of food in my life. Don't let it keep you from trying the cheese crisps. Just watch your thumbs.

MAKES 4 TO 6 SERVINGS

1 & 1/2 cups shredded Swiss cheese
1 sack (12 ounces) baby spinach or 3/4 pound from bulk bins
1 small red apple, cored and thinly sliced
1 wedge of lemon
3 or 4 sprigs fresh thyme, stripped from stems and chopped
1 rounded teaspoon Dijon mustard
1 & 1/2 tablespoons red wine vinegar (eyeball it)
1/4 to 1/3 cup extra-virgin olive oil (eyeball it)

T I D B I T

❝ Crisps may also be flavored with cracked black pepper and chopped thyme or other herbs, as the cheese melts in the skillet. ❞

Heat a nonstick skillet over medium-high heat. Add shredded Swiss in small, 1 & 1/2-inch piles to the hot skillet. When the cheese fries to a light golden color at the edges, about 2 minutes, and can be moved with a thin spatula, turn the cheese rounds, cook another 15 to 30 seconds, then remove from the skillet and transfer to a work surface to cool, in a minute or so. Repeat to form 12 to 16 crisps, 3 or 4 per salad.

Place spinach in a bowl. After slicing your apple, squeeze a wedge of lemon over the slices to keep them from browning and toss with spinach. For dressing, combine thyme, Dijon and vinegar with a whisk. Stream in olive oil while continuing to whisk dressing. Pour over the salad and toss to coat greens and apple evenly. Transfer greens to salad plates and top with Swiss crisps.

1

Everyday
Cioppino
(Fish Stew)
A Fine Kettle
of Fish

• • • • •

2

Mixed Greens
and Fennel
Salad

• • • • •

3

Nothin' to Fret
About Apple
Fritters

• • • • •

Everyday Cioppino (Fish Stew)—A Fine Kettle of Fish

MAKES 4 HEALTHY SERVINGS

1/4 cup extra-virgin olive oil (3 times around the pan)

1 teaspoon crushed red pepper flakes (eyeball the amount and crush in your palm)

1 tin flat fillets of anchovies, drained

6 cloves garlic, crushed

1 bay leaf, fresh or dried

2 ribs celery, chopped

1 medium onion, chopped

1 cup good quality dry white wine

1 container (14 ounces) chicken stock (paper container or canned such as Kitchen Basics)

1 can (28 ounces) chunky-style crushed tomatoes

4 sprigs fresh thyme, stripped (about 1 tablespoon)

A handful chopped fresh flat-leaf parsley

1 & 1/2 pounds cod, cut into 2-inch chunks

Salt and freshly ground black pepper, to taste

8 large shrimp (ask for deveined, easy-peel, or peel and devein)

8 sea scallops

16 to 20 raw mussels, scrubbed

A loaf of fresh, crusty bread, for mopping

In a large pot over moderate heat combine oil, crushed pepper, anchovies, garlic, and bay leaf. Let anchovies melt into the oil. They act as natural salt and will break up into the pepper-infused oil, providing heat in the flavor. Chop celery and onion near stove and add to the pot as you work. Sauté vegetables a couple of minutes to begin to soften and add wine to the pot. Reduce 1 minute, then add chicken stock, tomatoes, thyme, and parsley. Bring sauce to a bubble, then reduce heat to medium low. Season fish chunks with salt and pepper, add to sauce and simmer 5 minutes, giving the pot a shake now and then. (Don't stir with a spoon, you'll break the fish up). Add shrimp, scallops, and mussels and cover pot. Cook 10 minutes, giving the pot an occasional good shake. Remove lid and discard any unopened mussels. Carefully ladle stew into shallow bowls and pass bread at the table.

Mixed Greens and Fennel Salad

MAKES 4 SERVINGS

2 hearts romaine lettuce
1 medium head raddichio
1 small bulb fennel
Balsamic vinegar, a generous drizzle
3 tablespoons extra-virgin olive oil (3 times around the salad bowl)
Salt and freshly ground black pepper

Shred romaine and raddichio and discard cores. Trim tops of fennel bulb and quarter lengthwise. Remove core with an angled cut into each quarter. Slice fennel across into thin slices and add to salad. Dress with vinegar, oil, salt and pepper, to taste. Toss well and serve.

Nothin' to Fret About Apple Fritters

I learned of this fabulous, easy fruit fritter from my friend Rene. After trying it out at home, she became my good friend, Rene. Many thanks!

MAKES 20 APPLE FRITTER RINGS

Vegetable oil, for frying
4 Red or Golden Delicious apples
2 teaspoons lemon juice (a wedge will do)
2 cups complete pancake mix
1 & 1/2 cups water
1/2 teaspoon ground or freshly grated nutmeg
1/2 cup confectioners' sugar

Heat 1 inch vegetable oil over medium to medium-high heat. To test the oil temperature, add a 1-inch cube of bread to the hot oil. If it turns a deep golden brown while counting to 40, the oil is ready.

Core apples with an apple corer. Cut crosswise, forming 1/4-inch-thick apple rings. Sprinkle rings with the lemon juice to prevent browning. Combine pancake mix and water, season with nutmeg. Place some paper towels or brown paper sack on a work surface for draining fritters. Working in small batches of 5 to 6 slices, coat apple rings in batter and fry 2 to 3 minutes, until golden brown. Transfer to paper towels or paper sack to drain. When all the fritters are cooked, turn off oil and allow to cool before discarding.

Top fritters with confectioners' sugar (using a sifter or tea strainer) and transfer to a serving platter.

M E N U

1

Cheddar
Cheese and
Macaroni

• • • • •

2

Peas with
Onions and
Bacon

• • • • •

3

Apple Crisp

• • • • •

Cheddar Cheese and Macaroni

MAKES 4 ENTREE SERVINGS or 8 side servings

1 pound elbow macaroni, cooked 8 minutes or al dente to package
    directions

1 tablespoon vegetable or olive oil (once around the pan)
2 tablespoons butter
3 tablespoons flour
1 & 1/2 cups whole or 2% milk
3 cups shredded sharp white cheddar cheese
1/2 teaspoon nutmeg, ground or freshly grated
1/4 teaspoon ground cayenne pepper (a couple pinches)
Salt, to taste

Heat a medium-size deep skillet over medium heat. Add oil and butter. When
butter melts into the oil, stir in flour. Gently cook, whisking flour and butter,
together, until smooth and flour has had a chance to cook, about 3 minutes.
Slowly add milk while continuing to whisk. Gently bring milk to a bubble while
stirring frequently. Allow the milk to thicken a bit, then stir in 2 cups of shredded
cheddar cheese, a handful at a time. Season sauce with nutmeg and cayenne.
Taste and add a little salt, if you like. Add cooked pasta to the sauce and coat
completely by turning over and over in the cheese sauce. Transfer to a baking
dish, top with remaining cheese, and place under a hot broiler for a minute to
brown the top.

Peas with Onions and Bacon

MAKES 4 SERVINGS

3 slices bacon, cut into 1/2-inch pieces
1 small yellow onion, peeled and chopped
3 cups frozen peas
Salt and freshly ground black pepper, to taste

In a medium skillet over medium-high heat, brown chopped bacon, about
3 minutes. Add onion to the pan, and sauté another 3 minutes or so, until onions
are just tender. Add peas and reduce heat to medium. Season with salt and pepper and cook peas, 5 minutes. Transfer to a shallow bowl and serve. This recipe
is also wonderful made with steamed fresh or frozen sugar snap peas.

Apple Crisp

MAKES 4 TO 6 SERVINGS

6 McIntosh apples, peeled and diced into 1/2-inch pieces
The juice of 1/2 lemon
1 teaspoon ground cinnamon
1/2 teaspoon nutmeg, ground or freshly grated
2 tablespoons granulated sugar
1/2 cup flour or fine graham cracker crumbs
1/2 cup brown sugar
1/2 stick butter
1 pint vanilla ice cream

Preheat oven to 400°F.

In a 9 x 12 baking dish, combine apples, lemon juice, cinnamon, nutmeg, and sugar. In a small bowl, mix flour or graham cracker crumbs, brown sugar, and butter together using the tines of a fork and your fingers, working until small even crumbles form. Sprinkle this mixture evenly over apples and bake, 15 to 20 minutes until they are just tender and topping is golden brown. Serve apple crisp with small scoops of vanilla ice cream. YUM!

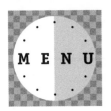

M E N U

1

Chicken Fried
Steaks with
Creamed Pan
Gravy and
Biscuits
• • • • •

2

Southern
Green Beans
• • • • •

3

Quick
Chocolate
Banana Cream
Pie
• • • • •

Chicken Fried Steaks with Creamed Pan Gravy and Biscuits

When I asked around about chicken fried steaks, EVERY Southerner I know had strong feelings and lots of advice on this roadside diner classic. Many like a traditional white milk gravy, others a deep brown gravy. Some prefer a red-eye gravy and still others like their fried steaks plain and crispy. When I sat down to come up with my recipe, I decided to fence-sit and make mine with a creamed brown pan gravy, on the side. I like the results.

MAKES 4 SERVINGS

1 & 1/2 pounds round steak, 1/2-inch thick
1 cup plus 2 tablespoons flour
1/3 cup cornmeal
1 teaspoon sweet paprika
1 teaspoon salt (1/3 palmful)
1/2 teaspoon freshly ground black pepper (eyeball it)
2 eggs, beaten
2 tablespoons water (2 splashes)
4 tablespoons vegetable oil
2 tablespoons flour
1 & 1/4 cups beef broth or stock
1/4 cup half-and-half or cream
1 package bake off biscuits (such as Pillsbury) prepared to directions
Wax paper

Preheat large, heavy skillet over medium-high heat

Set steaks on a wax-paper-lined work surface and cover with another piece of wax paper. Pound steaks to a 1/4-inch thickness. Set steaks to the side. Line work surface with more wax paper. Pour 1/2 cup flour into each of two piles on opposite ends of this work space. Add cornmeal, paprika, salt, and pepper to one pile of flour. Beat eggs and water in a pie plate or shallow dish.

Cut steaks into 4 portions and coat first in plain flour, then in egg, and then in the seasoned flour and cornmeal mixture.

Add 2 tablespoons oil to hot skillet and brown 2 steaks at a time. As they brown, remove from the pan, and add more oil, as needed. When the last 2 portions are browned, add the first two back to the pan. Cover pan, lower heat to medium-low and cook covered, 15 minutes. Remove steaks to serving platter and pour off all but 2 to 3 tablespoons of drippings. Add 2 tablespoons flour to the drippings, and cook, 2 minutes. Whisk in broth and season with salt and pepper. Add half-and-half or cream and whisk into gravy. When gravy bubbles, remove from heat. Serve steaks and warm biscuits with gravy on top.

Southern Green Beans

MAKES 4 SERVINGS

1 & 1/4 pounds green beans, trimmed and chopped into 1-inch pieces
2 slices bacon, chopped
1 small onion, minced
2 tablespoons red wine vinegar
2 teaspoons sugar

Cook green beans in a medium-size skillet in an inch of simmering water, covered, for 6 minutes. Drain and set aside. Return skillet to stove and set burner to medium high. Add bacon and brown. When fat begins to render, add chopped onions and cook with the bacon until tender. Return cooked green beans to the pan and turn to coat in bacon drippings and onions. When the beans are hot, bacon crisp at edges, and onions translucent, add vinegar to the pan and season with sugar. Allow the vinegar to evaporate and the sugar to combine with pan drippings, 1 or 2 minutes, then serve.

Quick Chocolate Banana Cream Pie

MAKES 8 SLICES

1 frozen pie shell, pricked several times with tines of a fork
1 package instant chocolate pudding, prepared to package directions
2 ripe bananas, thinly sliced on an angle
Whipped cream (spray-type is fine here)
1 dark chocolate candy bar

Preheat oven to 425°F. Bake pie shell 10 to 12 minutes, until golden. Remove from oven and let cool.

Line pie shell with half of the prepared chocolate pudding. Add a layer of bananas. Top with remaining pudding and banana slices. Cover with a giant swirl of whipped cream, starting at the center and working out. Shave a chocolate bar with a vegetable peeler and top pie with shavings. Serve immediately.

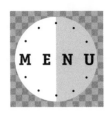

MENU

1

Veal Ragu with Campanelle Pasta
· · · · ·

2

Sicilian Chunk Vegetable Salad
· · · · ·

3

Assorted Italian Cookies and Citrus Rings with Brandy
· · · · ·

Veal Ragu with Campanelle Pasta

This recipe tastes like a marriage of Osso Buco and Lasagna Bolognese, yet it's made on the stovetop. Campanelle is a ruffled pasta that resembles small lasagna noodles. I find this cut in imported brands, such as Barilla. If you can't find campanelle, any curled short pasta or rigatoni may be substituted.

MAKES 6 SERVINGS

2 tablespoons extra-virgin olive oil (twice around the pan)

1 & 1/4 pounds ground veal

1 carrot, chopped

1 onion, chopped

2 cloves garlic, chopped

1 bay leaf, fresh or dried

Salt and freshly ground black pepper, to taste

1/2 cup dry white wine

1/2 cup chicken, beef or vegetable broth

1 can (28 ounces) crushed tomatoes

12 to 15 leaves fresh basil, torn or shredded

1 pound campanelle pasta, curly small lasagna shapes, cooked al dente*

1/2 cup grated Parmigiano Reggiano cheese, plus some for passing at table

Heat a large deep skillet over medium-high heat. Add oil and brown the veal, 2 or 3 minutes. Add carrot, onion, garlic, and bay leaf, and season with salt and pepper. Cook mixture 4 or 5 minutes more, stirring frequently, to soften veggies and combine flavors. Deglaze the pan with 1/2 cup white wine, 1 minute or 2. Add broth to the skillet and reduce heat to medium-low. Stir in tomatoes and bring sauce to a bubble. Simmer ragu sauce until ready to serve. Add torn basil and wilt the leaves into the hot sauce and remove bay leaf. Toss hot cooked pasta with 1/2 cup grated cheese. Combine hot pasta and cheese with the veal ragu in a large serving bowl or platter. Serve extra cheese for topping. Garnish platter with additional basil leaves.

*Note: Steam green beans for vegetable salad in a colander (covered) over the pasta water for about 5 minutes.

Sicilian Chunk Vegetable Salad

MAKES 6 SERVINGS

1/2 to 1/3 pound fresh green beans, trimmed
4 ribs celery, chopped
1/2 European or English "seedless" cucumber, diced
2 vine-ripe tomatoes, seeded and chopped
1/2 medium red onion, chopped
8 hot peppers, small cherry peppers or pepperoncini peppers
1 small jar (6 to 8 ounces) marinated mushrooms, drained
1 tin flat anchovies, drained and chopped
12 large green olives, pitted and coarsely chopped
1 & 1/2 tablespoons red wine vinegar (eyeball it)
1/4 cup extra-virgin olive oil (eyeball it)
Salt and coarse freshly ground black pepper, to taste

Steam green beans over pasta water (if preparing the previous recipe), or simmer
beans in an inch of boiling water for 3 minutes. Drain and chop them into thirds.
Combine all salad ingredients in a bowl and toss. Dress with vinegar and oil, salt
and pepper and serve.

Assorted Italian Cookies and Citrus Rings with Brandy

**My friend Vicky serves a cookie tray from our favorite bakery and sliced
oranges with brandy after her special family dinners. I am so happy to be a
part of her family, too.**

MAKES 6 SERVINGS

1 & 1/2 pounds assorted Italian cookies
2 or 3 navel oranges, washed and dried
1 Sicilian blood orange (optional)
2 to 3 shots brandy

Arrange the cookies on a serving tray. Slice whole oranges into discs and arrange
them in a shallow dish. Douse the orange slices with brandy, using 1 shot of
brandy for each sliced orange. To eat the oranges, break the skin and "unroll"
each slice. Easy. Delicious. For grown-ups only.

MENU

1

Winter
Vegetable
Stew
· · · · ·

2

Potato and
Smoked Gouda
Pancakes
· · · · ·

3

Ice Cream
S'mores Cups
· · · · ·

Winter Vegetable Stew

MAKES 4 SERVINGS

2 tablespoons extra-virgin olive oil (twice around the pan)
3 cloves garlic, smashed and skin pulled away
1 pound crimini mushrooms (16 to 20) halved
1 medium zucchini, quartered lengthwise and cut into 1-inch pieces
1 medium onion, chopped
Salt and freshly ground black pepper, to taste
1 can (15 ounces) chick peas (garbanzo beans), drained
1 & 1/2 teaspoons ground cumin (half-a-palmful)
1 can (28 ounces) diced tomatoes
2 tablespoons fresh rosemary, finely chopped

In a medium pot over moderate heat, sauté garlic and mushrooms in olive oil, 2 or 3 minutes. Add zucchini and onion and season with salt and pepper. Sauté another 5 minutes. Add garbanzo beans, cumin, tomatoes, and rosemary. Bring stew to a bubble, reduce heat to low and simmer, 10 minutes.

Potato and Smoked Gouda Pancakes

MAKES 4 SERVINGS

Olive or vegetable oil, for frying
2 pounds all-purpose potatoes, such as russets (about 3 large potatoes), peeled and shredded
Several dashes salt and freshly ground black pepper
1 small onion, grated
3 tablespoons all-purpose flour
1 & 1/4 cups shredded smoked Gouda cheese, the yield of an 8-ounce piece

TIDBIT

❝ Make these potato cheese pancakes in mini 2-inch rounds for your next cocktail party as a snack! ❞

Heat a nonstick skillet over medium-high heat. Add a thin layer of olive or vegetable oil, just enough to coat the bottom. In a large mixing bowl, combine potatoes with salt and pepper, onions, flour, and shredded cheese. Mix well and spoon piles of potato and cheese mixture into the pan, making 3-inch rounds, 1 inch apart. Cook pancakes until golden and crispy, about 4 minutes on each side. Remove to warm platter and repeat process.

Arrange pancakes, 3 per person, on dinner plates and ladle on the Winter Vegetable stew.

Ice Cream S'mores Cups

MAKES 4 DESSERT CUPS

1 cup graham cracker crumbs (available in baking aisle)
2 tablespoons melted butter
4 scoops vanilla or chocolate ice cream
1 bittersweet chocolate bar
4 large marshmallows

Combine graham cracker crumbs and butter. Spoon 1/4 of the crumbs into each dessert cup pressing them into the sides and bottom of each cup. Fill with vanilla or chocolate ice cream. With a vegetable peeler, shave curls of bittersweet chocolate over cups. Thread marshmallows onto a metal skewer, and hold over a burner at high heat to toast. Using a towel to grip the hot skewer, remove toasted marshmallows by running a fork over the skewer and push off. Top each cup with a toasted marshmallow and serve.

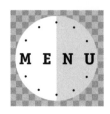
1

Stuffed Pork
Chops with
Cream Cheese
Potatoes and
Sugar Snap
Peas

· · · · ·

2

Pound Cake
with Vanilla
Ice Cream and
Chocolate
Sauce

· · · · ·

Stuffed Pork Chops with Cream Cheese Potatoes and Sugar Snap Peas

MAKES 4 SERVINGS

POTATOES
2 & 1/2 pounds potatoes, such as russets or Idaho, peeled and cut into chunks
1/2 cup milk
4 ounces cream cheese
1 small onion, finely chopped
Salt, to taste
2 tablespoons chopped fresh chives (optional)

STUFFED PORK CHOPS
1 tablespoon olive or vegetable oil, plus some for drizzling
2 slices bacon, chopped
1 small McIntosh apple, chopped
2 ribs celery from the heart, finely chopped
1 small onion, chopped
2 tablespoons fresh sage, chopped, or 1 teaspoon ground sage
2 tablespoons fresh thyme, chopped, or 1 tablespoon dried leaves
Salt and freshly ground black pepper, to taste
2 store-bought corn muffins
8 thin-cut boneless center-cut pork loin chops

SUGAR SNAP PEAS
2 pounds sugar snap peas
1 cup chicken broth or water
1 tablespoon butter
Salt, to taste

In a large pot, cover potatoes with water and season with salt. Cover pot to bring potatoes to a quick boil, and cook until tender, about 12 minutes. Drain potatoes and return them to the hot pot to dry. Set aside. In a small saucepan, heat milk, cream cheese and onion over medium-low heat until cream cheese melts and mixture bubbles. Pour into the potatoes and mash to desired consistency. Add a little extra milk for softer potatoes. Season with salt and transfer to a serving dish. Garnish with chopped chives.

STUFFING FOR PORK CHOPS: Preheat a medium skillet over medium-high heat. Add oil and bacon to the skillet and cook, 2 minutes. Add apple, celery, and onion and season the mixture with herbs, salt and pepper. Reduce heat to medium. Cook vegetables, 5 minutes, stirring frequently. Crumble corn muffins into the pan and combine to complete the stuffing.

PORK CHOPS: Preheat a large skillet or grill pan over medium-high heat. Drizzle chops with oil and season with salt and pepper. Cook chops 3 to 4 minutes on each side. Do not overcook. The chops should be firm, but still giving off juices.

Into a medium saucepan, over medium-high heat, place snap peas and broth and 1 tablespoon butter. When the liquid boils, cover the pan and reduce heat to low. Simmer, 3 to 5 minutes, until tender but still green. Drain and season with salt, if needed, and serve.

To assemble "stuffed" chops, set a cooked chop on serving plate. Mound the pork chop with stuffing, allowing some to spill onto plate, then top with a second chop. The end result will look like a stuffed, thick-cut pork chop, but these took 1/3 the time. Repeat with 3 remaining servings. Pass potatoes and snap peas to complete the meal.

Pound Cake with Vanilla Ice Cream and Chocolate Sauce

This is our old standby dessert on Sundays. Yummy.

MAKES 4 SERVINGS

4 slices pound cake, 1-inch thick
1 pint vanilla bean ice cream
Chocolate syrup, such as Hershey brand

Top pound cake slices with a generous scoop of softened vanilla bean ice cream and drizzle liberally with chocolate syrup. A classic.

MENU

1

Asparagus and
Green Beans
with Tarragon
Lemon Dip

· · · · ·

2

French Dip
Roast Beef
Sandwiches

· · · · ·

3

Chocolate
Fondue

· · · · ·

Asparagus and Green Beans with Tarragon Lemon Dip

MAKES 4 SERVINGS

1 pound fresh asparagus, trimmed
1 pound fresh green beans, trimmed

TARRAGON LEMON DIP
1 cup mayonnaise
The zest and juice of 1 lemon
1 small shallot, finely chopped
2 tablespoons chopped fresh tarragon (4 sprigs)
2 tablespoons chopped fresh flat-leaf parsley
A few grinds fresh black pepper

Sprigs of tarragon and parsley, for garnish

In a large skillet cook asparagus spears and green beans in 1 inch of salted boiling water, covered, 3 or 4 minutes. Drain and cool the vegetables and arrange them on a serving plate. Combine dip ingredients in a small bowl and garnish with sprigs of parsley and tarragon and set alongside vegetables on serving dish.

French Dip Roast Beef Sandwiches

MAKES 4 SERVINGS

2 tablespoons butter
1 shallot, chopped
1 & 1/2 tablespoons flour
1 shot dry sherry (optional)
2 cans (14 ounces each) beef consommé
1 & 1/2 pounds deli-sliced roast beef
Steak seasoning blend such as Montreal Seasoning by McCormick OR coarse salt and freshly ground black pepper to taste
4 torpedo sandwich rolls, split

In a large, shallow skillet over moderate heat, melt butter. Sauté shallots in the butter 2 minutes. Add flour and cook 1 minute longer. Whisk in sherry and cook liquid out. Whisk in consommé in a slow stream. Bring sauce to a bubble and allow to simmer over low heat until sandwiches are ready to serve.

Pile roast beef loosely across a large work surface, and season with grill seasoning or salt and black pepper. Gather 4 ramekins or small soup cups for dipping sauce, and 4 split torpedo rolls. Using tongs to help you assemble, dip meat into sauce and pile into rolls. Set ramekins with extra sauce next to the sandwiches.

Chocolate Fondue

MAKES 4 TO 6 SERVINGS

FONDUE
3/4 cup heavy whipping cream (reserve 1/4 cup to thin fondue, if necessary)
4 bittersweet chocolate bars (3 & 1/2 ounces each), chopped
2 tablespoons Frangelico or Amaretto liqueur (optional)
1/4 cup finely chopped hazelnuts or almonds (optional)

SUGGESTED "DIP-ABLES," CHOOSE 3 OR 4 OF THE FOLLOWING:
• Hazelnut or almond biscotti
• Salted pretzel sticks
• Cubed pound cake
• Sliced bananas
• Stem strawberries
• Sectioned navel oranges
• Ripe fresh pineapple, diced

Heat cream in a heavy nonreactive saucepan over moderate heat until cream comes to a low boil. Remove pan from heat and add chocolate, allowing it to stand in hot cream, 3 to 5 minutes to soften, then whisk together with the cream. Stir in liqueur and/or chopped nuts and transfer to a fondue pot or set the mixing bowl on a rack above a small lit candle. If fondue becomes too thick, stir in reserved cream, 1 tablespoon at a time, to desired consistency. Arrange your favorite "dip-ables" in piles on a platter alongside chocolate fondue with fondue forks, bamboo skewers or seafood forks as dipping utensils.

1

30-Minute
Southern
Classic:
Country
Captain
Chicken with
White and
Wild Rice

· · · · ·

2

Bourbon
Street Candy
Balls with
Pecans

· · · · ·

30-Minute Southern Classic: Country Captain Chicken with White and Wild Rice

MAKES 4 TO 6 SERVINGS

RICE
2 & 2/3 cups water
1 tablespoon butter
1 & 1/2 cups white and wild rice or long-grain rice

CHICKEN
2/3 cup flour (eyeball it)
1 rounded tablespoon sweet paprika
4 pieces (6 ounces each) boneless, skinless chicken breast
3 boneless, skinless chicken thighs
Salt and freshly ground black pepper
2 tablespoons extra-virgin olive oil (twice around the pan)
2 tablespoons butter
1 green bell pepper, seeded and chopped
1 red bell pepper, seeded and chopped
1 medium onion, chopped
2 or 3 large cloves garlic, chopped
1 tablespoon curry powder or mild curry paste
1 cup chicken broth
1 can (28 ounces) diced tomatoes or chunky-style crushed tomatoes
1/4 cup golden raisins or currants (a couple handfuls)
2 ounces (1 small pouch) sliced almonds, lightly toasted
3 scallions, chopped, for garnish

Bring water to a boil in a medium saucepan; add butter and rice and return to a boil. Reduce heat to low, cover pot, and cook rice, 20 minutes or until tender. Turn off heat and fluff rice with a fork.

Combine flour and paprika in a shallow dish. Season chicken with salt and pepper. Cut each chicken breast and thigh in half on an angle. Coat chicken pieces in paprika-seasoned flour.

Heat a large skillet over medium-high heat and add oil. Brown chicken pieces 3 minutes on each side and remove from the skillet. Add butter to the pan, then stir in peppers, onions, and garlic. Season veggies with salt and pepper and sauté 5 to 7 minutes to soften. Add curry, broth, tomatoes, and raisins or currants. Slide chicken back into the skillet and simmer over moderate heat, 5 minutes to combine flavors and finish cooking the chicken through. Garnish with sliced almonds.

Place skillet on a trivet and serve the chicken from the pan. Transfer rice to a serving dish and garnish with chopped scallions.

Bourbon Street Candy Balls with Pecans

MAKES 24 TO 30 BALLS

1 & 1/2 cups crushed Nilla wafers or other vanilla flavored wafer cookies
1 cup confectioners' sugar
4 shots bourbon
2 cups chopped pecans, ground in food processor
3 tablespoons light Karo syrup
Softened butter

Combine all ingredients in a bowl. Coat fingertips with a little softened butter to help you roll. Shape mixture into balls 1 & 1/2 inches in diameter. Arrange balls on a dessert platter and serve. Ask for help rolling. Four hands make very quick work of this dessert! Obviously, a grown-ups only treat!

M E N U

1

Green
Minestrone

• • • • •

2

Tomato Basil
Panzanella

• • • • •

3

Lemon
Coconut Angel
Food Cake

• • • • •

Green Minestrone

Minestrone is literally a BIG soup. This one tastes as if it simmered all day. For a strictly vegetarian minestrone, omit the pancetta or prosciutto, and use a vegetable broth or stock instead of the chicken.

MAKES 4 SERVINGS

2 tablespoons extra-virgin olive oil (twice around the pan)

4 slices pancetta or 1/4 pound thick-cut prosciutto, chopped

1 medium onion, chopped

2 ribs celery, chopped

2 large cloves garlic, crushed

1 bay leaf, fresh or dried

1 medium zucchini, diced

Salt and freshly ground black pepper

1 can (15 ounces) white cannellini beans

1 can (15 ounces) garbanzo beans

8 cups chicken broth or stock (two 1-quart paper containers)

1 cup ditalini pasta or mini penne pasta

1/2 pound green beans, trimmed and cut into 1-inch pieces

10 ounces triple-washed spinach, stems removed and coarsely chopped

1/2 cup Parmigiano Reggiano or Romano cheese, plus extra to pass at the table

12 to 16 leaves fresh basil, torn or shredded OR 1/4 cup chopped fresh flat-leaf parsley

TIDBIT

❝ Storebought
stocks have
come a long
way. Look for
handy, paper,
1-quart
containers of
low-sodium
stocks on your
soup aisle. ❞

Heat a soup pot over medium-high heat. Add oil and pancetta or prosciutto. Sauté 2 minutes, then add onions, celery, garlic, bay leaf and zucchini to the pot, and season with salt and pepper, to taste. Sauté another 5 minutes, stirring frequently. Add white beans, garbanzo beans and chicken broth to the pot, cover, and bring to a boil. Add pasta and green beans and cook 8 minutes, or until pasta is just tender. Stir in spinach to wilt, 1 minute. Stir in grated cheese and ladle soup into bowls. Top with basil or chopped parsley.

Tomato Basil Panzanella

MAKES 4 SERVINGS

1/2 pound day-old chewy farm-style bread, cubed
Bottled spring water, to cover bread
4 vine-ripe tomatoes, seeded and chopped
1/2 medium red onion, chopped
1 cup loosely packed basil leaves, torn or shredded
2 tablespoons red wine vinegar
1/4 cup extra-virgin olive oil
Salt and freshly ground black pepper, to taste

Place bread in a medium mixing bowl, cover with water, and allow it to soak, 3 to 5 minutes. In small handfuls, remove bread from the water and wring it out without mashing or tearing bread. You do not want wet bread, so wring it carefully.

Combine tomatoes with onions and basil in a second bowl and dress with vinegar, oil, salt and pepper. Add bread to tomato salad and combine. Adjust seasonings and serve.

Lemon Coconut Angel Food Cake

MAKES 6 SLICES

1 storebought prepared angel food cake
1 jar (9 to 11 ounces) lemon curd (found on the jam and jelly aisle)
The zest of 1 lemon
1 cup shredded coconut

Place a cake ring on a serving plate. Warm lemon curd over low heat and stir in lemon zest. Pour the warm sauce down over the cake in a slow stream to glaze it. Sprinkle shredded coconut liberally over the lemon-glazed cake and serve.

TIDBIT

❝ Panzanella is a great use for leftover, good quality, chewy bread. The combination of vegetables can be as simple as tomato and basil or as varied as everything your garden grows. ❞

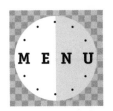

M E N U

1

Herb and
Cheese
Chicken
Tenders
Parmigiana
with Spaghetti
• • • • •

2

Antipasto
Salad Toss
• • • • •

T I D B I T

❝ To ease your
clean up, try
using disposable
pie tins for the
flour, egg and
bread
crumbs❞

Herb and Cheese Chicken Tenders Parmigiana with Spaghetti

This recipe is so versatile; serve these tenders hot or cold. Cold, pair them with pasta salad. Hot, they're good as is with a simple mixed green salad. Or, top with tomato sauce and cheese and serve with a side of spaghetti for an extra-tender quick Chicken Parm.

MAKES 4 BIG SERVINGS

Light olive oil, for frying
1 & 1/2 pounds chicken tenders
Salt and freshly ground black pepper, to taste
1 cup all-purpose flour
2 large eggs, beaten with 1/4 cup water

BREADING
1 & 1/2 cups Italian-style bread crumbs (eyeball it)
1/2 cup shredded Parmigiano Reggiano cheese (2 to 3 handfuls)
6 sprigs fresh thyme leaves, stripped and chopped (2 to 3 tablespoons)
6 sprigs fresh rosemary, finely chopped (3 tablespoons)
2 handfuls chopped fresh flat-leaf parsley
4 cloves garlic, finely chopped
1 teaspoon crushed red pepper flakes

Preheat oven to 350°F. Place a nonstick cookie sheet in oven with a foil liner.

Heat 1/2 inch oil in a large nonstick skillet over medium to medium-high heat.

Season chicken tenders with salt and pepper. Place flour in a shallow dish. Beat eggs with water in a second dish. In a third dish, combine the remaining ingredients. Coat chicken in flour, then egg, then breads and cheese mixture.

Add chicken to the skillet and cook until deeply golden on each side, 3 to 4 minutes. Transfer to hot cookie sheet already in oven and bake for another 5 minutes. Cook 5 or 6 tenders at a time in a single layer, adding additional oil if necessary. If chicken browns too quickly, lower heat slightly. Serve chicken hot or cold with green salad, or complete as a Parmigiana.

SIMPLE TOMATO SAUCE FOR CHICKEN PARMIGIANA

1 pound spaghetti
2 tablespoons extra-virgin olive oil
1 small white onion, finely chopped
3 cloves garlic, minced
1 can (14 ounces) chunky-style crushed tomatoes
1 can (28 ounces) crushed tomatoes
1 cup chicken broth or stock
A handful fresh basil leaves, torn into small pieces
Coarse salt, to taste
1 cup shredded provolone (optional)
1/2 cup grated Parmigiano Reggiano cheese

TIDBIT

❝ Served cold, these chicken tenders are a tailgate GREAT!❞

Set a large pot of salted water on for the pasta.

Preheat a large skillet over medium-low heat. Add extra-virgin olive oil, onions and garlic, and sauté for 10 minutes, stirring occasionally.

To the onions and garlic, add both cans of tomatoes and a cup of chicken broth and bring to a bubble. Reduce heat to simmer until ready to serve, then stir in torn basil and salt to taste.

Coat the chicken tenders in the 3 steps outlined in the previous recipe. Sauté chicken and finish in oven as directed. Remove from heat and set aside until pasta and sauce are ready.

When sauce simmers, cook pasta, drain and place in serving dish, coating it lightly with some sauce. Set chicken tenders on top of pasta and dot them with a little sauce as well. For a cheesy finish, cover the chicken with shredded provolone and Parmigiano Reggiano cheeses and either serve as is, or brown under a hot broiler for a minute or so.

Antipasto Salad Toss

This salad travels well in warm months because it's mayo-free. Pile salad into Italian rolls for a tailgate GREAT sandwich too.

MAKES 4 SERVINGS

TIDBIT

❝ Giardiniera can be found on the Italian foods aisle in jars, or in bulk bins near olive section. ❞

2 hearts romaine lettuce, chopped

1/2 pound Genoa salami, diced (ask for it in one chunk at deli counter)

2 cups giardiniera, hot pickled vegetable salad, coarsely chopped

12 pitted black olives, such as Kalamata, coarsely chopped

12 jumbo pitted green olives, coarsely chopped

1 small jar (8 ounces) roasted red peppers, drained and diced

1 small jar (6 ounces) marinated artichoke hearts, drained

2 tablespoons balsamic vinegar (eyeball it)

1/4 cup extra-virgin olive oil (eyeball it)

Salt and freshly ground black pepper

Combine lettuce, salami, chopped hot pickled vegetables, olives, red peppers, and artichoke hearts in a salad bowl. Drizzle with vinegar and oil. Toss, season with salt and pepper to taste, and serve.

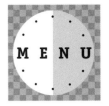

M E N U

1

Potato,
Spinach, and
Tomato Soup

· · · · ·

2

Panini with
Prosciutto,
Roasted
Peppers, and
Mozzarella

· · · · ·

Potato, Spinach, and Tomato Soup

MAKES 4 SERVINGS

3 cloves garlic, crushed or finely chopped

1 large onion, chopped

2 tablespoons extra-virgin olive oil

2 quarts chicken stock

3 pounds all-purpose potatoes, such as russets, peeled and thinly sliced

1 pound fresh triple-washed spinach, stems picked and coarsely chopped

1/4 teaspoon nutmeg, grated or ground

Salt and freshly ground black pepper

1 can (28 ounces) chunky-style crushed tomatoes or diced tomatoes

1/2 cup grated Parmigiano Reggiano or Romano cheese

In a deep pot, sauté garlic and onion in oil for 2 or 3 minutes. Add broth and bring to a boil. As you slice potatoes, add them carefully to the broth, and cook 20 minutes, stirring occasionally. The potatoes will begin to break up and thicken the soup as it cooks. Stir in spinach in bunches, adding another handful as it wilts into the soup. Season with nutmeg, salt and pepper, to taste. Stir in tomatoes and heat through, 1 or 2 minutes. Remove from the stove to a trivet. Stir in grated cheese and serve.

Panini with Prosciutto, Roasted Peppers, and Mozzarella

MAKES 4 PANINI

8 thin slices chewy, crusty Italian bread from a large loaf

1/3 pound prosciutto di Parma, thinly sliced

1 jar (16 ounces) roasted red peppers, drained well

1 pound fresh or fresh smoked mozzarella, sliced

Extra-virgin olive oil, for drizzling

Preheat a grill pan or large nonstick griddle over medium to medium-high heat. Build your sandwiches: place 2 or 3 slices of prosciutto on one piece of bread. Top with an even layer of roasted pepper and an even layer of sliced mozzarella, top with another slice of bread. Drizzle the tops of your assembled sandwiches with olive oil. Place that side face down on the griddle and drizzle the up side with additional olive oil. Weight the sandwiches down with a foil-covered brick or a heavy skillet filled with a sack of flour or heavy canned goods. Brown the sandwiches, 2 or 3 minutes on each side, then serve immediately.

MENU

1

Shrimp Cocktail with Rach's Quick Rémoulade

· · · · ·

2

One Great Gumbo with Chicken and Andouille Sausage

· · · · ·

3

Tossed Salad with Snap Peas, Radishes and Sweet Red Pepper Relish Dressing

· · · · ·

Shrimp Cocktail with Rach's Quick Rémoulade

MAKES 6 SERVINGS

1 lemon, halved

2 bay leaves, fresh or dried

1 tablespoon coriander seeds (a palmful)

1 tablespoon mustard seeds (a palmful)

30 large to jumbo raw shrimp, peeled and deveined (ask for these at fish counter)

RÉMOULADE

1 & 1/2 cups mayonnaise

1/2 cup Creole mustard (eyeball it)

The juice of 1 lemon

2 teaspoons cayenne pepper sauce (eyeball it)

1 rib celery, finely chopped

2 scallions, thinly sliced

Fill a deep pot halfway with water and place on stove over high heat. Squeeze the juice of 1 lemon into the water, and drop lemon halves into the pot. Add bay leaves, coriander, and mustard seeds to the water. When the water boils, add shrimp, and boil, 3 minutes or until pink and tails curl towards the heads. Drain and cold shock under running water.

Combine mayonnaise, mustard, lemon, cayenne, celery, and scallions in a small bowl for the rémoulade. Arrange shrimp around sauce bowl on serving plate.

One Great Gumbo with Chicken and Andouille Sausage

MAKES 6 SERVINGS

My dad is from the South and it takes him hours to build a proper gumbo. It's really good. In restaurants I've sampled gumbos that take up to 3 days to make! They were delicious, too. My gumbo? It's pretty tasty. And oh, yeah, mine takes just under 30 minutes to make.

2 cups white enriched rice, prepared to package directions

2 tablespoons extra-virgin olive oil

3/4 pound chicken tenders, diced

3/4 pound boneless, skinless chicken thighs, diced (3 thighs)

Salt and freshly ground black pepper, to taste

2 teaspoons poultry seasoning

3/4 to 1 pound andouille sausage (4 links, with casings removed), diced

3 tablespoons butter

3 ribs celery from the heart of the bunch, chopped

2 green bell peppers, seeded and diced

1 large onion, peeled and chopped

2 bay leaves, fresh or dried

2 tablespoons cayenne pepper sauce (eyeball it)

3 tablespoons flour

1 quart chicken stock or broth

2 cups chopped okra, fresh or frozen, defrosted

1 can (14 ounces) crushed tomatoes

1 can (14 ounces) diced tomatoes

2 to 3 tablespoons fresh thyme leaves (several sprigs), chopped

5 scallions, thinly sliced on an angle

Preheat a large heavy-bottomed pot over medium-high heat. Add 2 tablespoons oil, twice around the pan, and the diced chicken. Season with salt and pepper and a sprinkle of poultry seasoning. Brown on all sides, about 2 or 3 minutes. Chop your veggies while it's working. Add the andouille to the pan and cook another minute or two. Transfer chicken and sausage to a dish.

Return pan to heat and add butter. When the butter melts, add chopped celery, peppers, onion and bay. Season with salt and pepper and hot sauce. Cook 3 to 5 minutes to begin to soften veggies. Add flour and cook for 2 minutes. Slowly stir in the broth and bring to a boil. Add okra to the boiling broth, then return the meats to the pot and stir in tomatoes and half of your fresh thyme. When it's bubbling, reduce heat and simmer for 5 minutes to combine flavors, then adjust your seasonings.

Scoop cooked white rice into the center of bowlfuls of gumbo using an ice cream scoop. Setting the rice on top of the gumbo will keep it from getting too wet. Top with remaining chopped thyme and lots of chopped scallions.

TIDBIT

❝ This gumbo can be made with all white or all dark chicken meat, too. Whatever pleases you. ❞

Tossed Salad with Snap Peas, Radishes and Sweet Red Pepper Relish Dressing

MAKES 6 SERVINGS

2 hearts romaine, chopped

2 cups mixed baby greens (a few handfuls) from a 5 or 6-ounce sack

4 red radishes, sliced

1 cup fresh sugar snap peas, chopped

1/2 cup shredded carrots or 1 carrot, thinly sliced, chopped, or curled with a vegetable peeler

4 scallions, sliced on an angle

DRESSING

3 tablespoons red wine vinegar (eyeball it)

1 rounded teaspoon sugar

1/2 cup red pepper relish (found on condiment aisle)

1/3 cup extra-virgin olive oil (eyeball it)

Salt and freshly ground black pepper

Combine chopped romaine and baby greens with radishes, snap peas, carrots, and scallions in a large salad bowl. Combine vinegar, sugar and relish in a small bowl. Whisk in oil in a slow stream. Toss salad with dressing, and season with salt and pepper to taste, and serve.

Rachael puts the finishing touch—yes, it's EVOO—on her Tomato Basil Panzanella, recipe on page 121.

recipes
on page
43

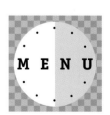

MENU

MAKE
YOUR
OWN
TAKE-OUT

1

Pecan-Crusted Chicken Tenders and Salad
with Tangy Maple Barbecue Dressing

••••

2

Cheddar and Chive Bread

••••

3

My Sister Maria's Easy Apple and
Cinnamon Cake and Ice Cream

••••

BIG
NIGHTS:
VERY
SPECIAL
DINNERS

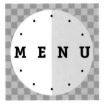

1

Tilapia with Tomatillo Sauce

....

2

Avocados with Creamy Maque Choux
(Corn and Peppers)

....

3

Margarita Granita

....

recipes
on page
206

recipes on page **196**

1

Sea Scallops with Vermouth

••••

2

Veal Scaloppini with Wine, Mushrooms,
and Green Olives

••••

3

Ripe Peaches with Port

••••

MENU

**BIG
NIGHTS:
VERY
SPECIAL
DINNERS**

FAMILY-
STYLE
SUPPERS

MENU

1

Green Minestrone
(shown below)
....

2

Tomato Basil Panzanella
....

3

Lemon Coconut Angel Food Cake
....

recipe
on page
120

recipes on page **64**

1

Lamb Chops with Mint and
Mustard Dipping Sauce

••••

2

Tomatoes Stuffed with Tabouleh Salad and
White Bean Salad with Thyme

••••

3

Limoncello Dessert

••••

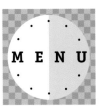

MENU

**MONDAY
THRU
FRIDAY
DINNER
SPECIALS**

MONDAY
THRU
FRIDAY
DINNER
SPECIALS

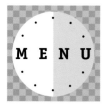
M E N U

1

Honey Mustard and Red Onion
Barbequed Chicken
····

2

Butter Bean Salad and Corn on the Cob
····

3

Fluffernutter Brownies
····

recipes
on page
86

recipe on page 121

1
Green Minestrone
····

2
Tomato Basil Panzanella (shown above)
····

3
Lemon Coconut Angel Food Cake
····

MENU

FAMILY-STYLE SUPPERS

DOUBLE-DUTY DINNERS

RACHAEL RAY 2
30-MINUTE MEALS

DOUBLE-DUTY DINNERS

What could be better than making a meal in 30 minutes? Getting A BIG head start on another meal while you're at it! In the following recipes, a double batch of one "base" recipe is prepared in under 30 minutes. It is then divided, and the first half prepared one way. The "leftover" half is refrigerated or frozen, and, on another occasion, it is transformed into an entirely different meal with new tastes and pleasures.

For example, have Chicken Divan tonight and Chicken Tetrazzini later in the week. Or, enjoy a light Poached Salmon supper this evening, then spicy Salmon Cakes for tomorrow's lunch. Here's one of my favorites: comforting Eggplant Caponata on creamy, cheesy polenta, followed by a zesty Caponata Pasta Bake later in the week.

Double Duty Dinners are all about having your cake and eating it, too—twice!

Poached Salmon with Dijon Dill Sauce and New Potatoes with Mint

This is my English friend Maggie's favorite simple supper.

MAKES 4 SERVINGS plus 4 reserved for salmon cakes

POTATOES

2 pounds small red-skinned new potatoes

Coarse salt

1 tablespoon butter

3 tablespoons finely chopped fresh mint (a handful of leaves)

1 teaspoon sugar

SALMON

7 portions (6 ounces each) Norwegian salmon (individually packaged in fish department; 7 portions will serve 8)

2 cups dry white wine

2 to 3 cups water

1 bay leaf, fresh or dried

Bouquet of fresh tarragon, dill and parsley sprigs, tied with kitchen string

GARNISH AND ACCOMPANIMENTS

2 cups sour cream

2 tablespoons prepared Dijon mustard

1/4 cup chopped fresh herbs: a few sprigs each tarragon, dill, and parsley

4 slices pumpernickel bread, quartered

1 bundle fresh watercress, washed and trimmed

1/2 English or seedless cucumber, thinly sliced

M E N U

1

Poached Salmon with Dijon Dill Sauce and New Potatoes with Mint
. . . . .

2

Double-Duty Lunch: Salmon Cakes on Mixed Baby Greens
. . . . .

TIDBIT

❝ Refrigerate salmon if using within 2 days, or freeze for next week's salmon cakes. ❞

Place potatoes in a pot, cover with water, put lid on, and bring to a boil. Add a few healthy pinches of coarse salt, reduce heat to medium and boil covered until tender, about 12 minutes.

Place salmon fillets in a large deep skillet. (You'll want the "extra" portions for salmon cakes on another night). Pour wine and water into the pan so that just the very top of the salmon is exposed. Add a bay leaf and a bouquet of a few sprigs each fresh tarragon, dill, and parsley to the pan and set it down into the liquid. Place over high heat and bring to a boil. Reduce heat to medium low and cover the pan. Poach salmon for 10 minutes, or until fish is firm and opaque.

To make the sauce for the salmon, combine sour cream with Dijon mustard and chopped herbs in a small bowl.

Drain potatoes and return them to the hot pot. Add butter and turn potatoes to coat them lightly, and sprinkle on the mint and sugar.

Remove salmon from the cooking liquid with a thin spatula. Set aside 4 portions, allow to cool, and refrigerate.

To serve, place a piece of salmon on each plate and garnish with sauce. Place pumpernickel squares, watercress, and sliced cucumber alongside fish. Add minted red potatoes to the plate and serve.

Double-Duty Lunch: Salmon Cakes on Mixed Baby Greens

MAKES 4 SERVINGS

Vegetable or canola oil, for frying

3 portions (6 ounces each) cooked salmon OR 3 cans (6 ounces each) salmon, drained well

1 to 1 & 1/2 cups cracker meal

2 large eggs, beaten

2 rounded teaspoons Old Bay Seasoning

1/2 red bell pepper, seeded and finely chopped

20 blades fresh chives, snipped or chopped

2 to 3 tablespoons fresh dill (a handful), finely chopped

1 teaspoon cayenne pepper sauce (Tabasco or other brand)

The juice and zest of 1 lemon

1 sack (10 ounces) mixed baby greens

Coarse salt, to taste

Extra-virgin olive oil, for drizzling

1/2 cup mayonnaise or reduced-fat mayonnaise

1/2 cup chili sauce

2 tablespoons dill pickle relish

Heat a large, heavy skillet with 1 inch of frying oil over moderate heat.

In a medium bowl, flake the cooked or drained canned salmon with a fork. Add about 1 cup cracker meal and work through the fish with your hands. Add the eggs, Old Bay Seasoning, bell pepper, chives, dill, cayenne pepper sauce, and the zest of one lemon and continue to blend well. If the mixture is wet, add more cracker meal. Form 3-inch patties about 1-inch thick. You should have 8 to 10 cakes. Fry in hot oil in a single layer until golden, 3 or 4 minutes on each side. Drain on a paper-towel-lined plate.

Toss salad greens with coarse salt and the juice of the lemon you zested. Drizzle the greens with a little olive oil and re-toss to coat.

Combine mayo, chili sauce, and relish in a small dish. To serve, place salmon cakes on a bed of baby greens, 2 cakes per person, and top with chili mayo.

MENU

1

**Eggplant
Caponata and
Herb Polenta**

• • • • •

2

**Double-Duty
Dinner:
Caponata
Pasta Bake**

• • • • •

Eggplant Caponata and Herb Polenta

MAKES 4 SERVINGS, plus caponata for a second dinner

EGGPLANT CAPONATA

2 tablespoons extra-virgin olive oil (twice around the pan)

4 cloves garlic, chopped

1/2 to 3/4 teaspoon crushed red pepper flakes

1 red bell pepper, seeded

1 Cubanelle Italian long green pepper, seeded

1 large sweet onion, peeled

2 ribs celery

1/2 cup large green olives, cracked away from pits

1/2 cup Kalamata black olives, cracked away from pits (from bulk bins
   in market)

1 jar (2 ounces) capers, drained

1/2 cup golden raisins (a couple handfuls)

1 medium firm eggplant, diced

Salt

1 can (28 ounces) diced tomatoes

1 can (14 ounces) crushed tomatoes

A handful chopped fresh flat-leaf parsley

HERB POLENTA

3 cups chicken stock

1 cup quick-cook polenta (found in Italian foods or specialty foods
   aisles)

4 sprigs fresh thyme, chopped

1 sprig fresh rosemary, finely chopped

1/4 cup grated Romano or Parmigiano Reggiano cheese

2 tablespoons butter

Salt and freshly ground black pepper, to taste

Preheat a big, deep pot over medium heat. Add oil, garlic, and crushed red pepper flakes. Place your cutting board near the stovetop, and toss the vegetables
into the pot as you chop them. Dice peppers, chop onion and celery. Then,
coarsely chop olives, and stir in along with the capers and raisins. Dice and salt
the eggplant and stir in. Increase the heat a bit, add diced and crushed tomatoes
and stir caponata well to combine. Cover pot and cook, 15 to 20 minutes, until
vegetables are tender. Stir in parsley and remove from heat.

Bring 3 cups chicken broth to a boil. Add quick-cooking polenta and stir
constantly until the cornmeal masses, about 3 minutes. Stir in herbs, cheese,
butter, salt and pepper.

Spread polenta out over a serving platter. Make a shallow well from the center out and fill with half the prepared caponata. This stands as a complete dinner on its own, so rich with vitamins and fresh vegetables. If you prepare a salad, make a simple one dressed with oil and vinegar, salt and pepper.

Double-Duty Dinner: Caponata Pasta Bake

MAKES 4 SERVINGS

1 & 1/2 quarts prepared caponata, half of the above recipe

1/2 pound penne or ziti rigate pasta, cooked al dente, about 8 minutes

1/2 cup grated Parmigiano Reggiano or Romano cheese (a couple handfuls)

1 & 1/2 cups shredded provolone cheese (available on dairy aisle of market)

1/2 teaspoon crushed red pepper flakes

Chopped fresh flat-leaf parsley, for garnish

Preheat broiler to high.

Reheat caponata in the microwave or on the stovetop. Cook pasta, drain and return to the hot pot. Toss with 1/2 cup grated cheese. Add hot caponata and combine. Transfer pasta and vegetables to a 9 x 13 baking dish. Top with shredded provolone cheese, crushed pepper flakes, and parsley. Place baking dish under broiler to brown and bubble cheese. Serve immediately.

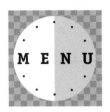

M E N U

1

A Divine
Chicken Divan
•••••

2

Double Duty
Dinner:
Chicken
Tetrazzini
•••••

A Divine Chicken Divan

MAKES 4 SERVINGS, plus chicken for tetrazzini

BASE CHICKEN RECIPE

1 quart chicken stock
8 pieces boneless, skinless chicken breasts (6 to 8 ounces each)
2 medium shallots, chopped
1 tablespoon extra-virgin olive oil
2 tablespoons butter
3 tablespoons flour
1 cup dry white wine
1/2 cup heavy cream
1/4 teaspoon ground nutmeg or the equivalent of freshly grated
Salt and freshly ground black pepper

DIVINE DIVAN

1 pound broccoli spears
2 cups grated Gruyère cheese (8-ounce brick), shredded

Bring 1 quart chicken stock to a boil in a wide, deep skillet with lid. Add chicken breasts and return stock to a boil. Reduce heat to medium low; cover and poach chicken, 8 minutes.

In a skillet, sauté shallots in oil and butter for 2 minutes. Sprinkle in 3 tablespoons flour and cook 1 minute. Whisk in 1 cup wine and reduce by half, about a minute. Ladle in chicken stock, whisking sauce as you do. Stir in 1/2 cup heavy cream. Season with nutmeg, salt, and pepper. Bring to a bubble and reduce heat to low. Slice chicken into 1/2-inch strips and add to the pan, coating them in sauce. At this stage remove half of the chicken in sauce and transfer to a container with a tight-fitting lid. Cool the chicken, cover, and freeze for the Tetrazzini next week.

DIVINE DIVAN: Preheat broiler.

To assemble, simmer broccoli spears in 1 inch of water, covered, for 5 minutes. Drain and transfer to a shallow baking or casserole dish. Layer on half the grated Gruyère and half of the base chicken recipe. Top with remaining Gruyère and brown until bubbling and golden under preheated broiler, about 2 minutes. Serve with salad greens with your favorite dressing and crusty bread.

Suggested side for both dinners

1 sack (10 ounces) baby salad greens
White wine vinegar and extra-virgin olive oil, for dressing
Salt and freshly ground black pepper
Crusty bread and butter

Double-Duty Dinner: Chicken Tetrazzini

MAKES 4 SERVINGS

1/2 pound wide egg noodles, cooked al dente, to package directions
Leftover chicken, half of base chicken recipe
2 tablespoons butter
12 mushrooms, sliced
1/2 cup bread crumbs
1/4 cup grated Parmigiano Reggiano cheese (a couple handfuls)
2 ounces slivered almonds, toasted

To assemble Tetrazzini, reheat the base chicken leftovers in microwave oven. Preheat broiler. Melt 2 tablespoons butter in a small pan. Sauté mushrooms, 5 minutes, until tender. Toss drained hot egg noodles with chicken and mushrooms. Transfer mixture to a baking dish and top with bread crumbs and cheese. Brown under preheated broiler, about 6 inches from heat source, about 2 to 3 minutes. Remove from broiler, sprinkle with toasted almonds, and serve with dressed salad greens and bread.

MENU

1

Spanish Beef
and Rice

• • • • •

2

Spicy Chopped
Salad with
Tortillas

• • • • •

3

Double-Duty
Dinner:
Stuffed Chilies
with Beef,
Rice, Spinach,
and Cheese

• • • • •

Spanish Beef and Rice

MAKES 4 SERVINGS, plus 4 reserved for stuffed peppers

2 cups beef stock
1 & 3/4 cups water
1 tablespoon butter
2 cups white enriched rice
1 tablespoon extra-virgin olive oil (once around the pan)
1 & 2/3 pounds ground sirloin
Salt and freshly ground black pepper, to taste
1 large onion, finely chopped
4 cloves garlic, chopped
1 green bell pepper, seeded and finely chopped
1 tablespoon Worcestershire Sauce
2 cups tomato sauce
1/4 teaspoon ground cloves
2 teaspoons ground cumin (2/3 palmful)
1/4 cup chopped fresh flat-leaf parsley (a couple handfuls)

Bring beef stock, water, and butter to a full boil in a medium-size pot. Add rice, reduce heat and cover pot. Cook 20 minutes, until rice is tender and liquid absorbed.

Heat a large, deep skillet over medium-high heat. Add oil and beef and season with salt and pepper. Brown meat, 2 or 3 minutes. Add onion, garlic, bell pepper, and Worcestershire. Cook 5 to 7 minutes, until veggies are just tender. Add tomato sauce, cloves, cumin, and parsley. Bring up to a bubble, then reduce heat to low.

Combine cooked rice with meat mixture and serve with Spicy Chopped Salad with Tortillas and taco dressing, below. Reserve half of the beef and rice for stuffed peppers later in the week.

Spicy Chopped Salad with Tortillas

MAKES 4 SERVINGS

2 hearts romaine lettuce, chopped
3 tablespoons canned or jarred sliced jalapeños, drained
3 tablespoons salad olives, Manzanilla with pimento, drained
1 vine-ripened tomato, seeded and chopped
1/2 red onion, chopped
1 cup broken tortilla chips (any variety)

2 tablespoons jarred taco sauce

The juice of 1 lime

2 tablespoons chopped cilantro or fresh flat-leaf parsley

1/4 cup olive oil (eyeball it)

Salt and freshly ground black pepper, to taste

Combine first five ingredients in a bowl, and toss with tortilla chip pieces. In a second bowl, combine taco sauce, lime juice, and cilantro or parsley. Whisk in olive oil in a slow stream until dressing is well combined. Toss salad with dressing to coat ingredients evenly, and serve.

Double-Duty Dinner: Stuffed Chilies with Beef, Rice, Spinach, and Cheese

MAKES 4 SERVINGS

4 long, mild to medium chili peppers, such as moderate-heat poblano or mild Italian Cubanelle

1 tablespoon extra-virgin olive oil, plus some for drizzling

1 clove garlic, cracked

10 ounces triple-washed spinach, stems removed and coarsely chopped

Salt and freshly ground black pepper, to taste

1/2 cup beef or chicken broth

3 cups leftover Spanish Beef and Rice

1 cup tomato sauce

2 cups shredded Monterey Jack, smoked cheddar or Pepper Jack cheese

Preheat a griddle or grill pan. Halve and seed chili peppers. Drizzle them with a little oil and grill over medium-high to high heat, 3 or 4 minutes on each side, until tender. Transfer peppers to a baking sheet, hollow-side up.

Place a medium skillet over medium heat and add 1 tablespoon olive oil (once around the pan) and a crushed clove of garlic. Sauté for a few minutes, then add spinach in bunches until it is all wilted. Season with salt and pepper. Remove spinach, drain liquid, and set aside.

Preheat broiler to high.

Combine broth and leftover beef and rice in the same skillet over medium heat. Add 1 cup tomato sauce and heat through.

Pile spinach and Spanish Beef and Rice into peppers. Top liberally with shredded cheese and melt under broiler, 3 to 5 minutes, then serve.

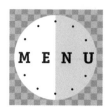

M E N U

1

Chicken and
Vegetable
Potage

· · · · ·

2

Double-Duty
Dinner:
Portuguese
Chicken and
Chorizo

· · · · ·

Chicken and Vegetable Potage

The following recipes are two fabulous one-pot meals!

MAKES 4 SERVINGS, plus 4 poached chicken breasts for your
Portuguese Chicken and Chorizo

8 pieces boneless, skinless chicken breast (6 ot 8 ounces each),
   cut 4 into large chunks, leave others whole

Salt, to taste

3 carrots, peeled and cut on an angle into 1/2-inch slices

3 ribs celery, cut on an angle into 2-inch pieces

2 small-to-medium onions, cut into 1 & 1/2-inch chunks

1 bay leaf, fresh or dried

4 sprigs fresh thyme

2 cups dry white wine

Water, to cover

10 blades chives, snipped or chopped

1/4 cup finely chopped fresh flat-leaf parsley (a couple handfuls)

Warm, crusty French baguette

Butter, room temperature, for passing

Season chicken with salt. Arrange pieces in a deep, large skillet. Cover chicken
with carrots, celery, and onions. Add bay leaf, thyme sprigs, white wine, and
water to cover veggies and chicken. Place over high heat and bring to a boil,
cover, reduce heat to simmer and cook, 20 minutes. Remove bay and thyme and
adjust salt to taste. Arrange chunks of chicken and vegetables in shallow serving
bowls, and cover with some of the broth. Garnish each serving with chives and
parsley. Serve with crusty bread and butter.

Double-Duty Dinner: Portuguese Chicken and Chorizo

4 all-purpose potatoes, such as russets, peeled and cut into quarters

4 carrots, peeled and cut into large pieces on an angle

3 ribs celery, cut into large pieces on an angle

1 large onion, cut into large chunks

1 cup dry white wine

2 teaspoons sugar

1 teaspoon salt

1 tablespoon extra-virgin olive oil (eyeball it)

2 cups chicken broth

3/4 pound chorizo, (casing removed, if preferred), cut on an angle into 1 & 1/2-inch slices

1 cup tomato sauce

4 pieces poached cooked chicken, leftover from potage, sliced on an angle into 1-inch strips

1/4 cup chopped fresh flat-leaf parsley

Crusty Portuguese bread or other chewy farm bread, for passing at the table

Place potatoes, carrots, celery, and onion in a pot. Add wine, sugar, salt, oil, and chicken broth. Cover pot and bring to a boil. Reduce heat and simmer, 15 minutes.

While vegetables cook, brown chorizo in a nonstick skillet over medium-high heat.

Uncover vegetables and add in the chorizo and the tomato sauce. Set cooked chicken into the pot and heat through for 5 minutes. Adjust seasoning. Ladle Portuguese Chicken into shallow bowls, garnish with parsley, and serve with crusty bread for dipping.

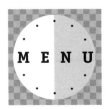

MENU

1

Boneless Roast
Leg of Lamb

• • • • •

2

Baby Potatoes
with Cumin

• • • • •

3

Watercress
and Mint Salad
with Lime
Dressing

• • • • •

4

Double-Duty
Lunch:
Lamb Pitas
with Tomato,
Scallions,
and Mint
Yogurt
Dressing

• • • • •

Boneless Roast Leg of Lamb

MAKES 2 TO 3 SERVINGS, plus leftovers for the Lamb Pitas

1 small boneless leg of lamb, 2 & 3/4 pounds (ask your butcher to
  butterfly the leg for you)
Extra-virgin olive oil, for drizzling
Coarse salt and freshly ground black pepper, to taste
6 cloves garlic, crushed
1 bunch fresh mint, washed
Wedges of lemon or grapefruit

Preheat oven to 400°F. Set top oven rack 6 inches from the broiler. Place lamb in
a shallow baking pan. Drizzle oil and rub evenly over lamb. Season both sides
with salt and coarse black pepper. Rub the boned side of the lamb with 2 cloves
crushed garlic, then pile the other cloves and a whole bundle of mint in the
center of the meat. Fold it over in half and roast, 20 minutes. Switch to the broiler
setting on high and brown the lamb, 5 minutes. Remove from oven. Let meat rest
5 to 10 minutes for juices to redistribute. Slice and serve. Squeeze a wedge of
lemon or grapefruit over the meat and enjoy. Reserve a little less than 1/3 of the
meat for the next day's recipe.

Baby Potatoes with Cumin

MAKES 3 SERVINGS

1 & 1/2 pounds very small potatoes, halve some, leave 1 & 1/2-inch
  potatoes whole
Extra-virgin olive oil, for drizzling
1 teaspoon cumin seeds, or 2 teaspoons ground (1/2 palmful)
Coarse salt, to taste

Preheat oven to 400°F.

Set potatoes on a cookie sheet and drizzle them with just enough oil to lightly
coat them, about 1 & 1/2 tablespoons. Toss potatoes with cumin seed or ground
cumin and roast, 20 minutes in a hot oven, then broil 5 minutes on high to
brown their edges. If you are making potatoes with the above recipe for lamb,
set the baking sheet with the potatoes in the oven alongside the lamb on the
same rack. Toss cooked potatoes with salt and serve.

Watercress and Mint Salad with Lime Dressing

MAKES 3 SERVINGS

1 bunch watercress, trimmed and coarsely chopped
4 sprigs fresh mint (2 tablespoons), chopped
A handful chopped fresh flat-leaf parsley
1 heart romaine, coarsely chopped
The juice of 1 lime
1 teaspoon sugar
3 tablespoons extra-virgin olive oil (eyeball it)
Coarse salt and freshly ground black pepper, to taste

Combine watercress, mint, parsley, and romaine in a small salad bowl. Combine lime juice and sugar in a small mixing bowl, and whisk in the oil in a slow stream. Pour dressing over the salad and season with salt and pepper.

Double-Duty Lunch:
Lamb Pitas with Tomato, Scallions, and Mint Yogurt Dressing

MAKES 4 PITAS, 2 servings

4 pita breads
1 pound leftover roast leg of lamb
1 cup chicken broth
1 tablespoon extra-virgin olive oil (once around the pan)
3 plum tomatoes, diced
4 scallions, thinly sliced on an angle
Salt and freshly ground black pepper, to taste
1 cup plain yogurt
1 teaspoon ground cumin (eyeball it)
1/2 teaspoon ground coriander (1/3 palmful)
2 tablespoons fresh mint (4 sprigs), finely chopped

Turn on oven to lowest setting.

Wrap pitas in foil and place in a warm oven. Thinly slice the cooked lamb. In a small skillet over moderate heat bring the chicken stock to a boil, then reduce the heat to low. Add the sliced lamb to reheat while keeping it moist.

To a second skillet over moderate heat, add oil, diced tomatoes and scallions, allowing them to heat through for about 2 minutes. Season with salt and pepper.

For the dressing, combine yogurt with cumin, coriander, and mint.

To assemble, remove pitas from oven and arrange on serving dish. Remove meat from warm broth with tongs and shake off excess. Arrange a few slices of lamb down the center of each pita. Top with a few spoonfuls each of tomatoes and scallions and the yogurt dressing.

PASSPORT
MEALS

RACHAEL RAY **2**
30-MINUTE MEALS

One of my favorite movies is, It's A Wonderful Life. My favorite scene is one of the most romantic notions I've ever seen put to celluloid. I cry every time. It is so real to me that I get flushed and sometimes have to watch through fingers covering my eyes. I feel I am intruding on George and Mary's most special moment. Can you guess the scene? George always wanted to see the world, but life got in the way. Mary is his new bride. They're poor. He's off, working late again, trying to save the Savings and Loan from mean, old Mr. Potter. It's pouring rain and cold outside. George, hopes dashed, wet, exhausted, drags himself up the steps to his leaky, dark house. And then he walks off a street in Pottersville and into a balmy night in the South Seas. Mary is all dolled up. The peeling wallpaper is hidden by travel posters of warm, far away islands with soft, white, powdery beaches and clear, blue-green waters. The air is filled with the aroma of a fire-roasted chicken. The rotisserie turns as the record player spins. George's friends hide beneath the window outside, singing island tunes and playing the ukulele. For a moment, George has the woman he loves alone on a deserted island, and a rotisserie chicken, too! Every man's fantasy come true! It's a Wonderful Life!

This scene still inspires me today whenever I sit down to write a Passport 30-Minute Meal. Passport Meals are menus that can take you away for a night. With 30 minutes and a little imagination you can go to Paris, Tuscany, Spain, Hong Kong or beyond, any night of the week! Take a tip from Mary and use these meals as a gift to someone you love. Or, show yourself a little love! If you can't afford either the time or money to run away to a fancy spa for a week, try a night in Morocco! Rent Casablanca and turn to page 174.

Southwestern Stuffed Peppers

MAKES 4 SERVINGS

2 cups vegetable broth
1 tablespoon butter
1 cup of white rice
2 long mild chili peppers, red or green (Cubanelle Italian peppers may be substituted)
1 tablespoon of extra-virgin olive oil (once around the pan)
1 small onion, chopped
1 cup frozen peas
1 cup mild or medium taco sauce
Salt and freshly ground black pepper, to taste
2 tablespoons chopped cilantro or fresh flat-leaf parsley, for garnish
2 scallions, thinly sliced, for garnish

Preheat a grill pan over high heat.

Bring 2 cups vegetable broth and butter to a boil in a small covered pot. Add rice, reduce heat to low and cook, 18 to 20 minutes, or until rice is tender and liquid absorbed.

Split peppers lengthwise and remove seeds, leaving stems intact. Grill peppers on hot grill pan for 3 to 5 minutes on each side. Remove from grill and let cool.

To a medium skillet over moderate heat, add olive oil and onion, and sauté, 2 or 3 minutes. Add cooked rice to the pan and stir in peas and taco sauce. Season with salt and pepper.

Load up pepper halves with seasoned rice. Place on serving dish and top with chopped cilantro or parsley, and scallions. Pile any extra rice on serving plates, nesting the stuffed peppers within.

M E N U

Meatfree
Fiesta Menu

1

Southwestern
Stuffed
Peppers
· · · · ·

2

Wild
Mushroom
Quesadillas
with Warm
Black Bean
Salsa
· · · · ·

3

Strawberry
Marg-alrightas
· · · · ·

Wild Mushroom Quesadillas with Warm Black Bean Salsa

MAKES 4 SERVINGS

2 tablespoons extra-virgin olive oil (twice around the pan), plus some for drizzling

16 crimini mushroom caps (baby portobellos) with stems trimmed and thinly sliced OR 4 portobello caps, halved and thinly sliced

16 shiitake mushrooms, stems removed and thinly sliced

Coarse freshly ground black pepper and salt, to taste

1 tablespoon fresh thyme, chopped, or 1 teaspoon dried

4 large flour tortillas, 12-inch diameter

2 cups shredded sharp white cheddar cheese

SALSA

1 tablespoon extra-virgin olive oil (once around the pan)

1 small onion, finely chopped

2 cloves garlic, finely chopped

1 jalapeño pepper, seeded and chopped

1 can (15 ounces) black beans, drained

1 cup frozen corn kernels

1/2 cup sun-dried tomatoes in oil, chopped

1/2 cup smoky barbecue sauce

Salt and freshly ground black pepper, to taste

TIDBIT

❝ Gently groom your 'shrooms. Clean mushrooms with a damp cloth. Do not run fresh mushrooms under water; they will discolor and toughen. ❞

Heat a medium nonstick skillet over medium heat. Add oil, then the sliced mushrooms. Season with pepper, salt and thyme, and sauté 10 minutes or until mushrooms are dark and tender. Remove from heat, and transfer to a dish.

For the salsa, return skillet to the stove over medium heat, and add another turn of olive oil. Add the onions, garlic and jalapeño pepper and sauté, 2 or 3 minutes, then add the beans and corn. Stir in sun-dried tomatoes and barbecue sauce. Season with salt and pepper, and transfer to a serving dish.

Heat a griddle pan or large nonstick skillet over medium to medium-high heat. Add a drizzle of oil to the pan and 1 tortilla. Cook tortilla 1 minute, then turn it over. Sprinkle 1/2 cup sharp cheddar over half the tortilla. Cover the cheese with 1/4 of the cooked mushrooms. Fold the plain half of the tortilla over top of the filling and gently press down with a spatula. Cook the filled quesadilla 30 seconds to a minute longer on each side to lightly brown and crisp the outside and melt the cheese. Remove the quesadilla to a large cutting board or transfer to a warm oven to hold, then repeat the process for the remaining quesadillas.

Cut each quesadilla into wedges and serve with warm salsa for topping.

Fresh Strawberry Marg-alrightas

2 pints ripe strawberries
The juice of 4 limes, plus 1 lime wedged to rim glass and for garnishing
8 rounded tablespoons sugar
1/2 cup orange juice
8 shots good quality tequila
2 trays of ice cubes
Coarse salt, to rim glasses

Reserve 4 strawberries with stems intact for garnish and split them. Trim remaining clean, dry strawberries.

To make one drink, add half a pint of strawberries to a blender. To that, add the juice of 1 lime, 2 rounded tablespoons sugar, a splash of orange juice, and 2 shots of tequila. Fill the blender with half a tray of ice and blend on high speed until the drink is icy but smooth.

Rim a cocktail glass with lime juice and salt and scoop in the frozen strawberry lime drink. Garnish glass with a wedge of lime and a split strawberry. Repeat with remaining ingredients.

Sunset Sangria

This sangria takes 5 to 10 minutes to assemble in a large pitcher. Prepare it in the morning so it has several hours to develop its fruity flavors. Take it out when dinner is ready to serve that evening.

MAKES 8 GLASSES SANGRIA

3 tablespoons sugar

3 tablespoons spiced dark rum

3 tablespoons Cointreau or other orange liqueur

1 navel orange, sliced

1 lemon, sliced

2 ripe peaches, cut into wedges

3 ripe plums, cut into wedges

2 cinnamon sticks

1 bottle red Rioja or other dry red wine

Sparkling soda water, for topping off sangria at table

Combine sugar, rum, orange liqueur, fruits and cinnamon sticks in a large pitcher. Cover with 1 bottle of Rioja wine and chill sangria several hours. To serve, spoon fruits into glasses or goblets. Pour in the sangria and top off with a splash of soda water.

Red Snapper with Olive Salsa and Green Beans

MAKES 4 SERVINGS

RED SNAPPER

4 red snapper fillets (8 ounces each)

Extra-virgin olive oil, for drizzling

1 & 1/2 teaspoons each (1/2 a palmful) ground cumin and sweet paprika

1 teaspoon each (1/3 palmful) coarse salt, freshly ground black pepper, and ground coriander

SALSA

3 plum tomatoes, seeded and chopped

A handful cilantro leaves, finely chopped (flat-leaf parsley may be substituted)

1/2 small red onion, chopped

12 large green olives, pitted or cracked away from pits with the flat of your knife, then coarsely chopped

The juice of 1 lime

1 teaspoon crushed red pepper flakes

GREEN BEANS

1 & 1/2 pounds fresh green beans, trimmed

1 tablespoon extra-virgin olive oil (once around the pan)

1 tablespoon butter

Salt, to taste

Toasted slivered or sliced almonds, for garnish

Preheat grill pan, cast-iron skillet or indoor electric grill to high heat. Drizzle snapper with olive oil. Combine spices in a small bowl, and rub fish with the mixture. Place fish on hot grill skin-side down. After 3 minutes, turn and cook fish 3 to 4 minutes longer.

Combine salsa ingredients in a small bowl and allow flavors to combine until ready to serve.

Cook green beans in 1 inch of boiling, salted water, covered, for 5 minutes, then drain. They should be bright green and still crisp. Return pan to heat and toss beans with oil and butter. Season with a little salt, transfer to a serving plate, and garnish with the toasted almonds.

To serve, place green beans alongside spiced snapper topped with a generous serving of salsa. Sunset Sangria makes a wonderful beverage for this meal.

TIDBIT

❝ Buy extra large, good quality green olives (such as Sicilian) for this recipe. Often found in the bulk olive bins in the appetizer/deli sections of your market. ❞

**Group Tour
to Spain**

1

**Paella for
Eight**
· · · · ·

2

**Spanish
Cheese and
Olives**
· · · · ·

3

White Sangria
· · · · ·

TIDBIT

❝ For deep
fruit flavor,
take 5 minutes
to prepare
Sangria in the
morning for
serving later in
the day. ❞

White Sangria

MAKES 8 GLASSES

3 tablespoons sugar
3 shots Calvados or other apple liqueur
1 lime, sliced
1 lemon, sliced
2 ripe peaches, pitted and cut into wedges
3 ripe green apples, cored and cut into wedges
1 bottle white Rioja Spanish wine or other dry white wine
1 pint raspberries
Sparkling soda water, for topping off sangria at table

Combine sugar, Calvados, lime, lemon, peaches, and apples in a large pitcher.
Cover with Rioja wine and chill sangria at least several hours. To serve, spoon
fruits into glasses or goblets, adding a few fresh raspberries to each glass. Pour
sangria over top of the fruit, topping glasses off with a splash of soda water.

Paella for Eight

MAKES 8 SERVINGS

3 tablespoons extra-virgin olive oil (twice around the pan)
3 cloves garlic, crushed
1/2 to 1 teaspoon crushed red pepper flakes
2 cups enriched white rice
1/4 teaspoon saffron threads
1 bay leaf, fresh or dried
1 quart chicken broth or stock
4 sprigs fresh thyme
1 & 1/2 pounds chicken tenders, cut into thirds
Salt and freshly ground black pepper, to taste
1 red bell pepper, seeded and chopped
1 medium onion, chopped
3/4 pound chorizo, casing removed (if preferred) and sliced on an angle
1 pound peeled and deveined large shrimp (about 24 shrimp)
18 mussels, cleaned (green-lipped, if available)
1 cup frozen peas
The zest of 2 lemons

GARNISH
1/4 cup chopped fresh flat-leaf parsley
4 scallions, chopped
Lemon wedges
Crusty bread for passing

Preheat a very wide skillet or paella pan over medium-high heat. Add 2 table-spoons olive oil, crushed garlic, red pepper flakes, and rice and sauté, 2 or 3 minutes. Add saffron threads, bay leaf, broth, and thyme and bring to a boil over high heat. Cover with lid or foil and reduce heat to simmer.

In a separate nonstick skillet, over medium-high heat, brown chicken on both sides in about 1 tablespoon olive oil. Season chicken with salt and pepper. Add red bell pepper and onion to the pan and cook 3 minutes longer. Add chorizo and cook another 2 minutes, then remove pan from heat.

After about 13 minutes, add shellfish to the paella pan, nesting them in the cooking rice. Pour in peas, scatter lemon zest over the rice and seafood, then cover the pan again. After 5 minutes, uncover and discard any unopened mussels. Stir rice and seafood and lift out bay leaf and thyme stems, now bare of their leaves. Arrange cooked chicken, peppers, onions and chorizo around the paella pan. Top with parsley and scallions and serve with wedges of lemon, and warm bread.

Spanish Cheese and Olives

MAKES 8 SERVINGS

1 package of your favorite type crackers
1/2 pound each: Manchego, Cabrales Blue and Mahon, or other assorted Spanish cheeses
4 ribs celery, halved lengthwise, then cut into 4-inch sticks
1 pound Spanish green olives (available in specialty olives case near deli section) or other mixed olives

Arrange crackers, cheeses, celery sticks, and a dish of olives on a cutting board or large serving platter and set out for guests to snack on while dinner cooks.

M E N U

Passport to
Mexico

1

Grilled Halibut
Tacos with
Guacamole
Sauce
• • • • •

2

Mexican Rice
• • • • •

3

Extra-Spicy
Refried Beans,
Lettuce,
Tomatoes, and
Lime
• • • • •

4

Crunchy Ice
Cream
• • • • •

Grilled Halibut Tacos with Guacamole Sauce

MAKES 4 SERVINGS, 3 fish tacos each

4 pieces fresh halibut, steak or fillets (6 to 8 ounces each)
Extra-virgin olive oil, for drizzling
Salt and freshly ground black pepper
The juice of 1 lime
3 small to medium ripe Haas avocados, pitted and scooped from skins with a large spoon
The juice of 1 lemon
1/4 teaspoon cayenne pepper (eyeball it)
1 cup plain yogurt
1 teaspoon coarse salt (eyeball it)
2 plum tomatoes, seeded and chopped
2 scallions, thinly sliced on an angle
1 heart romaine lettuce
12 soft 6-inch tortillas

Preheat a grill pan or indoor grill to high setting or prepare outdoor grill. Drizzle halibut on both sides with olive oil to keep fish from sticking to the pan or grill. Season with salt and pepper, to taste. Grill fish, 5 to 6 minutes on each side, or until opaque. Squeeze lime juice down over the fish and remove from the pan or grill. Flake fish into large chunks with a fork.

While fish is cooking, in a blender or food processor, combine avocado, lemon juice, cayenne pepper, yogurt, and salt. Process until smooth. Remove guacamole sauce to a bowl and stir in diced tomatoes and chopped scallions. Shred lettuce and reserve.

When fish comes off the grill pan or grill, blister and heat soft taco wraps. To assemble, pile some of the fish chunks into soft wraps and slather with guacamole sauce. Top with shredded lettuce, fold tacos over and eat!

Mexican Rice

MAKES 4 SERVINGS

2 tablespoons butter
1 cup enriched white rice
2 cups chicken broth
2 tablespoons each chopped cilantro and chopped pimiento
2 scallions, thinly sliced

Sauté rice in butter over medium-high heat, 2 or 3 minutes. Add broth and bring to a boil. Cover rice, reduce heat to simmer, and cook, 18 to 20 minutes. Fluff with a fork and add cilantro, pimiento and scallions. Stir to combine well and serve.

Extra-Spicy Refried Beans, Lettuce, Tomatoes, and Lime

MAKES 4 SERVINGS

2 cans (15 ounces each) refried beans
1 can (4 ounces) sliced jalapeños, drained and chopped
1 teaspoon cayenne hot pepper sauce
1 teaspoon garlic powder
2 hearts romaine lettuce, shredded
2 vine-ripe tomatoes, seeded and diced
Coarse salt, to taste
The juice of 1 lime
1 tablespoon extra-virgin olive oil

Heat refried beans in a medium nonstick skillet over medium heat. Stir in jalapeño, hot pepper sauce, and garlic powder and reduce heat to low and keep warm until ready to serve. Combine lettuce and tomatoes in a salad bowl, season with salt, and squeeze lime juice over the salad. Toss to combine. Drizzle olive oil over all and toss again. Serve refried beans alongside the salad.

Crunchy Ice Cream

Tastes like Mexican fried ice cream balls, but takes only minutes to prepare!

MAKES 4 SERVINGS

1 pint vanilla ice cream
2 teaspoons cinnamon sugar
2 tablespoons honey
1 cup crushed corn flakes
2 ounces chopped nut topping (found on baking aisle of market)
4 Maraschino cherries

Top large scoops of vanilla ice cream with a sprinkle of cinnamon sugar, a drizzle of honey, crushed corn flakes, chopped nut topping, and a cherry on top. Serve.

TIDBIT

❝ To get lime juices flowing, roll a whole lime on countertop, exerting pressure from the open palm of your hand, or place in microwave for 10 seconds only at high setting. ❞

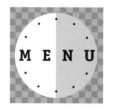

Passport to Greece: Guzaria Menu

1

Village Salad with Grilled Pita Bread
· · · · ·

2

Greek Meatballs in Wine Sauce
· · · · ·

3

Baked Gigantes Beans
· · · · ·

4

Grilled Shrimp
· · · · ·

Village Salad with Grilled Pita Bread

Guzaria, or Greek tapas, are enjoyed at a taverna: many little dishes that can be snacked on for a fulfilling meal. In Old Athens friends and townspeople would gather in small bars at the end of a hard day to talk and share food and drink at a leisurely pace over the course of the evening. Ouzo and cold beer are the suggested beverages with your Guzaria menu.

MAKES 4 SERVINGS

3 vine-ripe tomatoes, cut into chunks

1 medium red onion, thinly sliced

1/2 European seedless cucumber, cut into bite-size chunks

1 small red bell pepper, seeded and chunked

1 small green bell pepper, seeded and chunked

1 cup Kalamata black olives

1/2 cup chopped fresh flat-leaf parsley (a couple handfuls)

1/2 pound imported Greek feta cheese, sliced

1/4 cup extra-virgin olive oil (a couple glugs)

3 tablespoons red wine vinegar (3 splashes)

1 teaspoon dried oregano, crushed in palm of your hand

Coarse salt and freshly ground black pepper, to taste

Pita breads

Combine vegetables, olives, and parsley in a large bowl. Rest sliced feta cheese on top of the salad. Combine oil, vinegar, and oregano in a small plastic container with a lid. Shake vigorously to combine oil and vinegar and pour over salad and cheese. Season with salt and pepper and let the salad marinate until ready to serve. Serve with pita bread blistered and warmed on a hot griddle or grill pan.

Greek Meatballs in Wine Sauce

MAKES 4 SERVINGS

3/4 pound ground lamb

3/4 pound ground beef or veal

1 small yellow onion, minced or hand-grated

A handful fresh flat-leaf parsley, chopped

Salt and freshly ground black pepper, to taste

1 tablespoon butter

1 tablespoon extra-virgin olive oil (once around the pan)

1 cup dry white wine

1/2 lemon

Preheat a medium-sized skillet over medium-high heat.

In a large bowl, combine meats, onion, parsley, salt and pepper. Melt butter into oil in the pan and begin rolling the meat mixture into small, bite-size balls, adding to the pan as you roll them. Sauté, 10 to 12 minutes, shaking pan occasionally to brown equally on all sides. Deglaze pan with wine and allow it to reduce by half, 1 or 2 minutes. Remove pan from heat, squeeze the lemon juice over the meatballs in the skillet, and serve.

Baked Gigantes Beans

MAKES 4 SERVINGS

2 cans (15 ounces each) butter beans, drained
1 cup tomato sauce
A handful chopped fresh flat-leaf parsley
1/2 teaspoon dried oregano (eyeball the amount)
Extra-virgin olive oil, for drizzling
Salt and freshly ground black pepper, to taste

Preheat oven to 450°F.

In a small oven-safe casserole, combine beans with tomato sauce, parsley and oregano, crushing the oregano in your palm before you sprinkle it into the beans. Drizzle with a touch of oil and season with salt and pepper. Combine ingredients with a final toss. Bake in oven 12 minutes or until sauce is bubbling and beans are heated through.

Grilled Shrimp

MAKES 4 SERVINGS

16 uncooked jumbo shrimp in shell, deveined (ask for easy-peels at the
    seafood counter, or devein with small sharp knife)
Extra-virgin olive oil (about 1/2 cup) for brushing
Coarse salt and freshly ground black pepper, to taste
2 lemons, halved

Preheat griddle or grill pan over high heat.

Butterfly shrimp by slicing almost through lengthwise, but leaving shell on—this will keep the shrimp tender while grilling over such high heat. Brush shrimp with oil, season with salt and pepper and grill 2 minutes on each side, until shells are hot pink and shrimp is white. Place lemons cut-side down on grill at the last minute. The heat will release the juice from the lemons. To serve, squeeze grilled lemon halves over shrimp.

Olive Rosemary Crostini

MAKES 4 SERVINGS

2 cloves garlic, cracked away from skin
1/4 cup extra-virgin olive oil (eyeball the amount)
1 small loaf crusty bread, sliced
1/2 pound oil-cured black and Sicilian green olives, pitted and chopped
3 tablespoons capers, drained
1/2 teaspoon crushed red pepper flakes
2 sprigs fresh rosemary, leaves stripped from stems

Sauté 2 cloves garlic in oil over low heat in a small skillet. Toast bread slices under hot broiler on both sides. Using a pastry brush, dab charred bread with garlic oil. Place rest of oil in a small bowl with chopped olives. Pile garlic cloves on a cutting board together with capers, red pepper flakes, and rosemary leaves. Finely chop mixture, and combine with the olives and oil. To assemble crostini, spread this olive tapenade on toasts and enjoy!

Pesce Spada Rollotini (Rolled Swordfish)

When in Sicily, I have these swordfish rolls as a favorite lunch or late-night snack. Here, I use my grandfather's lemon, parsley, and garlic coating to bread my own fish rolls, and the results would make him proud!

MAKES 4 SERVINGS

1 & 1/2 pounds thin-cut swordfish steaks (ask at fish counter for
  3 steaks cut as thinly as possible, no more than 1/2-inch thick)
1 & 1/2 cups plain bread crumbs
A handful fresh flat-leaf parsley
1 large clove garlic, peeled
The zest of 1 lemon
Coarse salt
2 tablespoons extra-virgin olive oil

Pat dry swordfish steaks. Trim away skin and dark connective tissue, and place between wax paper sheets. Pound with rubber mallet, as you would chicken or veal cutlets. Cut the thin slices into several rectangular pieces, about 2 x 4 inches.

Place bread crumbs in a shallow dish. Pile parsley, garlic, lemon zest, and a little coarse salt on a cutting board. Finely chop the lemon-garlic mixture, then combine with plain bread crumbs. Gently press the fish slices into the crumb mixture, coating both sides. Roll up the coated fish strips tightly into small bundles.

Preheat a medium nonstick skillet over moderate heat, coat with a thin layer of olive oil (twice around the pan), and cook several swordfish rolls, 3 to 4 minutes on each side until just golden and firm. Remove from pan and serve swordfish with lemon wedges, Fennel Slaw Salad and Olive Rosemary Crostini.

Fennel Slaw Salad

MAKES 4 SERVINGS

A palmful golden raisins (2 tablespoons)
The juice of 1 navel orange
2 bulbs fresh fennel, trimmed of tops and fronds, cored and thinly
   sliced lengthwise
1 medium head radicchio lettuce, shredded
4 scallions, thinly sliced on an angle
A handful fresh flat-leaf parsley, chopped
A handful pignoli nuts, toasted (3 tablespoons)
2 tablespoons balsamic vinegar (eyeball the amount)
3 tablespoons extra-virgin olive oil (3 times around the bowl)
Coarse salt and freshly ground black pepper

Place raisins in a small dish, cover with the orange juice and 2 to 3 tablespoons hot water. Plump and soften the raisins, 5 minutes. Combine fennel, radicchio, scallions, and parsley in a bowl. Add plumped raisins in juice and the pignoli nuts to the slaw and toss with balsamic vinegar and olive oil to lightly coat. Season with coarse salt and pepper to taste.

M E N U

Passport to
Florence

1

Prosciutto di
Parma e
Melone
. . . . .

2

Ribollita-
Bread Soup
. . . . .

3

Rosemary
Grilled
Chicken with
Wild
Mushroom
Sauce
. . . . .

I've had many wonderful meals in Firenze—Florence, Italy. Some favorites, such as Bistecca Fiorentina I can only enjoy there. A steak cut from the back, it is traditionally cooked over hot hardwood or coals, hard to reproduce in my home kitchen.

In general, the Tuscan diet is simple. Meats are dark and prepared with little fuss: rabbit, boar, small wild fowl. The flavors are earthy. When I yearn for Florentine nights, I serve this hearty, satisfying menu.

Prosciutto di Parma is always the first course at one of my favorite restaurants in Florence, Il Latini. The owner, Torello (or Bull) physically looks the part, but dine here once and you will quickly learn that looks are deceiving. Torello is more lamb than bull, a welcoming, generous presence in his restaurant. He accepts no reservations, everyone is treated on a first-come, first-serve basis. Standing on line at Il Latini is part of the experience, and one not to be missed. Torello and his family bring out wine and cheese to soothe the crowds while they wait. It works! The line is filled with laughter, no grumbling heard!

Once inside, you can't believe your eyes! Prosciutto hams hang from every inch of available ceiling space and Torello greets each table with mounds of it thinly sliced and accompanied by platefuls of sweet hand melons. Wine produced on his local Tuscan land is served in great jugs, which are measured when you are greeted and again when you leave; the amount consumed per table fixes the modest price. Following the prosciutto, the next course, a ribollita is served in heavy silver tureens. A Tuscan specialty, ribollita is a soup thickened with stale bread. Torello's ribollita is a wonderful archetype: chicken stock with tomato, small white beans, and the soft, hearty consistency added by the bread. Bowlfuls are topped with very thinly sliced onion, a generous drizzle of dark green extra-virgin olive oil and spoonfuls of freshly grated Parmigiano Reggiano. This ribollita has become one of my favorite comfort foods, especially when I'm home. I often build a big fire while the soup simmers, as the two seem to complement each other so well.

The main course is always a selection of meats cooked on Torello's huge grills balanced over an open fire: rabbit with rosemary, pork chops, beefsteaks. Again, I can't duplicate this at home. For my main course, I use dark meat chicken with a complement of rosemary and a wild mushroom sauce. These mellow, deep-woods flavors and aromas take me far and away, back to Tuscany, recapturing my hearty dinners in the heart of Florence.

Prosciutto di Parma e Melone

2/3 pound prosciutto di Parma, thinly sliced
1 ripe cantaloupe

Transfer the prosciutto from the deli wrapper to a serving dish, separating the slices and ribboning them onto the plate. "Fluffed up" prosciutto is much easier to take from a serving plate.

To choose a ripe melon, give it a sniff and a good squeeze. Melon will be very fragrant and will give slightly to pressure. Cut a thin slice of the melon skin away where it attached to the vine. Trim a thin slice off the opposite end and stand the melon upright. Using a sharp knife, remove the skin by cutting strips top to bottom all the way around. Trim away any missed spots, cut it in half, from top to bottom, and scoop out the seeds. Cut cantaloupe into thin slices or wedges and arrange on a serving plate. Pile prosciutto onto melon slices and enjoy!

Ribollita-Bread Soup

MAKES 4 SERVINGS

2 tablespoons extra-virgin olive oil, plus some for drizzling at the table
4 large cloves garlic, chopped
1 medium onion, chopped
2 carrots, peeled and diced
2 ribs celery, chopped
1 fresh or dried bay leaf (fresh bay is available in herb section of larger markets)
Coarse salt and freshly ground black pepper, to taste
2 cans (15 ounces each) small white beans, such as Goya brand
6 cups chicken stock or broth
2 cups tomato sauce
3 cups stale chewy Italian bread, crust removed and bread torn into pieces (about half a loaf)
1 small white onion, thinly sliced or finely chopped, for garnish
1 cup grated Parmigiano Reggiano cheese

TIDBIT

ff Cannellini beans may be substituted but look for cans marked "small white beans" on international foods aisle of market. **JJ**

Heat a deep, heavy-bottomed pot over moderate heat. Add oil, garlic, onion, carrots, celery, and bay leaf to the pot. Season with salt and pepper and sauté until veggies begin to soften, 5 to 7 minutes. Add beans, stock, and tomato sauce. Cover pot and bring soup to a boil over medium-high heat. Remove lid and stir in torn stale bread. Continue stirring to incorporate bread as it breaks down. When soup becomes thick and bread is distributed evenly, adjust your seasonings and serve the soup in shallow bowls. Some ribollitas are so thick, the spoon can stand upright. Make yours as thick or thin as you like with either more or less bread or more or less stock or water.

Top shallow bowlfuls of soup with raw onion, a drizzle of olive oil, and a generous sprinkling of grated Parmigiano Reggiano.

Rosemary Grilled Chicken and Wild Mushroom Sauce

MAKES 4 SERVINGS

1 & 1/2 pounds boneless, skinless chicken thighs
Extra-virgin olive oil, for drizzling
Coarse salt and freshly ground black pepper, to taste
3 stems fresh rosemary, leaves stripped and chopped

SAUCE
1 cup chicken or vegetable stock
1 ounce dried porcini mushrooms
2 tablespoons extra-virgin olive oil
1/8 pound (4 slices) pancetta, chopped (available at your deli counter)
  OR 3 slices bacon, chopped
2 cloves garlic, crushed
1 large shallot, chopped
2 portobello mushroom caps, halved and thinly sliced
Coarse salt and freshly ground black pepper, to taste
1 tablespoon flour
1 cup dry red wine

Heat a grill pan over high heat. Drizzle chicken thighs with oil, season with salt, pepper and rosemary. Grill chicken 5 minutes on each side and remove from heat to rest for 5 minutes.

Place broth in a small bowl and cover. Heat in microwave on high for 2 minutes. Remove broth from microwave with oven mitt. Add dried porcinis to broth, replace the cover, and steep 5 to 10 minutes to reconstitute mushrooms. This may also be done on stovetop: simmer broth, add dried mushrooms and cook them in broth 10 minutes over low heat.

In a medium skillet, add olive oil and sauté pancetta, cracked garlic, and chopped shallot over medium heat for 3 minutes to crisp pancetta at edges. Add sliced portobello mushrooms, season with salt and pepper, and sauté 10 minutes, or until dark and tender. Add flour and cook 1 minute. Add red wine to the pan and reduce by half, 1 minute. Add reserved broth and porcini mushrooms and simmer together a minute or 2 longer.

Slice chicken thighs and fan out on a plate. Ladle thick mushroom sauce down over sliced chicken and serve.

M E N U

**Passport to
Vienna**

1

Veal Schnitzel

• • • • •

2

**Egg Noodles
with
Mushrooms**

• • • • •

3

**Warm Endive
Salad**

• • • • •

Veal Schnitzel

MAKES 4 SERVINGS

4 large veal scallops (6 ounces each)

3 disposable pie tins (optional, but it makes for easy clean up) or
   3 shallow dishes

1 cup flour

Salt and freshly ground black pepper

2 eggs

1 cup cracker meal (found near bread crumbs or at fish counter in
   market)

A drizzle extra-virgin olive oil

Butter, for frying

Whole nutmeg, for grating

Chopped fresh flat-leaf parsley, for garnish

1 lemon, cut into wedges

Heat a large skillet over moderate heat.

Cover work surface with a sheet of wax paper, and on it arrange scallops a few
inches apart. Top scallops with a second sheet of wax paper. Pound scallops out
to 1/4-inch thick using the bottom of small heavy skillet or a rubber mallet. Set
veal aside and set up 3 pie tins and a plate in a row. Place flour in one tin and
season with salt and pepper. In the second tin, beat eggs with a drizzle of water.
In the third tin, pour in about 1 cup of cracker meal.

Dredge veal lightly in flour. Then coat veal evenly in egg on both sides. Gently
press veal into cracker meal and set aside coated cutlets on a plate. When all
the veal is processed, discard tins—easy clean up! Add a drizzle of oil and
1 & 1/2 tablespoons butter to the skillet. When butter foams, add 2 pieces of
veal and cook 3 to 4 minutes on each side until golden brown. Remove to a
warm plate and grate a little nutmeg over hot schnitzel. Repeat with remaining
2 veal cutlets. Garnish with parsley and lemon wedges.

Egg Noodles with Mushrooms

MAKES 4 SERVINGS

1/2 pound wide egg noodles
2 tablespoons butter
8 white mushrooms, sliced
1 shallot, finely chopped
A handful fresh flat-leaf parsley, chopped
Salt, to taste

Boil egg noodles in salted water until just tender, about 6 minutes.

Sauté sliced mushrooms and shallot in 2 tablespoons butter over moderate heat until tender, about 3 or 4 minutes.

Toss noodles with mushrooms and parsley. Season with a little salt.

Warm Endive Salad

MAKES 4 SERVINGS

4 endives, trimmed and halved lengthwise, each half then split and
    fanned a bit
Oil for brushing greens: walnut, grapeseed or extra-virgin olive oil
Salt and freshly ground black pepper, to taste
2 tablespoons white wine vinegar

GARNISH
2 ounces chopped walnuts (available in small pouches on baking aisle)
12 large seedless red grapes, halved

Preheat grill pan or large nonstick skillet over medium-high heat.

Brush endive on both sides with oil, season with salt and pepper, then grill until tender and dark around the edges, about 3 minutes on each side. Arrange grilled endives on platter, and sprinkle with white wine vinegar, keeping a finger over the top of bottle to control the flow. Arrange walnut bits and grapes around the platter and serve. Simple and simply delicious!

Passport to
Belgium

1

Waterzooi de
Poulet

· · · · ·

2

Liège Waffles
with Berries
and Whipped
Cream

· · · · ·

T I D B I T

❝ Steamed
mussels may be
added to this
dish. The
chicken and
seafood
combination
only makes it
more
Belgian.❞

Brussels, the capital of Belgium, is considered by many to be the heart of
Europe. Belgians fervently defend their unique identity in all areas. They are
especially passionate and protective about their food. Mussels, waffles,
chocolate, fries and beer all have a Belgian passport. Hey France and
Germany, there will be no discussion here. As for me, I love eating my way
through all of Europe. And as for Belgian eats, Waterzooi, a rich yet mild,
stew-like concoction, is my favorite. Have it with a chilled Belgian Abby beer
in a frosty glass.

Waterzooi de Poulet

MAKES 4 SERVINGS

2 leeks
2 tablespoons butter
2 carrots, peeled and diced
2 all-purpose potatoes, peeled and diced
Salt and white pepper, to taste
1 fresh bay leaf or 2 leaves dried
4 sprigs fresh parsley, plus a handful chopped
4 sprigs fresh thyme
6 cups chicken stock or broth
4 boneless, skinless chicken breasts (8 ounces each)
1 cup heavy cream
1 large egg yolk
Crusty baguette, warmed

To clean and prepare leeks, trim rough tops and pull outer layer of the greens
and bulb away. Trim roots next. Cut leeks lengthwise, end to end, and lay halves
flat. Cut into 1/2-inch slices. Separate leeks and wash in colander under cold
water to remove all of the grit from between layers. Dry leeks and wipe down
cutting board.

In a deep pot over moderate heat, melt butter and sauté vegetables, 5 minutes.
Season with salt and white pepper. Tie together bay, parsley and thyme and add
to pot with stock, cover and bring to a boil. Add chicken, cover and reduce heat
to medium low. Poach the chicken 10 minutes, then remove and slice. Whisk
cream and egg together. Whisk in a ladle of broth into cream and egg to temper
it, then add mixture into the waterzooi and stir constantly, 2 to 3 minutes to
thicken. Add chicken back to the pot along with chopped parsley. Adjust seasoning. Ladle into warm shallow bowls and serve with crusty baguette for dipping.

Liège Waffles with Berries and Whipped Cream

Liège waffles are everywhere on the streets of Brussels. They're sugary and crunchy from the addition of pearl sugar to the waffle batter, and are eaten as a street snack in the late morning or late afternoon. At home, I combine storebought Belgian-style waffle mix with crushed sugar cubes to get an effect similar to Liège waffles with my small home waffle iron. I eat these as a simple dessert with sliced berries and a dab of whipped cream. They are equally delicious for Sunday brunch

MAKES 4 SERVINGS

2 tablespoons melted butter

Belgian-style waffle mix, prepared to package directions for 2 large waffles, 8 quarters

3/4 cup sugar cubes

1/2 pint ripe strawberries, sliced

Whipped cream in canister (from dairy aisle of market)

Heat waffle iron. Prepare waffle mix for 2 large waffles, 4 quarters each. Add sugar to a large food storage bag and crush cubes with a small heavy skillet or mallet. Add crushed cubes to prepared batter. Brush iron with melted butter. Add waffle mix and cook to waffle iron directions. Serve half a large waffle or 2 sections per person, topping with sliced berries and a rosette of whipped cream.

MENU

Passport to
Ireland

1

Loin Lamb
Chops
• • • • •

2

Braised Root
Vegetables
• • • • •

3

Colcannon-
Creamy Kale
and Potatoes
• • • • •

4

Soda Bread
with Sweet
Butter
• • • • •

Loin Lamb Chops with Braised Root Vegetables and Colcannon– Creamy Kale and Potatoes

MAKES 4 SERVINGS

BRAISED ROOT VEGETABLES

2 tablespoons butter
1 pound packaged baby carrots
1 medium rutabaga, peeled and diced
1 medium onion, diced
2 cups chicken or vegetable stock
Salt and freshly ground black pepper

CHOPS

8 loin lamb chops
Salt and freshly ground black pepper, to taste

COLCANNON

4 medium to large all-purpose potatoes, such as russet, peeled and cut
   into chunks
2 cups chicken or vegetable stock
1 head dark curly kale, trimmed of tough stems and chopped
2 tablespoons butter
3/4 cup whole milk (eyeball it)
1/4 teaspoon ground nutmeg, fresh or grated
1 teaspoon ground thyme
2 scallions, sliced
A handful chopped fresh flat-leaf parsley
Salt and freshly ground black pepper, to taste

Prepared, storebought Irish soda bread or brown bread, warmed
Butter

Preheat a skillet with a cover over medium to medium-high heat. Add butter, carrots, rutabaga, and onion. Cook veggies, stirring frequently, 5 minutes. Add broth or stock, reduce to a simmer, cover, and cook 15 minutes or until fork tender. Add salt and pepper, to taste. Remove from heat and set aside.

Preheat broiler to high for lamb, placing rack 6 to 8 inches from heat source

In a separate pot, boil potatoes 15 minutes in salted water. Drain, return to the hot pot and mash.

Passport
Dinners
• • • • •

168

Return broth to a simmer. Add kale, cover, and simmer 10 to 12 minutes.

Place chops in broiler, 5 minutes on each side. Remove and season chops with salt and pepper on both sides, and let them rest, 3 to 5 minutes.

In a large skillet over moderate heat, melt butter and add milk. Season with nutmeg and thyme and add scallions to the pan. With a slotted spoon, transfer kale from broth to the milk. To this pot, add mashed potatoes and stir 2 to 3 minutes or until nice and creamy, yet thickened. Adjust seasonings, to taste.

Irish soda bread or brown bread with butter makes a nice starter, side, or ending to this meal.

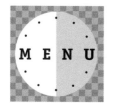
Passport to
France

1

Mushroom
Duxelles and
Paté with
Sliced
Baguette

• • • • •

2

Trout
Amandine,
Steamed
Asparagus, and
New Potatoes

• • • • •

3

Dessert
Cheeses and
Fresh Fruit

• • • • •

TIMING TIP: Set a deep pot half full of water on the stove for your potatoes. It will come to a boil while you prepare appetizer tray.

Mushroom Duxelles and Paté Platter with Sliced Baguette

MAKES 4 SERVINGS

1/2 pound crimini mushrooms, coarsely chopped

1 tablespoon extra-virgin olive oil

1 tablespoon butter

1 large shallot, finely chopped

1/2 teaspoon ground thyme

Salt and freshly ground black pepper

1/2 cup dry sherry

8 ounces paté (at specialty foods case of market, choose country or mousse-style, any flavor—ask for tastings)

1 baguette, sliced at bread counter

Cornichons, for garnish

Chopped fresh flat-leaf parsley, for garnish

Heat a skillet over moderate heat. Finely chop mushrooms in a food processor. Add oil and butter to the skillet, then shallots and mushroom bits. Season with ground thyme, salt and pepper, and sauté until mushrooms are deep brown, about 6 minutes. Deglaze pan with sherry. Transfer this mushroom duxelles to a small serving dish, and place on a platter alongside storebought paté. Garnish tray with sliced baguette, cornichons, capers, and a sprinkle of chopped parsley. Enjoy bread rounds with a slather of paté topped with mushrooms. Ooh, la, la!

Trout Amandine, Steamed Asparagus and New Potatoes

MAKES 4 SERVINGS

2 pounds small red potatoes, quartered

1 & 1/4 pounds thin asparagus spears

10 blades fresh chives, snipped or chopped

1 tablespoon extra-virgin olive oil, plus a drizzle for potatoes

8 trout fillets, lake or rainbow (4 to 6 ounces each)

1 egg

1 cup milk

1 cup flour

Salt and freshly ground black pepper

4 tablespoons butter
1 cup whole blanched almonds (about 6 ounces)
A handful fresh flat-leaf parsley, finely chopped
1 lemon, wedged

Turn oven on low and rest a platter on an oven rack.

Add potatoes to a deep pot of boiling salted water, just enough to cover them, and cook for about 12 minutes until fork tender.

Trim asparagus by holding an asparagus spear at each end, and bend to snap tip away from its tough end. Place trimmed spears in a colander and rest colander on top of the potato pot and cover. Do this the last 5 or 6 minutes that the potatoes are cooking, and the asparagus will steam at the same time.

Potatoes will be just about done when the last of your trout is going into the skillet (see below.) When the potatoes are tender, take a minute to drain them and return them to the warm pot. Leave asparagus covered and set aside. Dress potatoes with chives, a drizzle of olive oil and a little salt. Leave in warm pot until trout is on the table, then transfer to a serving bowl.

TROUT: Heat a large skillet over moderate heat. Combine egg and milk in a pie tin, and beat with a fork. Place a cup of flour in a second pie tin and season well with salt and sparingly with pepper. Coat trout fillets in egg and milk, then in seasoned flour. Collect fillets on a plate until all of them are dredged and ready to be cooked.

To the skillet add 1/2 tablespoon olive oil (half a turn of the pan in a slow stream), and 1 & 1/2 tablespoons butter. When butter foams, add trout and gently sauté 4 fillets for 2 or 3 minutes on each side, until golden. Transfer trout to warm platter in oven. Return pan to the stove and add remaining oil and 1 & 1/2 tablespoons butter, and sauté rest of trout. When all of the trout is cooked and added to serving platter, add last tablespoon of butter to the pan. When the butter melts, add almonds and brown until lightly golden, 1 to 2 minutes. Remove trout from oven and pour almonds over the platter. Garnish with chopped parsley, lemon wedges, and steamed asparagus spears.

Dessert Cheeses and Fresh Fruits

Place rinsed grapes and pears on a cutting board with your favorite dessert cheeses and sweet biscuits for a simple, elegant end to your meal. I like slightly sweet whole wheat biscuits by Carr's crackers and St. André triple-crème cheese. Ask for help from the cheese counter specialist in your market; they'll let you taste your pick of cheeses.

**Passport to
Paris:
Sidewalk
Bistro Menu**

1

**Oh-So-Good
Onion Soup**

• • • • •

2

Steak Frites

• • • • •

Oh-So-Good Onion Soup

MAKES 4 SERVINGS

1 tablespoon extra-virgin olive oil

2 tablespoons butter

6 medium onions, thinly sliced

Salt and freshly ground black pepper, to taste

1 teaspoon ground thyme or poultry seasoning

1 bay leaf, fresh or dried

1/2 cup dry sherry

6 cups beef stock

4 thick slices crusty bread

2 & 1/2 cups shredded Gruyère or Swiss cheese

A few sprigs of fresh thyme, leaves picked, for garnish

Heat a deep pot over medium to medium-high heat, and add oil and butter. Working next to the stove, slice onions, and add to the pot as you go. When all the onions are in, season with salt, pepper, ground thyme, and bay leaf. Cook onions, stirring frequently, 15 to 18 minutes, until tender, sweet and caramel colored. Add sherry to the pot and deglaze. Add 6 cups of stock, cover pot and bring up to a quick boil. Remove bay leaf.

Preheat broiler to high and toast bread slices. Arrange 4 small, deep soup bowls or crocks on a cookie sheet. Once soup boils, ladle it into bowls. Float toasted crusty bread on soup and top off with a mound of cheese. Sprinkle fresh thyme on cheese and place cookie sheet holding bowls under hot broiler until cheese melts and bubbles.

Steak Frites

MAKES 4 SERVINGS

Vegetable oil, for frying
3 medium russet potatoes, scrubbed and dried
Fine salt

1 tablespoon extra-virgin olive oil (once around the pan)
4 New York strip steaks, 3/4-inch thick (10 to 12 ounces each)
Salt and freshly ground black pepper, to taste
3 tablespoons butter, divided
1 large shallot, finely chopped
2 tablespoons flour
1 cup dry red wine

Heat 1 & 1/2 to 2 inches oil in a deep frying pan over medium heat. Cut potatoes into thin slices lengthwise. Cut each slice into thin shoestring strips. Lay cut potatoes on paper towels to dry a bit. Place about half of the potatoes at a time into hot oil, cook partially about 3 minutes, then transfer to a towel-lined plate. Potatoes will be limp and white. Do not panic! Double-frying is really the trick to crisp fries. So raise heat to medium-high and allow 2 to 3 minutes for oil to reach a higher temperature. Return potatoes to oil in 2 batches to crisp them to a deep, golden brown, another 2 to 3 minutes per batch. Remove potatoes to clean paper towels to drain, and season with fine salt.

For steaks, heat a large nonstick skillet over high heat, and add a little oil to coat pan. Sear steaks, 2 minutes on each side, reduce heat to medium and cook 3 to 5 minutes longer for medium rare, 7 to 8 for medium well. Remove steaks to a warm plate to rest. Add 2 tablespoons butter and the shallots to the pan, and cook 2 or 3 minutes. Stir in flour and cook a minute longer. Whisk wine into pan and scrape up pan drippings. Add the last pat of butter and remove pan from heat. Spoon wine and shallot sauce over the steaks and serve with hot, shoe-string potatoes. C'est fantastique!

TIDBIT

❝ Steak frites is often made with hanger steak and served without sauce. Make your own, as I do, and use a NY strip steak and oui, there is sauce! ❞

MENU

Passport to
Morocco

1

Vegetable
Couscous
• • • • •

2

Moroccan Rub
Lamb Chops
• • • • •

3

Garlic Chick
Peas and
Greens
• • • • •

Vegetable Couscous

A very friendly Moroccan cab driver in NYC told me how to make a 7-vegetable couscous that was the inspiration for this dish. I was so excited about the recipe that I wrote it out on my hand. Boy, was I hungry when I got out of that cab!

MAKES 4 ENTREE SERVINGS

2 tablespoons extra-virgin olive oil
1 bay leaf, fresh or dried
1 medium onion, chopped
1/2 medium zucchini, diced
1 small yellow squash, chopped
Salt and freshly ground black pepper, to taste
1/2 cup canned pumpkin
4 cups chicken or vegetable broth
1 & 1/2 teaspoons ground cumin (half a palmful)
1 teaspoon coriander seeds (1/3 palmful)
2 & 1/4 cups couscous
1 vine-ripe tomato, seeded and finely chopped
2 tablespoons each, chopped cilantro and fresh flat-leaf parsley
Mediterranean flat bread

Place a large saucepan over medium-high heat. Add the first five ingredients, and season with salt and pepper. Sauté, stirring frequently, 7 or 8 minutes. Add pumpkin and broth and stir to combine. Add cumin and coriander, and bring broth to a boil. Stir in couscous, cover and remove from heat. Let stand 5 minutes, then remove lid and fluff couscous with a fork. Remove bay leaf and add finely-chopped tomato, cilantro and parsley. Toss again and transfer to a serving platter. Serve with warm Mediterranean flat breads.

Moroccan Rub Lamb Chops

MAKES 4 SERVINGS

12 loin lamb chops
1 tablespoon extra-virgin olive oil
1 tablespoon ground cumin (a palmful)
2 teaspoons ground turmeric (eyeball it)
1 teaspoon sweet paprika (1/3 palmful)
1 teaspoon coriander seeds
1 teaspoon garlic salt
1/2 teaspoon hot red pepper flakes
1 lemon, wedged

Preheat grill pan to high. Brush chops with a little olive oil. Mix dry spices in a small container, cover and shake to combine. Rub spice blend into the chops on both sides, and grill them 7 to 8 minutes, turning once, for medium rare; 10 to 12 minutes for medium to medium-well. Serve with wedges of lemon.

Garlic Chick Peas and Greens

MAKES 4 SERVINGS

2 tablespoons extra-virgin olive oil (twice around the pan)
6 cloves garlic, crushed
1 pound mustard greens, trimmed and coarsely chopped
Salt and freshly ground black pepper, to taste
1 cup vegetable broth
2 cans (15 ounces each) chick peas, drained

Preheat a skillet over medium heat. Add oil and crushed garlic, sauté 2 minutes, then add greens. Turn and wilt greens in garlic oil and season with salt and pepper. Add vegetable broth to the pan, and bring to a boil. Cover pan, reduce heat and simmer greens, 7 or 8 minutes. Uncover the pan, and stir in chick peas, combining well with the stewed greens. Adjust salt and pepper and serve.

TIDBIT

❝ Other dark greens such as dandelion, collards, or chard may be substituted for the mustard greens. ❞

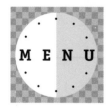

M E N U

Passport to Russia

1

Chicken Kiev
· · · · ·

2

Potatoes and Onions
· · · · ·

3

Red Radish Salad
· · · · ·

TIDBIT

❝ If you don't have a frying thermometer, drop a cube of white bread into hot oil and if it browns in a count of 40, the oil is ready. ❞

Chicken Kiev

MAKES 4 SERVINGS

Vegetable oil, for frying

4 pieces boneless, skinless chicken breasts (6 to 8 ounces each)
   OR 4 thin-cut chicken cutlets (6 ounces each) available in some markets

1 clove garlic, finely chopped

10 blades fresh chives, chopped (about 2 tablespoons)

A palmful fresh parsley, finely chopped (about 2 tablespoons)

A palmful fresh dill, finely chopped (about 2 tablespoons)

6 tablespoons chilled butter

1 cup flour

2 eggs

1 cup unseasoned bread crumbs

A wedge of lemon

Salt and freshly ground black pepper

Round toothpicks

To a large deep skillet over medium heat, add 1 & 1/2 inches of vegetable oil. Oil must reach 360°F for frying.

On work surface covered with waxed paper, lay out chicken breasts. To butterfly small breasts, place on cutting board. Cover with one hand, and with a sharp knife make a lateral cut from one side of the breast almost to the other and open it up like a book. (Thin-cut 6-ounce breasts may just be placed on waxed paper, covered with a second sheet, and pounded out to 1/4-inch thickness with a mallet or a small heavy skillet, being careful not to tear the meat.) Roll up breasts and set aside. Combine chopped garlic and herbs on work surface. Cut cold butter into 4 equal pieces and coat each piece liberally with the herb-garlic mix.

In 3 disposable pie tins: set out flour in first, eggs beaten with a splash of cold water in the second, and bread crumbs in the third. Unroll chicken, squeeze a lemon wedge over it, and season with salt and pepper. Place an herbed butter pat on each piece of chicken, roll up tightly, and secure with a toothpick. Roll stuffed breasts in flour, then egg, then bread crumbs.

Fry the Kiev bundles 7 to 8 minutes on each side until a deep golden brown all over.

Potatoes and Onions

MAKES 4 SERVINGS

1 & 1/2 pounds white thin-skinned potatoes (about 3 potatoes)
1 large sweet onion
Coarse salt
1 tablespoon vegetable oil (once around the pan)
2 tablespoons butter

Heat a heavy 10-inch skillet over medium-high heat. Slice potatoes and onions very thinly, and salt them. Add oil and butter to the pan. When the butter foams, add potatoes and onions. Place a dinner plate on top of potatoes and weight it with any heavy object: a sack of flour, heavy canned goods, etc. Let the potatoes and onions crust, 2 to 3 minutes, then turn them, replace weights and let other side crust. Keep turning the potatoes and onions for about 20 minutes, until they are evenly golden and crusted.

Red Radish Salad

MAKES 4 SERVINGS

2 teaspoons sugar
The juice of 1 lemon
1/2 cup sour cream
8 red radishes, thinly sliced
2 Red Delicious apples, quartered, cored and thinly sliced
1/2 European seedless cucumber, thinly sliced
2 tablespoons chopped fresh dill
Salt and freshly ground black pepper, to taste

Combine sugar, lemon juice, and sour cream in a medium bowl. Add radishes, apple, and cucumber, turning them to coat. Season with dill, salt and pepper. Toss again and serve.

MENU

**Passport to
Hong Kong**

1

**Baked Crab
Spring Rolls**
•••••

2

Noodle Bowls
•••••

3

**Hot Tea,
Sectioned
Oranges and
Ginger Snap
Cookies**
•••••

Baked Crab Spring Rolls

I like spring rolls, but I don't want to fry them. The method used here is the same I use to make a spanakopita-like Greek spinach and feta roll that is one of my all-time favorite recipes. One night I was making the spinach and feta rolls and I thought, "Hmmm...this could be a cool, quick twist on an Asian spring roll, too!". The pastry roll-ups make a great party offering and the method can be adapted to incorporate cooked shredded pork or shrimp.

MAKES 4 SERVINGS

1 tablespoon vegetable oil or olive oil

1/2 red bell pepper, finely chopped

2 ribs celery from the heart, finely chopped

6 water chestnuts, finely chopped

1/2 small onion, finely chopped

1/4 cup fresh bean sprouts (a handful), chopped

2 cans (6 ounces each) lump crab meat, drained and flaked

2 tablespoons dark soy sauce, such as Tamari

1/2 teaspoon dried thyme leaves (eyeball it)

4 sheets defrosted phyllo dough (13 x 17 inches each)

3 tablespoons melted butter

Preheat oven to 400° F.

Add oil to a preheated skillet over medium to medium-high heat. Sauté pepper, celery, water chestnuts, and onion, 2 to 3 minutes. While veggies are still a little crunchy, transfer to a bowl. Add bean spouts, crab, soy sauce, and thyme. Combine well with a spoon. Paint half of a sheet of phyllo dough with melted butter and fold sheet in half, making almost a square. Pile a few spoonfuls of filling 2 inches from the bottom of sheet and leaving 2 inches at either side of sheet. Fold bottom flap up and side edges in, then roll up and over until you reach the top of the sheet. Your crab pastry will look like a spring roll. Dab the edges and sides of your roll with melted butter and place seam-side down on a pastry sheet. Assemble all and bake on center rack 15 minutes or until lightly golden all over.

Noodle Bowls

I discovered the wonders of noodle bowls at a restaurant in Portland, Oregon where they hand-pull their own noodles. The owner tried to teach me how to stretch my own homemade noodles. It was a bad scene. My noodles looked like a game of Cat's Cradle gone horribly wrong. In this recipe, storebought fresh pasta comes to the rescue. The noodle bowls can be adapted in tons of ways. Use shrimp, pork, beef or just veggies, whatever pleases you.

MAKES 4 SERVINGS

3 quarts vegetable stock or chicken broth

1 & 1/2 pounds fresh linguini (available on dairy aisle)

1 & 1/2 pounds chicken tenders, cut into bite-size chunks, or chicken breasts cut for stir-fry

8 scallions cut into bite-size pieces on an angle

2 cups shredded carrots (available in pouches in produce section)

1 package fresh shiitake mushrooms (about 24 mushrooms), coarsely chopped

1/2 head bok choy, trimmed and shredded

1/2 pound snow peas, cut in half on an angle

Chopped fresh cilantro and/or chives, for garnish (optional)

Bring 3 quarts of vegetable stock or chicken broth to a boil in a soup pot.

In a large separate pot of boiling salted water, cook fresh linguini 3 minutes. Drain pasta just before it's done, as it will finish cooking while it steeps in your soup bowls.

Divide cooked fresh pasta into 4 equal amounts and place into 4 deep bowls.

Add chicken to boiling broth, and poach chicken 5 minutes.

Add veggies to bowls of pasta. Ladle broth and chicken equally into the four bowls to cover vegetables and noodles. Cover bowls tightly with small plates and let the soup steep 5 minutes.

Uncover your noodle bowls and serve. SLURP away! Where this soup comes from, it is customary to slurp as you eat, using oversized spoons to drag the noodles up to your mouth. You might need a bib, but you will have fun! Garnish with cilantro and/or chives for extra zing, if you prefer.

Sectioned oranges and gingersnap cookies, accompanied by black tea, are great finishers.

M E N U

**Passport to
Greece:
Ode to the
Toga Menu —
It's All
Wrapped Up!**

1

**Spanakopita,
Sorta**
· · · · ·

2

**Greek Grilled
Chicken and
Salad
with Warm
Pita Bread for
Wrapping**
· · · · ·

3

**Bakla-Squares
and Ice Cream**
· · · · ·

Spanakopita, Sorta

Spanakopita is a triangle-shaped phyllo pastry filled with spinach and feta cheese. These Spanakopita Sortas are made in rolls for fast, easy preparation. Larger than the triangles, you need only allow 1 per person as a starter. For a light supper, 2 per person will do, when served with a simple, mixed green salad, dressed with lemon juice and EVOO. For parties, cut each roll into 2 or 3 pieces and serve.

MAKES 4 SERVINGS

1 & 1/2 teaspoons extra-virgin olive oil (half a turn around the pan)

1 small onion, finely chopped

1 package (10 ounces) frozen chopped spinach, defrosted and squeezed dry

Salt and freshly ground black pepper, to taste

1/4 teaspoon nutmeg, ground or freshly grated

4 ounces feta cheese with black pepper, or plain feta, crumbled into tiny bits

1 egg, beaten

3 tablespoons sour cream

4 sheets (13 x 17 inches each) defrosted phyllo dough

3 tablespoons melted butter

Preheat oven to 400°F with rack in center position.

Preheat a small pan over medium to medium-high heat. Add oil and onion and sauté, 5 minutes. Remove onion to a bowl. Add spinach to onion and season with salt, pepper, and nutmeg. Add feta and combine with spinach. Add beaten egg and sour cream and combine well with cheese, spinach, and onion.

On a large work surface, lay out one sheet of phyllo. Paint half of the sheet with a little melted butter. Fold sheet in half to make almost a square. Pile up to 1/4 of your spinach mixture into a log shape working 2 inches from bottom and each side of the pastry. Tuck bottom up and fold both sides in, then roll and wrap upwards until you reach the edge of the dough sheet. Each filled pastry will resemble an egg roll. Paint the seam and the ends of the roll with butter and set roll seam-side-down on a cookie sheet. Repeat and make 4 rolls. Bake 15 minutes or until lightly golden, and serve.

Bakla-Squares and Ice Cream

MAKES 4 SERVINGS

4 sheets (13 x 17 inches each) phyllo dough
4 tablespoons melted butter
1 & 1/2 cups chopped walnuts
1 cup sugar
2 tablespoons cinnamon
1 pint vanilla bean ice cream
Honey, for topping

Cover the surface of a cookie sheet with parchment paper, and on it spread a sheet of phyllo dough. Brush phyllo with a little butter and scatter over one-third of the walnuts. Combine sugar and cinnamon and sprinkle 1/3 cup over walnuts. Repeat the phyllo, butter, sugar-cinnamon and walnut steps twice again, finishing with the 4th sheet of phyllo. Cut pastry into 3-inch squares with a sharp paring knife. Cover the pastry with another sheet of parchment paper and another cookie sheet. Bake in hot oven at 400°F for 18 to 23 minutes or until golden. Remove from oven and serve warm pastry squares with ice cream and a drizzle of honey.

Greek Grilled Chicken and Salad with Warm Pita Bread for Wrapping

MAKES 4 SERVINGS

1 & 1/3 to 1 & 1/2 pounds chicken tenders
Salt and freshly ground black pepper, to taste
8 pita breads
The zest and juice of 1 lemon
3 tablespoon red wine vinegar (eyeball it)
1/2 cup extra-virgin olive oil (eyeball it)
2 tablespoons fresh oregano (4 stems) stripped of leaves and chopped
3 cloves garlic, chopped
2 hearts romaine lettuce, chopped
1/2 cup pitted Kalamata olives, coarsely chopped
8 ounces feta cheese, crumbled
2 vine-ripe tomatoes, seeded and diced
1/3 seedless or English cucumber, diced
1/2 red onion, chopped
1/2 cup fresh flat-leaf parsley (a couple handfuls), chopped

Preheat grill pan over high heat. Place chicken in shallow dish and season with salt and pepper.

Preheat oven to moderate heat or if you've already made the Bakla-Squares, the oven will already be hot. Wrap pita breads in foil, and place in warm oven until dinner is served.

Combine lemon zest and juice with vinegar in a bowl and whisk in oil. Add oregano, garlic and whisk again to combine well. Pour half the dressing over chicken tenders, and turn them to coat.

Combine veggies in a mixing bowl and toss well with the remaining dressing just until very lightly coated. Season with salt and pepper and transfer to a large serving platter.

Grill tenders, 4 to 5 minutes on each side, transferring them as they're done to the salad-lined serving platter. Remove pitas from oven and unwrap. Cut pitas in half and arrange around the edge of platter.

To serve, each person can pile grilled chicken and veggies onto a pita, wrap up and enjoy!

BIG NIGHTS: VERY SPECIAL DINNERS

RACHAEL RAY
30-MINUTE MEALS 2

Anyone can make a reservation. When you cook, you make an impression. When a special night comes up in your life, rather than maxing out your credit line at a restaurant, why not choose to stay in—in style! Pick a few recipes, shop, chop, and cook. In 30 minutes or less, you, a mere mortal, will transform a bag full of raw ingredients into an explosive, sensual expression of your inner self.

When it comes to date meals, an all-time favorite recipe of mine is 'penne alla vodka.' There is something about the velvety texture of this sauce. Sexy. The first time I cooked up my version of this dish, it was so delectable and foolproof that I told ten friends about it, ten friends who couldn't cook. Most called back with tales of great dates. The sauce was a hit! Two weeks later, I started to get a few panicked messages on my answering machine. The fallout? Those who were not into having serious relationships could not seem to shake the dinner guests!

My own testimony follows. The scene: I'm at a birthday party for a close girlfriend friend of mine. I meet a man named John. He's charming, good looking, interesting. We chat: we have everything in common. He tells me he loves to cook. Really? (I am a hard sell on this talking point. I cook on television. Men know this. Some men tend to exaggerate their talents in the kitchen because of it.) I probe. John goes on. He tells me that last night he prepared tilapia with tomatillos, peppers, onions, garlic, and beer. By the time he gets to the garlic, I am so excited I cut him off and exclaim, "that's wonderful!" He stops me. There's more: he garnishes with cilantro and serves the fish with maque choux, French for corn succotash, hold the limas. I almost pass out cold. Even virtual cooking can make one swoon. John remains unforgettable.

Decadent Duo for Decadent Duos: Chocolate Cups with Whipped Cream

Make your dessert first to allow these chocolate cups to set and chill: This recipe is a no-bake pôts de crème, no kidding.

MAKES 4 SERVINGS in demitasse cups

4 demitasse cups
2/3 cup whole milk
1 egg
2 tablespoons sugar
Pinch salt
1 cup semisweet chocolate chips
2 tablespoons Frangelico (hazelnut liqueur) or dark rum
1 cup whipping cream
2 tablespoons sugar
Edible flowers (found in produce department) or candied violets, for garnish (optional)

Heat milk in a small pan over moderate heat until it comes to a boil. In a blender or food processor combine egg, sugar, a pinch of salt, semisweet chips and liqueur, using the low setting. Pour in boiling milk in a slow stream. The hot milk will cook the egg and melt the chocolate. Process or blend 1 minute, until smooth. Spoon into 4 demitasse cups and chill. After dinner, beat cream until soft peaks form. Add a little sugar and beat to combine. Top chocolate cups with a dollop of cream and garnish each cup with an edible flower or candied violet. Place cups on saucers and serve with demitasse spoons. If you use tea cups, this recipe will yield 2 cups, rather than 4.

MENU

1
Heart-y Salad
• • • • •

2
You-Won't-Be-
Single-For-
Long Vodka
Cream Pasta
• • • • •

3
Chocolate
Cups with
Whipped
Cream
• • • • •

You-Won't-Be-Single-For-Long Vodka Cream Pasta

This recipe will make enough for two couples. If you plan a romantic evening where more than two's a crowd, reserve half the sauce to refrigerate or freeze for another supper (omit the basil, adding fresh when you reheat later) and only cook 1/2 to 2/3 pound of penne.

TIDBIT

❛❛ I published a version of this entrée in my original 30-Minute Meals cookbook. It makes a return here for a reason: a fan of the show wrote to say that she made this menu for her boyfriend who had seconds just before he proposed. Really. He said it was the second helping that did it. Ain't love grand! ❜❜

MAKES 4 SERVINGS (make it for 2 with seconds in mind)

1 tablespoon extra-virgin olive oil (once around the pan)
1 tablespoon butter
2 garlic cloves, minced
2 shallots, minced
1 cup vodka
1 cup chicken stock
1 can (28 ounces) crushed tomatoes
Coarse salt and freshly ground black pepper, to taste
1/2 cup heavy cream
12 ounces pasta, such as penne rigate
20 leaves fresh basil, shredded or torn
Crusty bread

Put large pot of salted water on to boil.

Heat a large skillet over moderate heat. Add oil, butter, garlic, and shallots. Gently sauté garlic and shallots, 3 to 5 minutes to develop their sweetness. Add vodka, 3 turns around the pan in a steady stream will equal about a cup. Reduce vodka by half, 2 or 3 minutes. Add chicken stock and tomatoes. Bring sauce to a bubble, then reduce heat to simmer. Season with salt and pepper.

While sauce simmers, cook pasta in salted boiling water until al dente, a bit firm to the bite. While pasta cooks, prepare your salad or other side dishes.

Stir cream into the vodka sauce. When sauce returns to a bubble, remove from heat. Drain pasta. Toss hot pasta with sauce and basil leaves. Serve immediately, along with crusty bread.

Heart-y Salad: Hearts of Romaine, Palm, and Artichoke

MAKES 2 SERVINGS

1 heart romaine lettuce, shredded
1 cup fresh flat-leaf parsley leaves (half a bundle)
1 can (14 ounces), hearts of palm, drained
1/4 pound prosciutto di Parma
1 can (15 ounces) quartered artichoke hearts in water, drained
1/4 pound wedge Pecorino, Romano or Asiago cheese
Balsamic vinegar and extra-virgin olive oil, for drizzling
Salt and freshly ground black pepper, to taste

Place romaine on a platter and toss with parsley. Wrap hearts of palm in prosciutto and cut into bite-size pieces on an angle. Arrange palm and artichoke hearts over the romaine greens. Shave cheese with a vegetable peeler into short ribbons, working over the salad plate. Drizzle with vinegar and oil; season with salt and pepper.

M E N U

1

Pasta with
Citrus Cream
Sauce
· · · · ·

2

Veal
Medallions
with Lemon on
a Bed of
Spinach
· · · · ·

3

Champagne
Freezes
· · · · ·

Pasta with Citrus Cream Sauce

One of my favorite restaurants in Florence, Italy is Trattoria Garga. When I dine at Garga, I must have this pasta, created by the owner, so I'm told. It is called Magnifico, and it is! The flavors are intoxicating: cream, citrus, mint, basil. Unreal! I have tried many times to make it at home, on special nights. This recipe is as close as I've ever gotten to the original.

MAKES 2 SERVINGS

1 cup heavy cream
2 tablespoons cognac or dry sherry
The zest of 1 lemon
The zest of 1 large navel orange
1/2 teaspoon coarse salt
2 tablespoons fresh mint, chopped (about 3 sprigs)
12 leaves fresh basil, shredded or torn
1/2 pound linguini, or 3/4 pound fresh linguini, cooked al dente
1/2 cup grated Parmigiano Reggiano cheese

In a skillet over medium-low heat, warm cream. Add cognac or dry sherry, zest of lemon and orange, salt. Simmer, 7 to 10 minutes. Add mint and basil. Toss hot, drained pasta with sauce and grated cheese. Transfer to serving dish or dinner plates.

Veal Medallions with Lemon on a Bed of Spinach

This is an Italian staple that takes under 15 minutes, start to finish. I think its soft, mellow flavors make it a great romantic date meal!

MAKES 2 SERVINGS

2 tablespoons extra-virgin olive oil (twice around the pan)
1 tablespoon butter
2 tablespoons flour
1/2 cup chicken broth
1/2 pound thinly sliced veal scallops
Salt and freshly ground black pepper, to taste
The juice and zest of 1 lemon
A handful fresh flat-leaf parsley, finely chopped
1/4 cup water
10 ounces baby spinach
1/4 to 1/2 teaspoon freshly grated or ground nutmeg

In a skillet over moderate heat, combine oil, butter, and flour. Cook 2 or 3 minutes. Whisk in broth. Turn sliced veal in thickened sauce, 3 or 4 minutes and transfer veal to a warm platter. Season with salt and pepper. Add lemon zest, lemon juice, and chopped parsley to the remaining sauce in the pan and remove from heat.

In a second skillet over medium-high heat, wilt spinach in a splash of water. Drain and season with salt, pepper, and nutmeg.

To assemble, divide spinach between 2 dinner plates and top with veal and pan sauce.

Champagne Freezes

This is a real Venetian treat! Sgroppino. Be careful. It goes straight to your head and it gets results!

MAKES 2 SERVINGS

4 scoops lemon sorbet
2 ounces chilled vodka, citrus vodka or limoncello (Italian lemon liqueur)
2 ounces Prosecco or other sparkling wine or champagne
2 sprigs fresh mint

Blend lemon sorbet on low speed and pour in vodka or lemon liqueur in a slow stream. Add Prosecco or champagne. Pour into chilled martini glasses and serve, garnished with a sprig of mint.

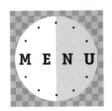

MENU

1

Brandy and
Orange
Chicken
Topped with
Stuffed
Shrimp
• • • • •

2

Fruited White
and Wild Rice
• • • • •

3

Maple Nut
Coffee Ice
Cream Dessert
• • • • •

Fruited White and Wild Rice

MAKES 4 SERVINGS

2 cups water
1 tablespoon butter
1 teaspoon salt (eyeball it)
1 cup white and wild rice blend
3 tablespoons golden raisins (a handful)
1/2 cup mandarin orange sections, drained, and chopped
1 package (2 ounces) sliced almonds (available on the baking aisle)
3 scallions, thinly sliced

Bring water to a boil, add butter and salt. Add white and wild rice blend and golden raisins, stir, return to a boil. Reduce heat, cover, and simmer, 20 minutes or until just tender. Fluff with a fork. Add chopped mandarins, almonds, and scallions. Toss to combine and serve.

Brandy and Orange Chicken Topped with Stuffed Shrimp

MAKES 4 SERVINGS

STUFFED SHRIMP
1 tablespoon extra-virgin olive oil (once around the pan)
2 tablespoons butter
1 rib celery, finely chopped
1 small onion, finely chopped
1/4 red bell pepper, finely chopped
6 ounces, drained weight, fresh lump crab meat (available at fresh fish counter) OR 2 cans (5 & 1/2 ounces each), drained
1/2 teaspoon ground thyme or poultry seasoning (eyeball it)
1 teaspoon sweet paprika (1/3 palmful)
Salt and freshly ground black pepper, to taste
2 thin slices white bread, toasted and buttered, then diced
A handful fresh chopped parsley (2 to 3 tablespoons)
3 tablespoons melted butter
8 jumbo shrimp, peeled and deveined, tails intact (ask for easy peels at the fish counter)

CHICKEN

4 pieces boneless, skinless chicken breast (6 to 8 ounces each)

1 teaspoon ground thyme or poultry seasoning

Salt and freshly ground black pepper, to taste

1 tablespoon extra-virgin olive oil

3 shots brandy (about 4 ounces total)

2 tablespoons butter

The zest of 1 large navel orange

Parsley sprigs and sliced navel oranges, for garnish

Preheat oven to 400°F.

To a small skillet over moderate heat add the olive oil and butter. When butter melts, add celery, onion, and red bell pepper and sauté 5 minutes. Add the crab and season with thyme or poultry seasoning, paprika, salt and pepper. Fold a few handfuls of diced toasted bread into the stuffing. Add parsley, and remove from heat.

Brush a baking dish with melted butter. Butterfly shrimp by cutting along the deveining line, into and almost through the shrimps. Place the open butterflied shrimp in your hand. Dab the shrimp with melted butter and place a rounded spoonful of crab stuffing on to the shrimp. Set the shrimp in the baking dish with the stuffing exposed and the tail upright. Bake in the preheated oven 6 to 8 minutes or until shrimp are pink and firm and stuffing is browned.

Season chicken breasts with poultry seasoning or ground thyme, salt and pepper. In a second skillet over medium-high heat, add olive oil and cook breasts, 5 minutes on each side, then remove to a serving plate. Add brandy to the pan and cook alcohol off, 1 minute. Add butter and orange zest, and spoon over the chicken, topping each breast with 2 stuffed shrimp. Garnish with sliced oranges and parsley sprigs.

Maple Nut Coffee Ice Cream Dessert

MAKES 4 SERVINGS

2 pints coffee ice cream

1 cup salted mixed nuts, coarsely chopped

1/2 cup medium to dark amber maple syrup, warmed

Rolled wafer cookies, for garnish

Top 2 scoops of coffee ice cream with chopped salted mixed nuts. Drizzle nuts and ice cream with warm maple syrup. Garnish with rolled wafer cookies and serve.

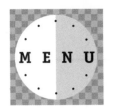

MENU

1
Great Grilled
Vegetables
• • • • •
2
Bruschetta
with Tomato
and Basil
• • • • •
3
Fettuccini
all'Alfredo
• • • • •

Great Grilled Vegetables

MAKES 4 SERVINGS

1 small eggplant, cut into 1/4 inch strips, lengthwise
1 small zucchini, cut into 1/4 inch slices, lengthwise
1 Cubanelle (light green) Italian pepper, cut into strips, lengthwise
1 small red onion, thinly sliced
8 medium crimini (baby portobello) mushrooms, trimmed
1/2 cup extra-virgin olive oil, for brushing
Coarse salt and freshly ground black pepper, to taste
2 tablespoons chopped fresh thyme or 1/2 teaspoon (a sprinkle) dried
    thyme or dried Italian seasoning

Preheat grill or grill pan over moderate to high heat. Assemble cut veggies on a platter; as you place them on the grill, brush each side with a little oil and season with salt and pepper. Cook until are just tender, 3 to 5 minutes on each side, depending on the vegetable. Arrange grilled veggies on a platter and garnish with a generous sprinkle of chopped fresh thyme.

Bruschetta with Tomato and Basil

Bruschetta just means charred bread that is rubbed with garlic cloves, then drizzled with olive oil, and seasoned with salt and pepper. The toppings for it are only limited by your imagination. Tomato and basil is at the top of the most requested list. When served with such toppings—cheese, shrimp, anchovies—they are known as crostini or little toasts.

MAKES 8 PIECES

1/2 baguette or crusty long loaf bread, sliced (8 pieces)
2 large cloves garlic, cracked away from skin
Extra-virgin olive oil, for drizzling
3 small plum tomatoes, halved and seeded
20 fresh basil leaves
Coarse salt, to taste

Preheat broiler to high. Place bread slices on your broiler pan. Toast bread on each side under hot broiler—keep an eye on it! Rub toasts with cracked garlic and drizzle with oil. Chop seeded tomatoes and place in a small bowl. Pile basil leaves on top of one another and roll into a log. Thinly slice basil into a green confetti and loosely combine with tomatoes. Add a drizzle of oil and a little coarse salt to the bowl and gently toss tomatoes and basil to coat. Place bowl on serving platter with a serving spoon and arrange toasts around the platter.

Fettuccine all'Alfredo

Legend has it that Mary Pickford and Douglas Fairbanks had this dish created for them by a restauranteur named Alfredo who would toss the molten center of a 40-kilo wheel of aged Parmigiano Reggiano together with hot pasta and butter at their tableside in Rome. This simple, yet glamorous supper has all the romance of Rome and Hollywood combined. Have it for a Dinner and a Flick night and make your own movie magic.

MAKES 4 SERVINGS, but I always make it for 2 of us. It's addictive.

1 package (12 ounces) egg fettuccine
3 tablespoons butter
1 cup heavy cream or half-and-half
1 cup grated Parmigiano Reggiano cheese (3 healthy handfuls)
1/4 teaspoon freshly grated or ground nutmeg
Coarse salt and freshly ground black pepper, to taste

Bring salted water to a rolling boil for your pasta and cook to package directions. Drain well.

Preheat a large skillet over moderate heat, add butter and melt. Add cream or half-and-half, and stirring constantly, add cheese and cook, 1 minute. Season with nutmeg, pepper and a pinch of salt. Turn off heat and add drained pasta to the skillet, tossing until sauce coats the pasta evenly. Adjust seasonings and serve.

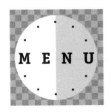

M E N U

1

Sage Veal
Chops

• • • • •

2

Wild
Mushroom
Fricassee over
Polenta

• • • • •

3

Arugula Salad
with Blue
Cheese, Pears,
and Apricot
Vinaigrette

• • • • •

A true food lover's menu full of earthy, rich flavors.

Sage Veal Chops

MAKES 4 SERVINGS

4 veal chops, each 1-inch thick
Salt and freshly ground black pepper, to taste
6 sprigs fresh sage, chopped (about 4 tablespoons)
1 tablespoon extra-virgin olive oil (once around the pan)
2 tablespoons butter
1/2 cup dry white wine (eyeball it)

Heat a heavy-bottomed skillet over medium-high heat. Season chops with salt and pepper and rub them each with about 1 tablespoon of chopped sage, rubbing well into both sides of the chops. Add oil to the pan. Melt butter into the oil and add chops to the pan. Cook 5 minutes on each side, remove to warm platter, and let rest. Add wine to the pan and scrape up the drippings. Spoon over the chops and serve.

Wild Mushroom Fricassee Over Polenta

MAKES 4 SERVINGS

POLENTA
3 cups chicken broth
1 cup quick-cooking polenta (found in Italian or specialty foods aisles)
2 tablespoons butter
1/4 cup grated Romano or Parmigiano Reggiano cheese
Salt and freshly ground black pepper, to taste

FRICASSEE
2 tablespoons extra-virgin olive oil (twice around the pan)
1 tablespoon butter
4 portobello mushroom caps, halved, then thinly sliced
16 fresh shiitake mushrooms, coarsely chopped
Coarse salt and freshly ground black pepper, to taste
2 tablespoons balsamic vinegar
1/2 cup beef stock or broth
2 scallions, thinly sliced on an angle

Bring 3 cups chicken broth to a boil in a covered pot. While the broth is coming to a boil, start fricassee. Heat a large nonstick skillet over medium-high heat. Add oil and butter. When butter melts into oil, add mushrooms and season with salt and pepper. Cook, stirring frequently, 10 minutes or until mushrooms are all dark and tender. Add vinegar and stir to coat. The vinegar will cook away in about 1 minute. Add broth and scallions. Toss to combine.

Stir quick-cooking polenta into boiling chicken broth until it masses. Stir in butter and cheese and season with salt to taste.

Serve polenta topped with Mushroom Fricassee alongside Sage Veal Chops.

Arugula Salad with Blue Cheese, Pears, and Apricot Vinaigrette

I often have a salad of arugula, pears, blue cheese, and dried apricots at Thalia in New York. When I make it for myself at home, I put the apricot flavor right into the dressing—delicious with the cheese and fruit in the salad.

MAKES 4 SERVINGS

2 bunches arugula, washed and dried, stems trimmed
1 head Bibb lettuce, torn
The juice of 1/2 lemon
1 ripe pear, thinly sliced
8 ounces Maytag or other blue cheese, crumbled

DRESSING
1 small shallot, minced
2 tablespoons white wine vinegar
1/4 cup apricot all-fruit spread (found near jams and jellies)
1/3 cup extra-virgin olive oil (eyeball the amount)
Salt and freshly ground black pepper, to taste

Combine arugula and lettuce in a salad bowl. Squeeze a little lemon juice over pear slices to keep them from browning. Arrange them on top of the lettuce and arugula. Top with blue cheese crumbles.

To make the dressing, combine shallots, vinegar, and apricot spread in a bowl. Stream in oil as you whisk. Add to salad, season with salt and black pepper and serve.

TIDBIT

❝ Look for 5 or 6-ounce sacks or wrapped bundles of washed and trimmed arugula, available in some markets ❞

Cooking with
Wine

1

Sea Scallops
with Vermouth

• • • • •

2

Veal
Scaloppini
with Wine,
Mushrooms,
and Green
Olives

• • • • •

3

Ripe Peaches
with Port

• • • • •

One of my top 5 favorite menus in this book. It must be those wines!

Sea Scallops with Vermouth

MAKES 4 SERVINGS

3 tablespoons extra-virgin olive oil
1 shallot, chopped
2 cans (14 ounces) quartered artichoke hearts in water, drained
Salt and freshly ground black pepper, to taste
A handful chopped fresh flat-leaf parsley
2 tablespoons capers, drained
16 sea scallops, drained and trimmed
1/2 cup dry vermouth

Heat large nonstick skillet over medium-high heat. Add about 2 tablespoons olive oil, then the chopped shallots to the pan. Cook a minute or so, add artichoke hearts and toss to heat through. Season with salt and pepper and combine with parsley and capers. Transfer to a serving dish.

Wipe out pan and return to stove, raising heat a bit. Season scallops with salt and pepper. Add one turn of olive oil to the very hot pan and immediately place the scallops in the pan. Sear the scallops in a single layer, causing them to caramelize, 2 minutes on each side. Add vermouth and cook out the alcohol, 1 to 2 minutes. Arrange over top of the artichokes and serve.

Veal Scaloppini with Wine, Mushrooms and Green Olives

MAKES 4 SERVINGS

3/4 pound linguini
1/4 cup extra-virgin olive oil (4 times around the pan), plus some for drizzling)
3 slices pancetta or bacon, chopped
1 small onion, chopped
16 crimini or button mushrooms, chopped
1 pound veal scaloppini, cut into 1-inch strips
Salt and freshly ground black pepper, to taste
2 cloves garlic, smashed
1 cup dry white wine

16 pitted, large green olives, coarsely chopped

A handful chopped, fresh flat-leaf Italian parsley

1 tablespoon butter, cut into pieces

1/3 cup grated Parmigiano Reggiano or Romano cheese (a couple handfuls)

In a big pot, bring water to boil, add salt, and cook linguini 8 minutes, to al dente.

Preheat a large heavy skillet over medium to medium-high heat. Add 1 tablespoon olive oil and the pancetta or bacon. Cook 1 to 2 minutes, then add onions and cook, another 2 to 3 minutes. Add mushrooms and cook, another 3 to 5 minutes.

While vegetables are cooking, season veal strips with salt and pepper. In a second skillet preheated over medium-high heat, add 1 & 1/2 tablespoons olive oil and 1 clove smashed garlic. Quick-fry half of the veal, searing each side of the strips, 1 to 2 minutes. Transfer to a plate and repeat. When done, add all of the veal and garlic to the onions and mushrooms, then add wine to the veal pan and scrape up all of the drippings. Cook wine down (and alcohol out), 2 to 3 minutes. Stir olives and parsley into veal and mushrooms, and serve on a bed of hot linguini tossed with a drizzle of olive oil, butter, and grated cheese.

Ripe Peaches with Port

MAKES 4 SERVINGS

4 ripe peaches

2 teaspoons sugar

4 shots (about 6 ounces total) port wine

4 scoops vanilla ice cream

Slice peaches and place in a bowl. Sprinkle with sugar and add good quality port. Toss to coat and let stand, 15 minutes. Spoon into dessert dishes and top with a small scoop of vanilla ice cream.

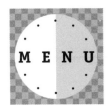

MENU

1
Veal Marsala
with Egg
Fettuccini
· · · · ·

2
Broccoli with
Garlic and
Asiago
· · · · ·

3
Quick Tiramisu
· · · · ·

Veal Marsala with Egg Fettuccini

MAKES 4 SERVINGS

1 & 1/4 pounds veal cutlets for scaloppini, from the butcher counter
Salt and freshly ground black pepper, to taste
1/2 cup flour (a couple scoops)
1/4 cup extra-virgin olive oil (4 times around the pan)
4 tablespoons butter
1 large or 2 small shallots, chopped
24 crimini (baby portobello) mushrooms, thinly sliced
1 cup Marsala wine
1/2 cup beef broth
1 box (12 to 14 ounces) egg fettuccini, cooked al dente
Finely chopped fresh flat-leaf parsley, for garnish

TIMING NOTE: Assemble any side dishes or salad first. Then, begin cooking the Veal Marsala just before your Egg Fettuccini goes into cooking water; the veal will take 12 minutes, the pasta 7 or 8.

Season veal with salt and pepper. Place a large piece of plastic wrap on a cutting board or work surface. Arrange veal with an inch or two between cutlets on the plastic wrap. Cover veal with additional plastic wrap and a sheet of wax paper. Gently pound out veal with meat mallet or a small, heavy frying pan. Fold the veal up in its plastic and wax paper wrapper and set aside.

Preheat a large skillet over medium-high heat. Create an assembly line between the veal and the hot pan: veal, shallow dish with flour, butter, and olive oil, pile of shallots and sliced mushrooms, Marsala and beef broth. Place a large platter over low heat on the burner adjacent to your veal pan. Warm it, then turn off the heat.

Dredge the veal lightly in flour. Sauté cutlets in a single layer, 2 minutes on each side. For each batch of veal, sauté in 1 tablespoon olive oil and 1 tablespoon butter. Transfer cooked cutlets to the warm serving platter.

Add another tablespoon olive oil and butter to the skillet. Add half of the chopped shallots and all of the sliced mushrooms, season with salt and pepper, and sauté, 5 minutes. Add Marsala to the pan and scrape up pan drippings. Add 1/4 cup beef broth and when it bubbles, add 1 tablespoon butter to the pan to gloss your sauce. Spoon mushrooms and Marsala over the veal. Return the pan to the stove, and add remaining olive oil, butter, and shallots, and cook a minute or two. Add remaining 1/4 cup beef broth and add the cooked and drained egg fettuccini to the pan. Toss with broth and butter and season with salt and chopped parsley. Transfer to a serving dish and serve with warm Veal Marsala.

Broccoli with Garlic and Asiago

MAKES 4 SERVINGS

1 large head broccoli, cut into long, thin spears
2 tablespoons extra-virgin olive oil (twice around the pan)
4 cloves garlic, finely chopped
1/4 pound Asiago cheese, shaved with vegetable peeler

Simmer broccoli in 1/2-inch boiling, salted water in a shallow, covered skillet for 3 or 4 minutes. Drain and remove from pan. Return pan to stovetop over medium heat, add oil and garlic, and sauté 3 minutes. Add broccoli spears and coat with the oil. Transfer to a serving dish and garnish with curls of Asiago cheese.

Quick Tiramisu

MAKES 4 SERVINGS

1 package ladyfingers (sponge cakes)
1/2 cup strong black coffee or espresso
2 ounces (shots) coffee liqueur (Kahlúa)
2 cups Mascarpone cheese (available in specialty cheese aisle)
1/2 cup powdered confectioners' sugar
1/4 cup cocoa powder
1/4 teaspoon ground cinnamon

Open the ladyfingers and separate them. Paint the ladyfingers with coffee combined with the coffee liqueur using a pastry brush. Line 4 martini glasses with a single layer of ladyfingers, letting the cakes overlap a bit at the stem. Press the cakes down to fit the lines of the glass. Beat Mascarpone and sugar together, 2 or 3 minutes and spoon into the glasses. Top glasses off with a cap of coffee and liqueur-soaked ladyfingers. Dust each completed dessert with cocoa powder combined with a touch of cinnamon.

MENU

1

Delmonico
Steaks with
Balsamic
Onions and
Steak Sauce
.....

2

Oven Steak
Fries
.....

3

Blue Cheese
and Walnut
Spinach Salad
with Maple
Dressing
.....

Delmonico Steaks with Balsamic Onions and Steak Sauce

MAKES 4 SERVINGS

4 Delmonico steaks, 1-inch thick (10 to 12 ounces each)
2 teaspoons extra-virgin olive oil
Steak seasoning blend such as Montreal Seasoning by McCormick OR
   salt and freshly ground black pepper, to taste

ONIONS
1 tablespoon extra-virgin olive oil (once around the pan)
2 large yellow onions, thinly sliced
1/4 cup balsamic vinegar (eyeball it)

STEAK SAUCE
1 & 1/2 teaspoons extra-virgin olive oil (half a turn around the pan)
2 cloves garlic, chopped
1 small white boiling onion, chopped
1/4 cup dry cooking sherry (eyeball it)
1 cup canned tomato sauce
1 tablespoon Worcestershire sauce (eyeball it)
Freshly ground black pepper, to taste

Heat a heavy grill pan or griddle pan over high heat, and wipe it with olive oil.
Cook steaks 4 minutes on each side for medium, 7 to 8 minutes for medium
well. Season with steak seasoning or salt and pepper and remove to a warm
platter.

ONIONS: Heat a medium nonstick skillet over medium-high heat. Add oil and
sliced yellow onions and cook, stirring occasionally, 10 to 12 minutes, until onions
are soft and sweet. Add balsamic vinegar to the pan and turn onions until vinegar cooks away and glazes onions a deep brown, 3 to 5 minutes.

STEAK SAUCE: Heat a small saucepan over medium heat. Add oil, garlic and
white onions and sauté, 5 minutes until tender. Add sherry to the pan and combine with onions. Stir in tomato sauce and Worcestershire and season with black
pepper.

To serve, top steaks with onions and drizzle a little steak sauce down over the
top, reserving half to pass at table.

Oven Steak Fries

MAKES 4 SERVINGS

5 russet potatoes, with skins, cut into thin wedges
3 tablespoons extra-virgin olive oil
1 teaspoon dried thyme (eyeball it)
1 teaspoon dried oregano (eyeball it)
1 tablespoon steak seasoning blend such as Montreal Seasoning by
    McCormick OR salt and freshly ground black pepper, to taste

Preheat oven to high. Cut potatoes and spread out on a cookie sheet. Coat
potatoes with olive oil, dried herbs, and steak seasoning or salt and pepper.
Spread potatoes to the corners of the cookie sheet and cook in a very hot oven,
25 minutes, turning them once, halfway in the cooking process. Serve fries hot
from the oven.

Blue Cheese and Walnut Spinach Salad with Maple Dressing

MAKES 4 SERVINGS

1 sack (10 ounces) baby spinach
1/3 pound blue cheese, crumbled
1 can (6 ounces) walnut halves, toasted
1/4 cup maple syrup, warmed
1 & 1/2 tablespoons cider vinegar
1/4 cup extra-virgin olive oil
Salt and freshly ground black pepper

Place spinach on a large platter. Top with blue cheese and walnuts. Warm maple
syrup in a small saucepan. Pour vinegar into a small bowl. Whisk oil into vinegar
in a slow stream, then whisk in maple syrup slowly. Pour dressing over the salad
and serve. Season with salt and pepper, to taste.

M E N U

1

Broiled Lamb
Chops with
Balsamic
Reduction
• • • • •

2

Gemelli Pasta
with Roasted
Red Pepper
Sauce
• • • • •

3

Broccoli Rabe
with Garlic
and Lemon
• • • • •

4

Crème de
Menthe
Parfaits
• • • • •

Gemelli Pasta with Roasted Red Pepper Sauce

MAKES 4 SERVINGS

1 pound gemelli pasta (thin twists)
1 jar (16 ounces) roasted red peppers, drained or 3 fresh roasted red peppers
2 tablespoons extra-virgin olive oil (twice around the pan)
2 cloves garlic, finely chopped
1 large shallot, finely chopped
1 cup dry white wine or chicken broth
1 can (28 ounces) crushed tomatoes
A handful chopped fresh flat-leaf parsley
Salt and freshly ground black pepper, to taste
Grated Romano cheese, for passing at the table
Crusty bread

Place a large pot of water on the stove and bring to a boil. Salt water and cook gemelli to al dente, with a bite to it, about 9 minutes.

Grind drained roasted peppers in a food processor.

Heat a large skillet over moderate heat. Add olive oil, garlic, and shallots to the pan and sauté 3 minutes, then stir in roasted peppers. Sauté 2 minutes, stir in wine or chicken broth and reduce liquid for 1 or 2 minutes. Stir in tomatoes and parsley. Season sauce with salt and pepper and simmer until ready to serve.

Toss hot pasta with sauce and transfer to a serving dish. Pass grated Romano cheese and crusty bread at table.

Broccoli Rabe with Lemon and Garlic

MAKES 4 SERVINGS

1 & 1/2 pounds broccoli rabe, trimmed of stems, then coarsely chopped
Coarse salt, to taste
2 tablespoons extra-virgin olive oil
3 cloves garlic, chopped
1/2 teaspoon crushed red pepper flakes
The zest and juice of 1 lemon

Bring 1-inch of water to a boil in a deep skillet. Add rabe, season with salt, and cover pan. Reduce heat and simmer for 10 minutes. Drain. Return pan to heat and sauté garlic and red pepper flakes in oil over moderate heat for 1 or 2

Big Nights:
Very Special
Dinners
• • • • •
202

minutes. Add rabe, coat in garlic oil, and cook 2 minutes and remove from heat. Squeeze the lemon over the pan and sprinkle in zest. Toss thoroughly and transfer to serving dish.

Broiled Lamb Chops with Balsamic Reduction

MAKES 4 SERVINGS

2 pounds rack of lamb, cut into chops
1 & 1/2 cups balsamic vinegar
3 tablespoons brown sugar
3 sprigs fresh rosemary, finely chopped
2 cloves garlic, crushed and peeled
Salt and freshly ground black pepper, to taste

Preheat broiler. Arrange chops on broiler pan.

In a small pot, combine vinegar, sugar, rosemary, and garlic. Bring to a boil and reduce heat to low. Simmer 10 minutes to reduce and thicken sauce. Remove garlic.

Broil chops 5 minutes on each side for medium rare. Season with salt and pepper, and transfer to warm serving platter and drizzle with balsamic rosemary reduction.

Crème de Menthe Parfaits

MAKES 4 SERVINGS

Crème de Menthe liqueur, for drizzling
Softened French vanilla ice cream, 1 pint per 4 servings
Suggested garnish: fresh mint leaves, raspberries or edible flowers

In parfait cups or cocktail glasses, layer crème de menthe with French vanilla ice cream. Garnish parfaits with edible flowers or raspberries and fresh mint leaves.

M E N U

1

Red Snapper
Livornese
.....

2

Penne with
Parsley and
Walnut Pesto
.....

3

Cauliflower
with Red,
Black, and
Green Confetti
.....

Red Snapper Livornese

MAKES 4 SERVINGS

4 red snapper fillets (8 ounces each)
Salt and freshly ground black pepper
1 tablespoon extra-virgin olive oil (once around the pan)

SAUCE
1 tablespoon extra-virgin olive oil (once around the pan)
3 cloves garlic, finely chopped
1 cup dry white wine
1 can (14 ounces) diced tomatoes in juice
1/4 cup chopped fresh flat-leaf parsley (a couple handfuls)

Heat a large nonstick skillet over medium-high heat.

Score the snapper skins in a 1-inch crosshatch with a sharp knife. Season both
sides of the fish with salt and pepper. Add olive oil to skillet and cook skin side
down, 4 or 5 minutes until skin is crisp. Turn fillets and cook on reverse side
3 minutes or until fillets are firm and flesh is opaque. Transfer to a warm, shallow
serving dish. Reduce heat under skillet to medium. Add olive oil and garlic and
sauté, 2 minutes. Add wine and reduce by half, about 2 minutes. Add tomatoes
and parsley and simmer, 2 minutes more. Pour sauce over fish and serve.

Penne with Parsley and Walnut Pesto

MAKES 4 SERVINGS

1/2 cup extra-virgin olive oil (eyeball it)
2 cloves cracked garlic
2 cups fresh flat-leaf parsley, stems removed
1/2 cup walnut pieces or 2/3 cup walnut halves, toasted
1/4 teaspoon ground or grated nutmeg
Salt and freshly ground black pepper, to taste
1/2 cup grated Parmigiano Reggiano cheese
1 pound penne rigate (with lines) pasta
1/3 pound fresh green beans, cut into thirds

In a small saucepan over medium heat cook garlic in oil, 5 minutes, then remove
pan from heat. Fill the food processor with parsley leaves, loosely packed. Add
walnuts and 1/2 of the warm oil and both cloves of garlic to the parsley in the
processor. Add nutmeg, salt and pepper, set lid in place and pulse grind the mixture into a thick paste. Add any remaining parsley and pulse to combine. Transfer

to a large pasta bowl. Stir in remaining oil and cheese. Adjust seasonings to taste.

While cooking penne to package directions for al dente, watch the time. After about 6 minutes, add green beans to the pasta pot. The beans will cook along with the pasta for the last 2 or 3 minutes. Drain pasta and beans together in a colander, then transfer to the pasta bowl with the pesto. Toss for 1 to 2 minutes to combine. Serve immediately.

Cauliflower with Red, Green, and Black Confetti

Another of my friend Vicky's creations!

MAKES 4 SERVINGS

1 head cauliflower, separated into bite-size florets
Coarse salt
2 tablespoons extra-virgin olive oil (twice around the pan)
3 to 4 large cloves garlic, chopped
4 anchovy fillets (optional)
1/2 teaspoon crushed red pepper flakes
1 jar (14 ounces) roasted red peppers, drained and diced into small bits
16 oil-cured olives, drained and chopped into small bits
1/2 cup fresh flat-leaf parsley, finely chopped
Salt and freshly ground black pepper, to taste

Cook cauliflower in 1-inch of boiling water, covered, for 6 to 8 minutes until tender. Drain and return pan to stove, uncovered. Set heat at medium and add oil, garlic, anchovies (optional, unless you are dining with Vicky) and crushed red pepper flakes to the pan. Break up anchovies with the back of a wooden spoon until they melt into oil. Add roasted peppers, olives, and parsley and combine. Add cooked, drained cauliflower and toss to distribute the red, green, and black confetti. Season with salt and pepper and serve.

M E N U

1

John's Fish:
Tilapia with
Tomatillo
Sauce

· · · · ·

2

Avocados
with Creamy
Maque Choux
(Corn and
Peppers)

· · · · ·

3

Margarita
Granita

· · · · ·

John's Fish: Tilapia with Tomatillo Sauce

MAKES 4 SERVINGS

4 fillets Tilapia (1 & 1/4 to 1 & 1/2 pounds)
Salt and freshly ground black pepper, to taste
1 teaspoon ground cumin (eyeball it)
1/2 teaspoon sweet paprika (eyeball it)
2 tablespoons extra-virgin olive oil (twice around the pan)
The juice of 1 lime
1/2 medium red onion chopped
1 jalapeño or serrano pepper, seeded, and finely chopped
2 or 3 large cloves garlic, finely chopped
8 to 10 tomatillos, peeled and diced with juice
Coarse salt, to taste
1/2 bottle pale beer
2 tablespoons chopped cilantro (a palmful), plus a few sprigs for garnish

Avocados with Creamy Maque Choux (Corn and Peppers)

MAKES 4 SERVINGS

1 tablespoon extra-virgin olive oil (once around the pan)
1/2 red onion, chopped
1 jalapeño pepper, seeded and finely chopped
1 small red bell pepper, seeded and chopped
4 ears fresh corn on the cob, husked
A sprinkle of sugar
Dash cayenne pepper
Dash salt
2 tablespoons butter
2 ripe avocados
The juice of 1 lime
Coarse salt

T I D B I T

❝ Orange
roughy or
flounder are
good
substitutes for
tilapia. ❞

Season tilapia on both sides salt, pepper, cumin, and paprika. Preheat a nonstick skillet over medium-high heat. Add 1 tablespoon olive oil to the hot skillet and sauté tilapia 3 minutes on each side, turning carefully with a thin spatula. Squeeze the juice of 1/2 lime over the fish, and transfer fillets to a warm serving platter.

Return skillet to the stove over medium-high heat. Add 1 tablespoon olive oil, red onion, jalapeño, and garlic, and sauté, 1 minute or 2, then add tomatillos. Season with salt and pepper, and sauté, another 1 or 2 minutes. Add beer and the juice of 1/2 lime, and bring sauce to a boil. Reduce heat to low and simmer, 5 minutes.

While sauce is simmering, get a second skillet hot over moderate heat. Add olive oil, onion, jalapeño, bell pepper, and sauté, 2 or 3 minutes. Working on a plate to catch the milky juices, scrape corn off the cob. Break up kernels and pour into the skillet. Combine with peppers and onions. Season with sugar, cayenne, and salt. When mixture bubbles, reduce heat to a simmer. Cut butter into pieces, stir into corn mixture, and simmer until creamy, 5 to 7 minutes.

Cut avocados in half lengthwise and remove pits. Squeeze lime juice over the avocados to keep them from browning and season with a little coarse salt.

Back to the sauce for fish: Add cilantro, and adjust salt and pepper, to taste. Spoon hot tomatillo sauce over the fish and garnish with sprigs of cilantro.

To serve, set 1/2 an avocado per person alongside a serving of fish, topped with tomatillo sauce. Fill the avocado with maque choux, allowing the corn to spill down and over the sides. The ripe avocado is spooned away from its skin with bites of creamy, warm corn and peppers.

TIDBIT

❝ Two cups of frozen corn may be substituted for the fresh corn. However, the results will not be as creamy as when made with the sweet, fresh corn kernels. ❞

Margarita Granita

These icy, frozen treats, a combination after-dinner drink and dessert, are refreshing following a spicy meal.

MAKES 4 COCKTAILS

The juice of 2 limes
1 tray ice cubes
1 pint lime sherbet (4 large scoops)
4 shots good quality tequila
2 shots Cointreau, or other orange liqueur

Combine all ingredients in a blender and blend on high, 1 or 2 minutes or until smooth and frothy. Spoon into glasses and serve.

1

A Different
Surf and Turf
for Two:
Baked Scallops
and Seared
Tournedos
with Artichoke
Hearts and
Asparagus Tips
• • • • •

2

Nuts and
Berries
Parfaits
• • • • •

A Different Surf and Turf for Two: Baked Scallops and Seared Tournedos with Artichoke Hearts and Asparagus Tips

MAKES 2 SERVINGS (...on Valentine's Day, 2 is just enough.)

BAKED SCALLOPS

8 large sea scallops, trimmed at base of each scallop

2 tablespoons melted butter

2 cloves garlic, minced

1 shallot, chopped

1/4 teaspoon nutmeg, freshly grated or a few pinches ground

Salt and freshly ground black pepper

2 tablespoons extra-virgin olive oil

1/2 cup Italian bread crumbs

A handful fresh flat-leaf parsley, chopped

SEARED TOURNEDOS

A drizzle olive oil

1 tablespoon butter

2 tournedos (fillet mignon steaks, each 1 to 1 & 1/4-inch thick) at room
temperature

Grill seasoning blend such as McCormick Montreal Steak Seasoning OR
coarse salt and cracked black pepper, to taste

2 slices white slicing bread, toasted and buttered

1/2 cup Madeira or dry sherry

1 tablespoon fresh tarragon, chopped (2 sprigs)

ARTICHOKES AND ASPARAGUS TIPS

1 pound thin asparagus spears, tips cut into 2-inch pieces

1 can (15 ounces) quartered artichoke hearts, drained

A drizzle extra-virgin olive oil

The juice of 1/4 lemon

Salt and freshly ground black pepper, to taste

Edible flowers (available in fresh herb section of produce department),
for garnish

Preheat oven to 425°F.

Toss scallops with melted butter, garlic, shallots, nutmeg, and salt and pepper in
a medium bowl. Transfer to a shallow casserole dish. Combine oil and bread
crumbs, scatter over scallops and place casserole in oven. Bake, 10 to 12 minutes
or until bread crumbs are deep golden and scallops opaque.

Heat a small skillet over medium to medium-high heat. Coat pan with oil and butter and add steaks to sear. Cook 4 minutes on each side for medium-well. Season with grill seasoning or coarse salt and pepper after meat is fully cooked (this keeps the salt from drawing out juices prematurely). Let meat rest 5 minutes on warm platter, to allow juices to redistribute. Return pan to heat and deglaze with the Madeira or sherry, scraping up any of the pan drippings. When liquid is reduced by half, remove from heat, add tarragon, and set aside.

Steam asparagus in 1/4-inch boiling water for 3 minutes and drain. Return to warm pan and combine with drained artichoke hearts, olive oil, lemon juice, salt and pepper. Heat mixture through and remove from stove.

To serve, place steaks on buttered toast and drizzle with Madeira (or sherry) sauce. Gently transfer 4 baked scallops to each plate. and arrange the lemon-dressed artichoke hearts and asparagus tips on the plate. Edible flowers make a delicate, colorful garnish. The no-bake Nut and Berry Parfaits add a grand finale to your dining-in Valentine's celebration.

Nuts and Berries Parfaits

MAKES FIXINS FOR 4, so 2 can have it twice!

1 pint vanilla bean ice cream
1/2 pint fresh raspberries
Hazelnut (Frangelico) or almond (Amaretto) liqueur, for drizzling
Whipped cream in spray canister (available on the dairy aisle)
2 ounces chopped toasted hazelnuts or slivered almonds (available in small pouches on baking aisle)
Maraschino cherries

Alternate layers of ice cream in fancy glasses with whole raspberries and hazelnut or almond liqueur. Top with swirls of whipped cream, toasted hazelnuts or almonds and, of course, a cherry.

1

**Tenderloin
Steaks with
Gorgonzola**
· · · · ·

2

**Roast Potatoes
with Rosemary**
· · · · ·

3

**Green Beans
and Portobello
Mushroom
Sauté**
· · · · ·

4

**Orange
Creamsicle
Liqueur
Dessert**
· · · · ·

Roast Potatoes with Rosemary

MAKES 4 SERVINGS

2 pounds small potatoes, baby Yukon gold or red skin
6 cloves garlic, cracked away from skin
2 to 3 tablespoons extra-virgin olive oil (enough to just coat potatoes)
2 tablespoons fresh rosemary leaves, chopped
Salt and freshly ground black pepper, to taste

Preheat oven to 500°F or highest setting.

Halve potatoes and place on a cookie sheet. Combine with garlic. Coat potatoes and garlic with oil and season with rosemary, salt, and pepper.

Place on lower rack of oven and roast 20 to 25 minutes, turning potatoes once after about 12 minutes. Continue roasting until golden and crisp at edges.

Green Beans and Portobello Mushroom Sauté

MAKES 4 SERVINGS

1 & 1/4 pounds green beans, trimmed and cut in half
Coarse salt
2 tablespoons extra-virgin olive oil (twice around the pan)
1 tablespoon butter
1 medium onion, chopped
2 portobello mushroom caps, halved and thinly sliced
Coarse salt and freshly ground black pepper, to taste
1/2 cup dry sherry

Simmer green beans in a skillet in salted boiling water, 5 minutes. Drain and set aside. Return skillet to moderate heat. Add oil, butter, and onions and sauté, 2 to 3 minutes. Add mushrooms, season with salt and pepper, and sauté, 3 to 5 minutes. Return green beans to the pan. Heat through while adding sherry. Reduce sherry for 1 or 2 minutes, and transfer vegetables to a serving plate.

Tenderloin Steaks with Gorgonzola

MAKES 4 SERVINGS

4 beef tenderloin steaks, each 1 & 1/2-inches thick, at room temperature
1 tablespoon extra-virgin olive oil (eyeball it)
Salt and freshly ground black pepper, to taste
3/4 pound gorgonzola cheese
4 leaves fresh sage, thinly sliced

Place a large, flat griddle or skillet over high heat. When it is hot, using a pair of tongs and a folded paper towel, wipe cooking surface with oil and place steaks on hot pan. Caramelize both sides of the tenderloin steaks, 2 minutes on each side. Reduce heat to moderate and cook 4 to 5 minutes longer. Season meat with salt and pepper.

Preheat broiler to high.

Arrange steaks on a baking sheet and top each with 3 ounces cheese. Place sheet 6 inches from broiler and heat just long enough to melt the cheese. Remove from the oven and top with sage. Let meat rest, up to 5 minutes, allowing the juices to redistribute, then serve.

Orange Creamsicle Liqueur Dessert

MAKES 4 SERVINGS

1 pint vanilla ice cream
4 ounces orange liqueur, such as Cointreau or Grand Marnier
The zest of 1 orange
4 thin slices navel orange, for garnish
8 vanilla wafer or butter cookies

Scoop vanilla ice cream into dessert cups. Top with 1 ounce orange liqueur per serving. Garnish with orange zest, slices of orange, and cookies.

T I D B I T

❝ Take the chill off: Let meat rest 10 minutes at room temperature before preparation and again, once removed from heat. ❞

M E N U

1

Grilled
Shrimp Cocktail
with
Horseradish
Cream Dipping
Sauce
· · · · ·

2

Steak Au
Poivre and
Arugula-Stuffed
Tomatoes
· · · · ·

Grilled Shrimp Cocktail with Horseradish Cream Dipping Sauce

MAKES 4 SERVINGS

1 & 1/2 pounds jumbo shrimp (20 shrimp), deveined, peel intact
1 teaspoon coarse salt
3 tablespoons butter, melted
The juice and zest of 1 lemon

SAUCE
1/2 cup plain bread crumbs (3 handfuls)
1/2 cup prepared horseradish
1/2 cup half-and-half or light cream
1/2 teaspoon salt (eyeball it)
1 teaspoon cayenne pepper sauce or 1/4 teaspoon cayenne pepper
1 cup sour cream
2 tablespoons fresh chopped parsley, for garnish
4 leaves romaine hearts

Preheat a grill pan over medium-high heat.

Loosen shells of shrimp and butterfly them by cutting along the vein on the back of the shrimp. Toss shrimp with salt. Combine melted butter with lemon juice and zest. Using a pastry brush, brush shrimps with lemon butter and set on hot grill, and grill, 3 to 4 minutes on each side, until pink and firm.

Meanwhile, in a bowl, combine bread crumbs, horseradish, cream, and salt. Let the cream soak into the bread crumbs, 2 minutes. Loosen bread crumbs with a fork. Stir in cayenne sauce or ground cayenne and combine with sour cream. Spoon equal amounts of sauce into ramekins on individual plates or a dip bowl in the center of one large platter.

Arrange the 4 romaine lettuce leaves on platter and place 5 grilled shrimp down the center of each leaf. Serve with seafood forks alongside dipping sauce.

T I D B I T

❝ Ask for
"easy-peel"
jumbo shrimp at
the fish counter.
They are raw,
deveined and in
the shell. ❞

Big Nights:
Very Special
Dinners
· · · · ·

Steak Au Poivre and Arugula-Stuffed Tomatoes

MAKES 4 SERVINGS

TOMATOES

4 vine-ripe tomatoes, red or yellow, tops trimmed and seeded
Extra-virgin olive oil, for drizzling
Salt and freshly ground black pepper, to taste

STUFFING

1/2 cup bread crumbs or 1 slice (1/2-inch thick) stale crusty bread, torn
1/2 cup grated Parmigiano Reggiano cheese
1/2 teaspoon crushed red pepper flakes
1 clove garlic, chopped
2 cups arugula leaves
1 tablespoon extra-virgin olive oil (eyeball it)

STEAKS

4 New York strip steaks (1-inch thick each), at room temperature
3 tablespoons coarsely ground black pepper
Olive oil to coat skillet
1/4 cup good brandy
2 tablespoons butter

TIDBIT

❝ How to seed tomatoes: Trim off top, invert over garbage bowl and squeeze gently to remove seeds and pulp. ❞

Remove steaks from refrigerator and allow them to come to room temperature for about 10 minutes.

Preheat oven to 400°F.

Arrange tomatoes on a broiler pan and drizzle with oil and season with salt and pepper. Combine bread crumbs, cheese, red pepper flakes, garlic, arugula, and oil in food processor and pulse grind to form stuffing. Stuff tomatoes to the rims with arugula mixture and place in the center rack of the oven. Bake 10 to 12 minutes. Let tomatoes stand 5 minutes to set before serving.

Place a heavy-bottomed skillet over medium-high to high heat. Coat steaks liberally on both sides with coarse black pepper. To a very hot pan, drizzle oil to thinly coat the cooking surface. It will smoke. Add steaks immediately. Sear and seal the steaks, cooking them 4 minutes on each side. Remove and let stand 5 minutes for medium-rare steaks. Reduce heat a bit and cook 5 minutes longer for medium to medium-well. Add brandy to the skillet and warm, then ignite. Add butter, then spoon pan juices over steaks. Serve stuffed tomatoes alongside steaks.

M E N U

1

Individual
Beef
Wellingtons
with
Broiled Plum
Tomatoes and
Steamed
Broccoli Spears

· · · · ·

2

Chocolate
Mint Parfaits

· · · · ·

Individual Beef Wellingtons with Broiled Plum Tomatoes and Steamed Broccoli Spears

MAKES 4 SERVINGS

1 tablespoon extra-virgin olive oil (once around the pan), plus some for drizzling

1 tablespoon butter

1 large shallot, chopped

1/2 pound button mushrooms and stems, cleaned and finely chopped or processed

4 sprigs fresh thyme, finely chopped (about 1 tablespoon) or 1 teaspoon dried thyme

Salt and freshly ground black pepper, to taste

2 tablespoons dry sherry (2 splashes)

4 tournedos, fillet mignon steaks (1-inch thick)

8 ounces mousse paté (available in specialty cheese and appetizer cases of larger markets)

1 sheet frozen prepared puff pastry, 11 x 17 inches, defrosted

1 egg, beaten with a splash of water

4 plum tomatoes

1 large head broccoli, trimmed and sliced into spears

Preheat oven to 425°F.

Heat a small skillet over medium heat. Add oil and butter, shallots, and chopped mushrooms, and thyme. Season with salt and pepper and sauté, 5 minutes. Add sherry and let the liquid evaporate. Remove mushrooms from heat.

In a nonstick skillet over high heat, sear meat 2 minutes on each side in a drizzle of oil. Remove skillet from the heat and season meat with salt and pepper.

Cut paté into 4 pieces, 2 ounces each. Spread the puff pastry sheet out onto a cookie sheet covered with parchment paper. Quarter the dough with a sharp knife. On each rectangle of dough, place 1/4 of the cooked mushrooms. Top mushrooms with 2 ounces paté and 1 tournedo of beef. Wrap dough up and over the meat, trim excess dough, and seal the dough with egg wash, using a pastry brush.

Leftover dough bits may be used to decorate the tops of your Wellingtons. Turn the wrapped Wellingtons over and cover with egg wash. Bake 10 minutes or until golden. Let stand 5 minutes, then serve.

Preheat broiler to high. Split plum tomatoes in half lengthwise. Drizzle with olive oil and salt and pepper. Broil 5 minutes, then transfer to a serving dish.

Steam broccoli spears in 1 inch simmering salted water, covered, for 5 to 6 minutes, or until just tender. Transfer to a serving plate and serve alongside Wellingtons and broccoli spears.

Chocolate Mint Parfaits

MAKES 4 SERVINGS

4 shots crème de menthe liqueur (about 1 & 1/2 ounces each)
1 pint mint chocolate chip ice cream or chocolate ice cream
4 chocolate mint candies, such as Andes or peppermint patties
4 sprigs fresh mint

Using 4 parfait or cocktail glasses, pour half a shot of crème de menthe into each glass. Top with scoops of ice cream, then drizzle another half a shot per parfait of crème de menthe over ice cream. Garnish with mint candy and fresh mint sprigs.

MENU

1
Spinach and Mushroom Stuffed Chicken Breasts

· · · · ·

2
Spaghetti with Zucchini and Garlic

· · · · ·

3
Sambucca Cake with Strawberries, Whipped Cream and Shaved Bitter Chocolate

· · · · ·

Spinach and Mushroom Stuffed Chicken Breasts

I am not much for gadgets and tools. My food processor is my most exotic kitchen accessory, and I wasn't convinced and only started using one in the late '90s! I am a kitchen minimalist by practice and of necessity. I have a tiny kitchen in my cabin in the woods. Tiny kitchens have tiny cabinets. No room for clutter.

MAKES 4 SERVINGS

4 boneless, skinless chicken breasts (6 ounces each)

Large plastic food storage bags or wax paper

1 package (10 ounces) frozen chopped spinach, defrosted (in microwave)

2 tablespoons butter

12 small mushroom caps, crimini or button

2 cloves garlic, cracked

1 small shallot, quartered

Salt and freshly ground black pepper, to taste

1 cup part-skim ricotta cheese

1/2 cup grated Parmigiano Reggiano or Romano cheese (a couple handfuls)

1/2 teaspoon freshly grated or ground nutmeg

Toothpicks

3 tablespoons extra-virgin olive oil (three times around the pan)

SAUCE

2 tablespoons butter

2 tablespoons flour

1/2 cup white wine

1 cup chicken broth

Place breasts in a plastic food storage bag or in the center of 2 large sheets of wax paper. Pound the chicken from the center outward using a heavy-bottomed skillet or mallet.

Defrost spinach and transfer to a kitchen towel. Twist towel around spinach and wring it out until very dry. Transfer to a medium mixing bowl.

Place a nonstick skillet over moderate heat. When skillet is hot, add butter, mushrooms, garlic, and shallot. Season with salt and pepper and sauté, 5 minutes. Transfer to a food processor. Pulse grind the mushrooms and add to the spinach in the mixing bowl. Add ricotta, grated cheese, and nutmeg to the bowl and stir to combine.

Return skillet to the stove over medium-high heat.

Place a mound of stuffing on each chicken breast and roll breast over the stuffing. Secure with toothpicks. Add 3 tablespoons oil to the pan, add breasts, and brown on all sides, cooking 10 to 12 minutes. The meat will cook quickly because it is thin. Remove breasts to a warm platter.

To make the sauce, add butter and flour to the pan and cook for a minute, then whisk in wine and reduce for another minute. Whisk in broth and return breasts to the pan. Reduce heat and simmer until ready to serve. Serve breasts whole, or remove from pan, slice on an angle and fan out on dinner plates. Top with generous spoonfuls of the sauce.

Spaghetti with Zucchini and Garlic

MAKES 4 SERVINGS

1 pound spaghetti, cooked al dente
2 small to medium zucchini
1/4 cup extra-virgin olive oil (4 times around the pan)
4 cloves garlic, finely chopped
Salt and freshly ground black pepper, to taste
1/2 cup grated Parmigiano Reggiano or Romano cheese

Pile up 2 or 3 layers of paper towels on a work surface. Using a box grater, hold the zucchini at an angle and shred onto the towels.

Heat a large skillet over moderate heat. Add the olive oil, then the chopped garlic. When garlic speaks by sizzling in oil, add shredded zucchini and season with salt and pepper. Sauté, 7 to 10 minutes. Add hot, drained pasta to the pan, and toss with zucchini. Add a couple of handfuls of grated cheese. Adjust seasonings and serve.

Sambucca Cake with Strawberries, Whipped Cream, and Shaved Bitter Chocolate

MAKES 4 SERVINGS

1 prepared pound cake (from bakery section or frozen foods, defrosted)
3 ounces Sambucca, or other anise liqueur
1/2 pint strawberries, halved or sliced
2 teaspoons plus 2 tablespoons sugar
1 pint whipping cream
Chocolate syrup, for drizzling
1 bar good quality dark bittersweet chocolate

Place 2-inch slices of pound cake on dessert plates. Douse cake slices with Sambucca or other anise liqueur.

Slice berries and sprinkle with a little sugar, then toss and reserve.

Beat whipping cream sweetened with 2 tablespoons sugar with a hand mixer until soft peaks form.

Top cake with berries and drizzle with zigzags of syrup. Top with whipped cream. Using a vegetable peeler, shave dark chocolate over each dessert and serve.

HEALTHY HUNGER BUSTERS

RACHAEL RAY 30-MINUTE MEALS 2

HEALTHY HUNGER BUSTERS

Atkins. The Zone. Low carb, high carb, no carb — whatever! We all want to be fit. But, we still need to eat! These are meals for you and your friends to share, guilt free! Go to the gym. Run through the park. Practice Pilates until you are uber-svelt. Then, cook up something good, and good for you, too.

I've always been of the mind that when you eat well, you get to eat more. In this chapter, I've tried to address specific situations. I looked at the kind of nights I enjoy in my life and I tried to fill each of them with healthful menus: date nights, having the girls over, movie-watching, too-pooped-from-working-out-to-cook nights. I think it's all in here.

I also thought about families or couples with one person dieting and the other(s) not. If you are watching what you eat, but those around do not have the same needs, here are some real problem-solving menus for all to enjoy! Don't make those close to you suffer with dry meats or plain Jane steamed dinners. The meals in this chapter are so full of big flavors that no one will ever guess that they are really healthy, too!

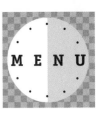

M E N U

1
Swordfish
Steaks
.....

2
Mango Salsa
.....

3
Curry
Couscous
.....

Swordfish Steaks

MAKES 4 SERVINGS

4 swordfish steaks, 1 & 1/2 inches thick (8 ounces each)
The juice of 1 lime
A drizzle extra-virgin olive oil
Salt and freshly ground black pepper, to taste

Mango Salsa

1 ripe mango, peeled and diced
1 small red bell pepper, seeded and diced
1 jalapeño or serrano pepper, seeded and finely chopped
1 inch fresh gingerroot, grated or minced
1/4 seedless European or English cucumber, peeled and chopped
20 blades fresh chives, finely chopped
The juice of 1 lime

Curry Couscous

2 cups chicken broth or water
2 teaspoons curry powder or 1 rounded teaspoon mild curry paste
1/2 teaspoon coarse salt
1 tablespoon extra-virgin olive oil
A handful raisins, dark or golden
1 cup couscous
2 scallions, sliced on an angle
1 carrot, shredded or grated
1 navel orange, peeled and chopped
1 pouch (2 ounces) sliced almonds (available on baking aisle)

Preheat grill pan or indoor electric grill to high heat. Squeeze lime juice over fish, and drizzle with a little oil, rubbing it into the fish to coat well. Season with salt and pepper, and cook steaks 3 to 4 minutes on each side.

SALSA: To assemble, combine all ingredients for salsa in a small bowl.

COUSCOUS: Bring broth or water to a boil with curry powder, salt, olive oil, and raisins. Place couscous in a bowl. Add boiling liquid, cover, and let couscous stand 10 minutes, then fluff with a fork and combine with scallions, carrot, orange bits, and almonds.

Top swordfish steaks with Mango Salsa and serve with generous portions of Curry Couscous.

TIDBIT

❝ Dicing mangos made easy: Cut mango away from the pit. Then score each inner half with a small, sharp knife making 1/2-inch cuts, vertically and horizontally. Push the skin of the mango halves almost inside out. The scored flesh will separate. Scrape off diced mango with your knife. ❞

MENU

1

Tuna Steaks
Au Poivre

• • • • •

2

White Beans
with Rosemary
and Roasted
Red Peppers

• • • • •

3

Bitter Greens
Salad

• • • • •

TIDBIT

❝ To roast red peppers: Preheat broiler to high. Halve and seed pepper and place skin-side-up close to hot broiler to blacken skins. Transfer pepper to a brown paper sack and seal to keep in the steam. When cool enough to handle, peel away charred skins. ❞

TIMING NOTE: If you are planning to roast your red pepper, rather than use storebought, place your pepper under broiler to blacken first. (See red pepper Tidbit, below.)

Tuna Steak au Poivre

MAKES 4 SERVINGS

4 tuna steaks, 1 & 1/2 inches thick (6 ounces each)
Coarse salt
Extra-virgin olive oil, for drizzling
Coarse freshly ground black pepper
Lemon wedges, for passing

White Beans with Rosemary and Roasted Red Peppers

MAKES 4 SERVINGS

2 tablespoons extra-virgin olive oil (twice around the pan)
2 cloves garlic, finely chopped
1 small onion, chopped
2 cans (15 ounces each) cannellini beans, rinsed and drained
1 roasted red pepper, storebought or homemade (see Tidbit), diced
2 sprigs fresh rosemary, leaves stripped and finely chopped
A handful chopped fresh flat-leaf parsley
Coarse salt and freshly ground black pepper, to taste

Preheat a large nonstick skillet or grill pan over high heat. Pat tuna steaks dry and season with a little coarse salt. Drizzle olive oil over tuna to lightly coat on both sides. Season one side of the steaks with a generous coating of coarse ground black pepper. When the pan is very hot, add steaks, peppered-side down. Sear and brown them 2 minutes, then turn and immediately reduce heat to medium. Loosely cover pan with a tin foil tent and allow steaks to cook 2 to 3 minutes for rare, 5 minutes for medium, and 7 minutes for well done.

In a second skillet over moderate heat, coat pan with olive oil, add garlic and onion and sauté, 3 minutes, to soften onion bits. Add beans and chopped roasted red pepper and heat through, 2 to 3 minutes. Stir in rosemary and parsley and season beans with salt and pepper.

Place a serving of beans on a dinner plate, top with Tuna Steak, and serve Bitter Greens Salad alongside.

Bitter Greens Salad

MAKES 4 SERVINGS

1 head escarole, core trimmed, then shredded
1 medium radicchio, shredded
The juice of 1 lemon
Extra-virgin olive oil, to coat
Coarse salt, to taste

Combine escarole and radicchio in a shallow dish. Coat with lemon juice, then a drizzle of oil. Season salad with coarse salt and toss well.

TIDBIT

❝ Juice halved lemons with cut side facing up, letting juice spill over the sides of the lemon. The seeds will stay with the lemon and not fall into your food. ❞

M E N U

1

Grilled
Mahi-Mahi
Fillets

· · · · ·

2

Asparagus
with Orange
and Sesame

· · · · ·

3

Star Anise
Blackberries
with Lemon
Sorbet

· · · · ·

When you are cooking light, it's important to please all the senses: make the food colorful, fragrant, and varied in texture. This menu does all of that. It's light, yet full of big flavors: citrus, ginger, sesame. The mahi-mahi uses less than a teaspoon of oil per portion, the asparagus is oil free. The fish is sturdy and hard to over or undercook. The dessert is simple, classy, and, except for the cookie garnish, fat-free.

Grilled Mahi-Mahi Fillets

MAKES 4 SERVINGS

4 portions mahi-mahi fillets (6 to 8 ounces each)
Salt and freshly ground black pepper, to taste
The juice of 2 limes
3 tablespoons Tamari dark soy sauce
2 inches fresh gingerroot, grated (about 1 & 1/2 tablespoons)
1 tablespoon vegetable or canola oil
20 blades fresh chives, chopped OR 3 scallions, thinly sliced, for garnish

Preheat grill pan over medium-high to high heat. Season mahi-mahi fillets with salt and pepper. Combine lime juice, dark soy, ginger, and a little vegetable or canola oil in a shallow dish. Turn fish in the citrus-soy marinade and let it "hang out" for 10 minutes. Grill 4 to 5 minutes per side or until fish is firm and opaque.

Asparagus with Orange and Sesame

MAKES 4 SERVINGS

1 to 1 & 3/4 pounds thin asparagus spears
2 navel oranges
1 inch fresh gingerroot, peeled
Salt
2 tablespoons toasted sesame seeds

Take one spear of asparagus and hold it at each end. Bend the asparagus until it snaps and breaks. Use this spear as your guide on where to trim the ends of your bundle of spears.

Cut the ends off two navel oranges and stand them upright on a cutting board. Remove skins in strips using a sharp knife to cut down from the top of the orange. Reserve the peels of 1 orange. When oranges are peeled and trimmed, slice into 1/4-inch rounds, and set aside.

In a skillet with cover, bring 1-inch of water to a boil with the peels of 1 orange and the gingerroot. When the water boils, add a healthy pinch of salt and asparagus spears. Simmer 3 to 5 minutes until just tender, then drain. Assemble a few spears on each dinner plate, crisscrossing the spears and orange slices. Finish with a sprinkle of sesame seeds and top with 1 portion of grilled mahi mahi. Garnish plates with chopped chives and serve.

Star Anise Blackberries with Lemon Sorbet

MAKES 4 SERVINGS

3/4 cup water
1/4 cup sugar
2 star anise
1 teaspoon lemon juice
1 pint blackberries
1 pint lemon sorbet
8 Piroline cookies or other wafer-style dessert cookie

In a small saucepan over moderate heat, combine water, sugar, star anise, and lemon juice. Stir and cook until sugar dissolves and water comes to a bubble. Add blackberries and cook 30 seconds. Remove pan from heat and let stand a minute or two, stirring occasionally. Remove star anise. Scoop lemon sorbet into 4 small dessert cups. Top with blackberries and garnish with 2 Piroline cookies or dessert wafers.

TIDBIT

❝ The flavor of the anise is another surprise. Star Anise is carried in most large supermarkets on the spice aisle. It's wonderful in poached pears as well. ❞

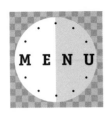
1

Pan-Seared
Shrimp and
Scallop
Skewers
· · · · ·

2

Orzo with
Spinach and
Tomato
· · · · ·

3

Fat-Free
Chocolate
Sorbet Banana
Splits
· · · · ·

Pan-Seared Shrimp and Scallop Skewers

MAKES 4 SERVINGS

8 bamboo skewers (6 to 8 inches)
16 jumbo shrimp, deveined and peeled
16 sea scallops
Salt and freshly ground black pepper, to taste
1 teaspoon sweet paprika (1/3 palmful)
1/2 teaspoon crushed red pepper flakes (eyeball it)
The zest and juice of 1 lemon
2 tablespoons chopped fresh flat-leaf parsley (a handful)
1 tablespoon extra-virgin olive oil (once around the pan)

Preheat a large nonstick skillet over medium-high to high heat.

Thread 4 shrimps each on 4 of the skewers, and 4 scallops on the other 4 skewers, and season with salt and pepper on both sides. Combine paprika, crushed pepper, lemon zest, and parsley in a small dish. Sprinkle over shrimps and rub in a bit. Add a generous teaspoon of extra-virgin olive oil (half a turn around the pan) to the hot skillet and sear the shrimps 3 minutes on each side or until curled and pink. Squeeze the juice of 1/2 lemon over the pan and remove skewers in the juice to a warm platter. Return pan to the heat and add remaining oil. Cook scallops 3 to 4 minutes on each side or until deep caramel in color. Squeeze the juice of 1/2 lemon over the pan and transfer skewers to serving platter alongside shrimp.

Orzo with Spinach and Tomato

MAKES 4 SERVINGS

1 sack spinach (10 ounces) triple-washed, stems removed
1 pint grape or cherry tomatoes, halved
The zest of 2 lemons
1 & 1/2 cups orzo, cooked al dente
1 tablespoon extra-virgin olive oil (once around the bowl)
24 basil leaves, torn or thinly sliced
Salt and freshly ground black pepper, to taste

Working in small piles, shred spinach into ribbons. Pile shredded spinach in the bottom of a medium-sized mixing bowl. Halve tomatoes and add them to the bowl, along with the lemon zest (save the lemons in the fridge to juice for another recipe.) Add hot orzo pasta to the mixing bowl. The heat of the pasta will wilt the spinach and warm the tomatoes at the bottom of the bowl and get the juices flowing from veggies. It also releases the flavor and oils in the lemon zest. Drizzle olive oil over the pasta and toss to combine the veggies and orzo. Add basil and salt and pepper and toss again. Taste your orzo to adjust seasonings and serve.

Fat-Free Chocolate Sorbet Banana Splits

MAKES 4 BANANA SPLITS

4 ripe bananas
2 pints chocolate sorbet
1/2 pint fresh raspberries
12 storebought meringues (available on packaged cookie aisle)

Split bananas lengthwise and line each of 4 sundae boats with 1 split banana. Place 3 small scoops of chocolate sorbet in each boat and garnish with raspberries and a meringue.

M E N U

1

Israeli Spice
Chicken

. . . . .

2

Two-Tomato
Salad

. . . . .

3

Zucchini with
Mint and
Parsley

. . . . .

Israeli Spice Chicken

My good friend Joshua went to Israel and brought me back a delicious spice rub for meats. It went on everything I baked, grilled, roasted or blackened for weeks. I even put it on my Thanksgiving bird. Then, sadly, it was gone. This is my attempt at replicating it. It still works on anything and everything! Make extra and store in a cool, dry place for up to 6 months.

MAKES 4 SERVINGS

4 boneless, skinless chicken breasts (1 & 1/2 to 2 pounds) split to make 8 pieces
Extra-virgin olive oil, for drizzling
4 tablespoons Israeli Spice Rub (a palmful, then half again)

ISRAELI SPICE RUB, FOR MEAT AND FISH
1 & 1/2 tablespoons sweet paprika (1 & 1/2 palmfuls)
1 & 1/2 tablespoons ground cumin (1 & 1/2 palmfuls)
1 teaspoon dried oregano (1/3 palmful)
1 teaspoon ground coriander (1/3 palmful)
1/2 to 1 teaspoon crushed red pepper flakes
1 & 1/2 teaspoons (1/2 palmful) coarse Kosher salt

Warm pita or flat bread, for passing

Place chicken in a shallow dish. Drizzle with extra-virgin olive oil to barely coat the meat. Rub chicken liberally with spice blend. Let stand 10 minutes.

Preheat grill pan or large nonstick skillet to medium-high. Grill chicken 6 or 7 minutes on each side or until juices run clear. Serve with tomato salad and green vegetable. Piling the salad and the chicken in a warm pita is a fun way to combine the flavors and textures of the two recipes.

Two-Tomato Salad

MAKES 4 SERVINGS

3 vine-ripe or Israeli red tomatoes
2 tomatoes, either yellow or orange
1 small onion, thinly sliced
1/2 cup fresh flat-leaf parsley leaves, chopped (2 handfuls)

DRESSING
3 tablespoons extra-virgin olive oil (a couple glugs)
The juice of 1 ripe lemon
1/2 teaspoon ground cumin
1/2 teaspoon ground coriander
1/2 teaspoon crushed red pepper flakes
Kosher salt, to taste

Seed and chop the tomatoes and combine with onion and parsley in a shallow bowl. Combine oil, lemon juice and spices in a small plastic container with a lid. Shake dressing to combine and pour over salad. Season with kosher salt and toss to combine well. Let stand 10 minutes and serve.

Zucchini with Mint and Parsley

MAKES 4 SERVINGS

4 small, tender zucchini (about 1 to 1 & 1/2 pounds)
3 tablespoons extra-virgin olive oil (3 times around the pan)
3 cloves garlic, minced
1/4 cup chopped fresh mint
1/2 cup fresh flat-leaf parsley tops, chopped (a couple handfuls)
Coarse salt and freshly ground black pepper, to taste

Heat a large skillet over medium heat. Cut small zucchini into 1/4-inch slices. Add oil, garlic, and zucchini to pan and sauté, 7 to 8 minutes, turning occasionally with a firm shake of the skillet, until just tender. Add mint and parsley, salt and pepper and cook 1 minute longer. Remove from heat and serve.

MENU

1 Too-Easy Chicken with Leeks
.....
2 Lemon Rice Pilaf
.....
3 Whatever-Your-Garden-Grows Salad
.....

Too-Easy Chicken with Leeks

MAKES 4 SERVINGS

2 leeks
4 pieces boneless, skinless chicken breasts (6 to 8 ounces each)
Salt and freshly ground black pepper, to taste
2 tablespoons extra-virgin olive oil (twice around the pan)
1 cup dry white wine

Trim leeks of tough green ends and roots. Split them lengthwise, then cut across into 1/2-inch slices. Place sandy slices of leeks into a colander. Run under cold water, separating the layers of each slice to free the grains of sand. Drain leeks very well and place within arm's reach of the stovetop.

Heat a large nonstick skillet over medium-high heat. Season chicken breasts with salt and pepper. Add olive oil to coat skillet, then add chicken breasts and brown, 3 to 4 minutes on each side, then transfer to a plate. Add a little more oil to the pan, then add leeks, and sauté, 5 minutes, until they become soft. Add 1 cup wine to the pan and nest chicken breasts down into leeks. Reduce heat to simmer for another 5 to 7 minutes. To serve, remove chicken from pan and slice on an angle. Fan and arrange sliced chicken breasts over a bed of sautéed leeks on each dinner plate or warm serving platter.

Lemon Rice Pilaf

MAKES 4 SERVINGS

1 tablespoon extra-virgin olive oil (once around the pan in a slow stream)
1 tablespoon butter
1 large shallot, finely chopped
1 & 1/2 cups long grain rice
1/2 cup dry white wine
A few sprigs fresh thyme, leaves stripped and chopped (about 1 tablespoon)
1 can (14 ounces) or 2 cups chicken broth or stock
1 cup water
The zest of 1 lemon
A handful chopped fresh flat-leaf parsley
Slivered almonds, toasted, for garnish

Healthy Hunger Busters
.....
230

Heat a medium saucepan over moderate heat. Add oil and butter and shallots to pan. Sauté, 2 minutes, then add 1 & 1/2 cups rice, and lightly brown, 3 to 5 minutes. Add wine and allow it to evaporate entirely, 1 to 2 minutes. Add thyme and chicken broth. Add a cup of water to pot and bring to a boil. Cover rice, reduce heat, and cook 20 minutes, until tender. Stir in the lemon zest and the parsley. Transfer to dinner plates or warm serving dish and garnish with toasted slivered almonds.

Whatever-Your-Garden-Grows Salad

As the title says, try any and every mix of veggies; substitutions encouraged!

MAKES 4 SERVINGS

1/4 pound fresh wax beans
1/4 pound fresh green beans
1 small yellow squash, cut into strips (julienne)
1 red bell pepper, cut into thin strips (julienne)
2 scallions, thinly sliced on an angle
2 cups baby spinach or arugula leaves, shredded

DRESSING
1 teaspoon Dijon mustard
2 tablespoons white wine or tarragon vinegar (a couple splashes)
The juice of 1/2 lemon
1/4 cup extra-virgin olive oil
2 tablespoons chopped fresh tarragon and/or fresh parsley
Salt and freshly ground black pepper, to taste

In a deep skillet bring 3 inches of water to a boil. Add trimmed wax and green beans and julienne-sliced yellow squash to the pot, and simmer for 2 minutes. Add red peppers and simmer, 1 minute longer. You want the vegetables to remain full of color and bite. Drain vegetables in a colander and cold-shock under running water. Place drained vegetables in a serving dish and combine with sliced scallions and shredded spinach or arugula.

Whisk together mustard, vinegar, and lemon juice. Add olive oil in a slow stream, whisking to get a nice emulsion. Add herbs, adjust salt and pepper to taste, and pour dressing over your salad, tossing to combine flavors and coat evenly.

TIDBIT

❝ To wash gritty greens such as arugula or spinach, fill sink with cold water, soak leaves and let sand fall to the bottom of the sink. Remove greens and dry on paper towels or on your dish rack. ❞

MENU

A Svelte Menu
for Friends
Trying to Get
Trim

1

Thai-
Vietnamese
Salad Bar
Supreme

• • • • •

2

Sorbet and
Fresh Fruit Bar

• • • • •

Thai-Vietnamese Salad Bar Supreme

MAKES 4 TO 6 SERVINGS

SALAD BAR FIXINS

3 hearts romaine lettuce, chopped

1 sack (10 ounces) mixed baby greens

2 cup fresh bean sprouts, any variety

1 cup thinly-sliced daikon or red radishes

2 cups shredded carrots (available prepped in plastic bags in produce case)

8 scallions, thinly sliced on an angle

1/2 seedless cucumber, halved lengthwise, then thinly sliced

1 pint yellow or red grape tomatoes

1 red onion, quartered and thinly sliced

1 bunch fresh mint leaves, trimmed

1 bunch fresh basil leaves, trimmed

2 packages (2 ounces each) chopped nuts (found on baking aisle)

CROUTONS

8 slices almond or anisette toast, such as Stella D'Oro brand, cut into 1-inch pieces

CHICKEN

1/4 cup Tamari dark soy sauce

2 tablespoons vegetable oil (eyeball it)

8 chicken cutlets (labeled "thin cut" breasts)

Salt and freshly ground black pepper, to taste

FISH

1 & 1/2 pounds mahi-mahi

Vegetable oil, for drizzling

1 lime, halved

Arrange salad bar ingredients in serving dishes and bowls as you prep them: romaine, baby mixed greens, bean sprouts, daikon, carrots, scallions, cucumbers, tomatoes, red onions, mint, basil, nuts, and sweet almond or anise "croutons."

Heat a grill pan over medium-high heat.

Combine soy and oil in a shallow dish. Add chicken, turn to coat, and season with salt and pepper. Drizzle fish with oil and season with salt and pepper. Grill chicken, 3 minutes on each side. Cut into strips on an angle and pile on a serving plate. Grill fish, 4 to 5 minutes on each side, until opaque. Squeeze lime over the fish and break into chunks as you transfer to a serving plate.

Healthy
Hunger Busters

• • • • •

Dressings

PEANUT DRESSING

3 tablespoons white vinegar or rice wine vinegar

1/2 cup white grape or apple juice concentrate

3 tablespoons peanut butter

2 inches fresh gingerroot, grated

1/2 teaspoon cayenne pepper

1/2 cup vegetable oil

CHILI GARLIC SWEET-HOT DRESSING

3 tablespoons white vinegar or rice wine vinegar

1/3 cup pepper jelly (available on condiment aisle)

2 cloves garlic, finely chopped

1 teaspoon freshly ground black pepper

2 teaspoons hot chili oil

1/2 cup vegetable oil

For peanut dressing, combine top 5 ingredients in a blender. Turn on for 30 seconds, then open lid and continue blending while streaming in oil. Transfer dressing to a serving dish and sprinkle in a spoonful of nuts from your salad bar to garnish. For chili garlic dressing, whisk together vinegar, pepper jelly, garlic, black pepper and chili oil. Stream in vegetable oil while continuing to whisk. When the oil is incorporated, transfer dressing to a small dish to serve.

Sorbet and Fresh Fruit Bar

MAKES 6 SERVINGS

1 pint mango sorbet

1 pint strawberry sorbet

1/2 cup toasted shredded coconut

2 ripe bananas, sliced

2 teaspoons lemon juice

1 pint strawberries, sliced

1 package wafer cookies or wafer roll cookies

Set out ice cream cups, sorbet selections, ice cream scoops, and coconut. Toss sliced bananas with a little lemon juice to retard browning, and set them in a bowl alongside dishes of sliced berries and cookies. Just like the salad bar, guests can have it their way.

❝ Save time all-week long! Wash and trim all of your produce when you bring it home from the supermarket. Store clean, dry greens in large plastic bags. Ready-to-use means less time in the kitchen for you! ❞

**Vegetable
Pizzas**

1

**Zucchini-roni
Pizza**

· · · · ·

2

**Asparagus and
Plum Tomato
Pizza**

· · · · ·

Pair up either of these HEALTHY pizzas with a simple salad of mixed greens for a fast, satisfying, and delicious dinner.

Zucchini-roni Pizza

MAKES ONE 12-INCH PIZZA

1 jar (14 ounces) roasted red peppers OR 2 medium home-roasted red
   peppers

1/2 pound refrigerated pizza dough

1 tablespoon flour or corn meal

1/2 pound smoked fresh mozzarella cheese, thinly sliced
   OR substitute 1 & 1/2 cups shredded smoked Gouda cheese

1/2 medium zucchini, very thinly sliced (think of pepperoni slices)

2 cloves garlic, minced

A drizzle extra-virgin olive oil (about 1 tablespoon)

1 teaspoon crushed red pepper flakes (eyeball it)

1 teaspoon dried Italian seasoning (eyeball it)

Coarse salt, to taste

Preheat oven to 400°F, along with a pizza stone if you have one.

If you are using jarred red peppers, drain them very well and pat dry with paper towel. Place peppers in a food processor and pulse-grind into a paste. Dust your pizza dough with flour or corn meal. Punch and spread the dough out onto a perforated pizza pan or onto a work surface to be transferred to a pizza stone. Spread red pepper paste in a thin layer onto the dough, and top with thin slices of smoked fresh mozzarella cheese.

Place very thinly sliced zucchini in a small bowl and combine with remaining ingredients, tossing well to evenly coat with seasonings. The zucchini will have a flavor similar to pepperoni. You've just made zucchinironi!

Arrange zucchinironi slices around your pie—as few or as many as you like—but don't overlap slices or pie will be wet.

Bake 10 minutes on the middle rack of preheated oven, or until cheese is bubbly and golden and edges of pizza are crisp.

Asparagus and Plum Tomato Pizza

MAKES ONE 12-INCH PIZZA

1/2 pound thin asparagus spears
1/2 pound refrigerated pizza dough
1 tablespoon flour or corn meal
1 cup prepared pesto sauce, homemade or storebought
1/2 pound fontina cheese, diced into small cubes (about 1 & 1/2 cups)
1 firm plum tomato, seeded and diced

Preheat oven to 400°F and place oven rack in middle position. If you have a pizza stone, preheat that as well.

Trim tough ends off asparagus, leaving 4- or 5-inch tender spears. Place tops in a small skillet in 1/2-inch of boiling water. Cover pan and steam, 2 minutes. Run under cool water and drain well. Cut spears on the diagonal into 1-inch pieces.

Dust dough with flour or corn meal. Punch out and spread your pizza dough onto a pizza tin or a work surface to transfer to a pizza stone. Spread dough with a thin layer of pesto sauce. Dot the pesto sauce with cubed fontina, and add a scattering of chopped asparagus and diced plum tomatoes.

Bake pie, 12 to 14 minutes in preheated oven on middle rack, or until fontina melts and edges of your pizza are crisp and dark golden.

MENU

Low Carbs
Power Supper

1

Spinach and
Roasted Red
Pepper
Salad with
Honey
Balsamic
Dressing
• • • • •

2

Lean Sirloin
Burgers
—Hold The
Bun—with
Sautéed
Mushrooms
• • • • •

3

Vine-Ripe
Tomatoes
with Herb
Gremolada
• • • • •

Spinach and Roasted Red Pepper Salad with Honey Balsamic Dressing

MAKES 4 SERVINGS

10 ounces triple-washed spinach, stems removed and coarsely chopped
1 jar (12 to 14 ounces) roasted red peppers, drained well

DRESSING
2 teaspoons grainy mustard
2 rounded teaspoons honey
2 tablespoons balsamic vinegar
1/3 cup extra-virgin olive oil (eyeball it)
Coarse salt and freshly ground black pepper, to taste

Arrange spinach on a platter or salad bowl. Slice well-drained red peppers into thin strips and arrange them over top of the salad. Whisk together mustard, honey, and vinegar in a bowl. Slowly stream in olive oil while continuing to whisk. Pour dressing in a slow stream, back and forth over the top of the salad, season with salt and pepper and serve.

Lean Sirloin Burgers—Hold The Bun— with Sautéed Mushrooms

MAKES 4 SERVINGS

1 & 1/2 pounds ground sirloin
Worcestershire sauce, for brushing
Steak seasoning blend such as Montreal Seasoning by McCormick OR salt and freshly ground black pepper, to taste
Olive oil, for drizzling
2 tablespoons extra-virgin olive oil (twice around the pan)
4 cloves garlic, crushed
1 pound crimini mushrooms, cleaned with a damp towel and quartered
Salt and freshly ground black pepper, to taste
1/4 cup dry cooking sherry
Grainy, stone-ground prepared mustard, for passing at the table

Let meat rest to take the chill off.

Preheat a nonstick skillet over medium-high to high heat.

Place the meat in a bowl and score it into 4 equal sections and form the meat into patties. Pour a few tablespoons of Worcestershire sauce into a small dish and, using a pastry brush, lightly baste the burgers with the sauce. Add steak seasoning blend or salt and pepper. Drizzle a little oil into the hot skillet, add the burgers, and cook for 2 minutes. Then turn and sear the reverse side to caramelize the meat. Lower the heat slightly and cook 3 to 5 minutes longer on each side, for medium-rare to medium-well burgers. Remove meat to a warm plate and return skillet to the stovetop, adding 2 tablespoons oil, the garlic, and the mushrooms. Season with salt and pepper, and sauté, 5 to 7 minutes until mushroom are just tender. Deglaze the pan with dry sherry and scrape up the pan drippings. Distribute the mushrooms equally over the burgers. Pass grainy mustard at the table.

Vine-Ripe Tomatoes with Herb Gremolada

MAKES 4 STUFFED TOMATOES

4 yellow or red vine-ripe tomatoes
Salt and freshly ground black pepper, to taste
2 cups fresh parsley tops, about 1 large bundle
1 small clove garlic, cracked away from skin
The zest of 2 lemons
1 teaspoon crushed red pepper flakes
1 teaspoon coarse salt
1/3 cup bread crumbs (a couple handfuls)
1 tablespoon red wine vinegar (a splash)
1 tablespoon extra-virgin olive oil (a good drizzle)

Cut the tops off the tomatoes and, with a spoon, hull them completely of seeds and liquid. Season the insides of the tomatoes with salt and pepper.

In a food processor, place parsley, garlic, lemon zest, red pepper flakes, salt, bread crumbs, vinegar and oil, and pulse until well combined.

Stuff 1/4 of the gremolada into each tomato and serve.

M E N U

1

Poached
Grouper with
Tomato and
Basil

• • • • •

2

Mediterranean
Succotash:
Butter Beans,
Corn, and Bell
Peppers

• • • • •

3

Melon with
Sorbet and
Berries

• • • • •

Mediterranean Succotash: Butter Beans, Corn, and Bell Peppers

MAKES 4 SERVINGS

2 tablespoons extra-virgin olive oil (twice around the pan)
2 cloves garlic, chopped
2 bell peppers, yellow, red or green, seeded and chopped
2 cups frozen corn kernels
1 can (15 ounces) butter beans, drained
Salt and freshly ground black pepper, to taste
A handful chopped fresh flat-leaf parsley

Heat a medium skillet over medium-high heat. Add oil, garlic, and peppers.
Sauté, stirring frequently, 5 minutes. Add corn, cook 2 or 3 minutes longer. Add
beans and heat them through, 1 or 2 minutes. Season with salt and pepper, then
stir in parsley. Transfer to individual dinner plates or serving bowl.

Poached Grouper with Tomato and Basil

MAKES 4 SERVINGS

4 grouper fillets (6 to 8 ounces each)
Salt and freshly ground black pepper, to taste
1 tablespoon extra-virgin olive oil
1 clove garlic, crushed
1 shallot, sliced
1/2 cup white wine (eyeball it)
1 can diced tomatoes, well drained
The juice of 1/4 lemon
20 leaves fresh basil, torn or rolled and shredded with your knife

Season fish with salt and pepper. To a large skillet, add the oil and fish, turning
fish to coat lightly in the oil. Then add garlic, shallots, and wine. Top each fillet
with 1/4 of the tomatoes. Place the pan on the stovetop and bring the liquid to
a boil over medium-high heat. Cover with a tight-fitting lid and reduce heat to
moderate. Cook fish, 8 to 10 minutes, until opaque and flaky, but not dry.
Carefully transfer fish topped with tomatoes to dinner plates or serving plate
with a thin spatula. Spoon pan juices over the fish. Squeeze lemon over the fish
and top with lots of torn or shredded basil. Serve immediately.

Melon with Sorbet and Berries

MAKES 4 SERVINGS

1 cantaloupe, quartered and seeded
1 pint mango or strawberry sorbet
1/2 pint raspberries
1/2 pint strawberries, sliced
2 teaspoons sugar

Cut a thin slice from the skin side of each melon wedge to give it a stable base on the plate. Top each melon "boat" with a scoop of mango or strawberry sorbet. Toss berries with a little sugar and spill them down and over the sorbet and melon.

MENU

1

Pan-Seared
Salmon
with Citrus
Vinegar Glaze
and Green
Beans

• • • • •

2

Orange and
Almond Salad

• • • • •

3

Mango Sorbet
with
Amaretto
and
Crystallized
Ginger

• • • • •

Orange and Almond Salad

MAKES 4 SERVINGS

2 hearts romaine lettuce, chopped
3 navel oranges (save rind)
1/4 cup slivered almonds (available on the baking aisle)
2 tablespoons chopped fresh tarragon (2 or 3 sprigs)
2 rounded teaspoons honey
2 tablespoons tarragon vinegar
A splash of orange juice
1/4 teaspoon dry mustard (a couple pinches)
1/3 cup extra-virgin olive oil (eyeball it)
Salt and freshly ground black pepper, to taste

Arrange chopped lettuce on a platter. To peel orange, trim a slice of skin from the top and bottom of the orange down to the flesh. Stand the orange upright and cut off the remaining peel, working from top to bottom around the orange. Cut orange in half lengthwise and slice into half-moon shapes. Arrange the sliced oranges around the chopped romaine. Lightly toast the almonds in a small skillet over moderate heat or in a toaster or conventional oven. Top the romaine and oranges with toasted almonds and chopped tarragon.

In a small bowl, combine honey, vinegar, orange juice, and mustard with a whisk. Stream in the olive oil while continuing to whisk to combine well. Pour the dressing evenly over the entire salad platter in a slow, thin stream. Season the salad with salt and pepper. The salad is pretty as is, no tossing.

TIDBIT

❝ Look for individually packaged salmon fillets from Norway near the fresh counter. They have skins removed and weigh exactly 6 ounces each. ❞

Pan-Seared Salmon with Citrus Vinegar Glaze and Green Beans

MAKES 4 SERVINGS

4 salmon fillets (6 ounces each)
Extra-virgin olive oil, for brushing fish
Salt and freshly ground black pepper, to taste
1/2 cup dry white wine
1/2 cup balsamic vinegar
2 tablespoons orange juice (a splash)
2 teaspoons lemon juice
2 tablespoons brown sugar
1/2 teaspoon coarse black pepper

1 pound green beans, trimmed
Orange and/or lemon rind slices

Preheat a cast-iron pan or heavy-bottomed skillet over medium-high heat. Brush the salmon fillets with oil. Season with salt and pepper. Cook salmon until just cooked through, about 3 minutes on each side.

While salmon cooks, bring wine, vinegar, citrus juices and brown sugar to a boil over high heat. Reduce glaze 3 or 4 minutes, until thickened. Remove from heat. Stir in 1/2 teaspoon coarse black pepper.

To a second skillet, add green beans, pieces of orange and/or lemon rind and 1/2 inch of water. Bring to a boil, cover, and cook 3 or 4 minutes. Drain the beans, toss with a drizzle of oil (optional) and season with salt and pepper.

Drizzle glaze over salmon fillets and serve with citrus green beans.

Mango Sorbet with Amaretto and Crystallized Ginger

MAKES 4 SERVINGS

1 pint mango sorbet
2 ounces Amaretto, or other almond liqueur
2 pieces crystallized ginger (available in Asian foods section)
8 gingersnap cookies
1/2 pint fresh raspberries

In cocktail glasses or small dessert cups, place 2 small round scoops of mango sorbet. Pour 1/2 ounce Amaretto over the sorbet. Using a small hand-held grater, grate the crystallized ginger over the sorbet to garnish. If you don't have a small grater, use a small paring knife to shave off small curls of ginger. Set 2 ginger snaps into each sorbet and top with a scattering of fresh red raspberries.

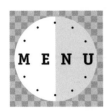

M E N U

1

Chicken
Scarpariello
• • • • •

2

Orzo with
Parsley and
Lemon Zest
• • • • •

3

Spicy Greens
with Warm
Balsamic
Dressing
• • • • •

Orzo with Parsley and Lemon Zest

MAKES 4 SERVINGS

1/2 pound orzo pasta
Coarse salt
1 tablespoon extra-virgin olive oil (eyeball it)
Freshly ground black pepper, to taste
The zest of 2 large lemons
1/4 cup fresh flat-leaf parsley, finely chopped (a couple handfuls)

Cook orzo in salted water, 7 to 8 minutes, al dente. Drain well, transfer to a
warm serving bowl, and drizzle with a tablespoon of olive oil. Season with salt
and pepper, add lemon zest and parsley, and toss to combine the flavors with
the orzo.

Chicken Scarpariello

MAKES 4 SERVINGS

1 & 1/2 pounds boneless, skinless chicken breast
Salt and freshly ground black pepper
1 teaspoon poultry seasoning
2 tablespoons extra-virgin olive oil (twice around the pan)
2 red bell peppers, seeded and cut into 1-inch pieces
3 hot cherry peppers, drained and chopped
4 cloves garlic, chopped or thinly sliced
1/2 cup dry white wine
1/2 cup chicken stock or broth
1/4 cup chopped fresh flat-leaf parsley (a couple handfuls)
2 tablespoons juice from a jar of hot peppers

Heat a large, heavy skillet over medium-high heat. Cut chicken into large chunks
and season with salt and pepper and poultry seasoning. Add 1 tablespoon olive
oil to the hot pan. Set chicken into pan and do not turn for 2 or 3 minutes or
you will tear the meat. Brown, 3 minutes on each side, then remove the chicken
to a warm plate. Add peppers, chopped hot peppers, and garlic to the pan.
Sauté for 5 minutes, tossing frequently. Add wine and reduce 1 minute, scraping
up the pan drippings. Add the chicken stock and bring up to a bubble. Set the
chicken back into the pan, toss in the parsley, and cook through, another 2 or 3
minutes. Scatter a little hot pepper juice over the pan and serve the Scarpariello
over a bed of lemon orzo. WOW!

Spicy Greens with Warm Balsamic Dressing

MAKES 4 SERVINGS

1 bunch arugula, trimmed and chopped
1 head radicchio, chopped
2 cups escarole (half a head), chopped
1/4 medium red onion, thinly sliced
1/4 cup extra-virgin olive oil
1 clove garlic, cracked
1/3 cup balsamic vinegar
Salt and freshly ground black pepper, to taste

Arrange salad greens and scatter red onion on a large platter. Heat oil and garlic in a small pan over moderate heat. Simmer garlic in oil to infuse the flavor. Remove the garlic and oil to a small bowl. Wipe the pan and return to heat. Add balsamic vinegar. Raise heat to high and reduce vinegar by half, 30 seconds. Stream oil into saucepan and whisk to combine with vinegar. Drizzle dressing over the salad and season with salt and pepper.

Index

almond(s):
  and orange salad, 240
  smoked, five-spice beef and pepper stir-fry and rice with, 48

amaretto, mango sorbet with crystallized ginger and, 241

andouille sausage, one great gumbo with chicken and, 126–27

angel food cake, lemon coconut, 121

antipasto salad toss, 124

apple(s):
  and cinnamon cake and ice cream, my sister Maria's easy, 42
  crisp, 107
  fritters, nothin' to fret about, 105
  grilled, maple mustard pork chops with, 88

apricot vinaigrette, arugula salad with blue cheese, pears and, 195

artichoke:
  spinach calzones, 55
  spinach pasta salad, 21

artichoke hearts:
  baked scallops and seared tournedos with asparagus tips and, 208–9
  Emmanuel's baked, 93
  hearts of romaine, palm and, 187

arugula:
  salad with blue cheese, pears, and apricot vinaigrette, 195
  -stuffed tomatoes, steak au poivre and, 213

Asiago, broccoli with garlic and, 199

asparagus:
  and green beans with tarragon lemon dip, 116
  with orange and sesame, 224
  pasta salad, 41
  and plum tomato pizza, 235
  steamed, trout amandine, new potatoes and, 170–71

asparagus tips:
  baked scallops and seared tournedos with artichoke hearts and, 208–9
  steamed, 82

avocados:
  chili lime, 25
  with creamy maque choux (corn and peppers), 206–7

bacon:
  crispy-topped baked beans with, 71
  and egg "coal miner's" pasta, 84
  peas with onions and, 106

bakla-squares and ice cream, 181

balsamic:
  chicken cutlets, grilled, over spinach salad with warm shallot vinaigrette, 74–75
  dressing, warm, spicy greens with, 243
  glazed vegetables, 63
  honey dressing, spinach and roasted red pepper salad with, 236
  onions, Delmonico steaks with steak sauce and, 200
  reduction, broiled lamb chops with, 203

banana(s):
  chocolate cream pie, quick, 109
  chocolate dipped, 100
  raita, 51
  splits, fat-free chocolate sorbet, 227

basil:
  bruschetta with tomato and, 192
  poached grouper with tomato and, 238
  tomato panzanella, 121

beans:
  crispy-topped baked, with bacon, 71
  salad, three, 89
  see also specific beans

beef:
  chicken fried steaks with creamed pan gravy and biscuits, 108
  marinated, 62
  and pepper stir-fry, five-spice, and rice with smoked almonds, 48
  Spanish rice and, 138
  stuffed chilies with rice, spinach, cheese and, 139
  Wellingtons, individual, with broiled plum tomatoes and steamed broccoli spears, 214–15

beet and red cabbage slaw salad with currant dressing, 71

berries:
  Liège waffles with whipped cream and, 167
  melon with sorbet and, 239
  and nuts parfaits, 209
  see also specific berries

bitter greens salad, 223

black and white shakes, 19

black bean(s):
  burrito filling, spicy, 38
  salsa, warm, wild mushroom quesadilla with, 148

blackberries, star anise, with lemon sorbet, 225

blue cheese:

arugula salad with pears, apricot vinaigrette and, 195

and walnut spinach salad with maple dressing, 201

boeuf bourguignon with butter and parsley egg noodles, 102–3

Bourbon Street candy balls with pecans, 119

braciole with mushroom tomato gravy, 59

brandy:

assorted Italian cookies and citrus rings with, 111

and orange chicken topped with stuffed shrimp, 190–91

breads:

cheddar and chive, 42

flat, *see* flat bread

soup—ribollita, 162

broccoli:

with garlic and Asiago, 199

pizza with chicken, sun-dried tomatoes and, 32–33

spears, steamed, individual beef Wellingtons with broiled plum tomatoes and, 214–15

broccoli rabe:

with golden raisins, 77

with lemon and garlic, 202–3

brownies, fluffernutter, 87

bruschetta with tomato and basil, 192

burgers:

Cajun pork, 22

harvest turkey, 31

jerky turkey, with island salsa, 24

portobello, with green sauce and smoked mozzarella, 20

sirloin, see sirloin burgers

burrito bar, make-your-own, 38–39

butter and parsley egg noodles, boeuf bourguignon with, 102–3

butter bean(s):

in baked gigantes beans, 157

corn, bell peppers and, 238

butter bean salad, 86–87

cabbage, red, and beet slaw salad with currant dressing, 71

Cajun pork burgers, 22

cake:

lemon coconut angel food, 121

my sister Maria's easy apple and cinnamon, and ice cream, 42

sambucca, with strawberries, whipped cream, and shaved bitter chocolate, 218

calzones:

sausage, 56

spinach artichoke, 55

candy balls with pecans, Bourbon Street, 119

caponata:

herb polenta and eggplant, 134–35

pasta bake, 135

cauliflower with red, green and black confetti, 205

champagne freezes, 189

cheddar cheese:

and chive bread, 42

and macaroni, 106

cheese(s)(y):

dessert, fresh fruits and, 171

and fruit board, 90

grilled 4, sandwiches, 101

and herb chicken tenders parmigiana with spaghetti, 122

orzo, 63

POPcorn, 33

Spanish olives and, 153

squares, cracked corn and, 79

stuffed chilies with beef, rice, spinach and, 139

see also specific cheeses

cherry(ies):

orange, and cranberry compote, warm, with vanilla ice cream, 77

sauce, Neapolitan ice cream with, 61

chicken:

brandy and orange, topped with stuffed shrimp, 190–91

breasts, spinach and mushroom-stuffed, 216–17

country captain, with white and wild rice, 118–19

curry, sweet 'n spicy, with fragrant basmati rice, 52

cutlets, grilled balsamic, over spinach salad with warm shallot vinaigrette, 74–75

divan, a divine, 136–37

Greek grilled, and salad with warm pita bread for wrapping, 182

honey mustard barbecued, 86

Israeli spice, 228

Kiev, 176

with leeks, too-easy, 230

marinated, 62

one great gumbo with andouille sausage and, 126–27

paillard, 66–67

parmigiana, simple tomato sauce for, 123

piccata pasta toss, 94

pizza with sun-dried tomatoes, broccoli and, 32–33
Portuguese chorizo and, 141
red peppers, and chorizo burrito filling, 38–39
rosemary grilled, and wild mushroom sauce, 163
scarpariello, 242
sesame, salad, 44–45
tetrazzini, 137
tikka with charred tomato chutney and warm flat
    bread, 50
and vegetable potage, 140
waterzooi de poulet, 166

chicken fried steaks with creamed pan gravy and
    biscuits, 108

chicken sandwiches:
grilled honey lime, 73
hot Buffalo, 46–47
smoky orange barbecued, 70

chicken tenders:
parmigiana, herb and cheese, with spaghetti, 122
pecan-crusted, and salad with tangy maple
    barbecue dressing, 43

chick peas and greens, garlic, 175

chili(es):
corn on the cob with lime and, 87
garlic sweet-hot dressing, 233
lime avocados, 25

chilies:
Southwestern stuffed peppers, 147
stuffed, with beef, rice, spinach, and cheese, 139

chive:
and cheddar bread, 42
lemon vinaigrette, romaine hearts with, 97

chocolate:
banana cream pie, quick, 109
bitter, shaved, sambucca cake with strawberries,
    whipped cream and, 218
cups with whipped cream, 185
dipped bananas, 100
fondue, 117
mint parfaits, 215
sauce, pound cake with vanilla ice cream and, 115
sorbet banana splits, fat-free, 227

chorizo:
chicken, and red pepper burrito filling, 38–39
Portuguese chicken and, 141

chutney, charred tomato, chicken tikka with warm flat
    bread and, 50

cilantro, roasted salsa with mint and, 38

cinnamon and apple cake and ice cream, my sister
    Maria's easy, 42

citrus:
cream sauce, pasta with, 188
white wine spritzer, 67

coconut lemon angel food cake, 121

compote, warm cherry, orange and cranberry, with
    vanilla ice cream, 77

cookies:
assorted Italian, and citrus rings with brandy, 111
and cream, sugared stone fruits with, 85

corn:
butter beans, bell peppers and, 238
on the cob with chili and lime, 87
cracked, and cheese squares, 79
and peppers (maque choux), creamy, with
    avocados, 206–7

couscous:
curry, 221
vegetable, 174

crab spring rolls, baked, 178

cranberry, cherry, and orange compote, warm, with
    vanilla ice cream, 77

cream, sugared stone fruits with cookies and, 85

cream pie, quick chocolate banana, 109

crème de Menthe parfaits, 203

crisp, apple, 107

crostini, olive rosemary, 158

cucumber, mixed baby greens with mandarin orange
    and, in sesame dressing, 49

cumin:
baby potatoes with, 142
potatoes with, 51

currant dressing, red cabbage and beet slaw salad
    with, 71

curry:
couscous, 221
in a hurry, chicken sweet 'n spicy, with fragrant
    basmati rice, 52

decadent duo for decadent duos: chocolate cups with
    whipped cream, 185

Delmonico steaks with balsamic onions and steak
    sauce, 200

dessert, see specific desserts

deviled potato salad, 27

different surf and turf for two, a: baked scallops and
    seared tournedos with artichoke hearts and
    asparagus tips, 208–9

dill sauce, poached salmon with Dijon, and new potatoes with mint, 131–32

dips:
French, roast beef sandwiches, 116
roasted garlic and feta walnut, with toasted flat bread, 98
tarragon lemon, asparagus and green beans with, 116

dressings:
chili garlic sweet-hot, 233
currant, red cabbage and beet slaw salad with, 71
honey balsamic, spinach and roasted red pepper salad with, 236
lime, watercress and mint salad with, 143
maple, blue cheese and walnut spinach salad with, 201
mint yogurt, lamb pitas with tomato, scallions and, 144
peanut, 233
sesame, mixed baby greens with mandarin orange and cucumber in, 49
sweet red pepper relish, tossed salad with snap peas, radishes and, 128
tangy maple barbecue, pecan-crusted chicken tenders and salad with, 43
warm balsamic, spicy greens with, 243

egg and bacon "coal miner's" pasta, 84

egg creams, NY, 19

egg noodles:
butter and parsley, boeuf bourguignon with, 102–3
with mushrooms, 165
veal marsala with egg fettuccini, 198

eggplant caponata and herb polenta, 134–35

eggplant caponata pasta bake, 135

Elsa's jumbo shrimp with sage and pancetta, 68

Emmanuel's baked artichoke hearts, 93

endive salad, warm, 165

fat-free chocolate sorbet banana splits, 227

fennel:
and mixed greens salad, 105
slaw salad, 159

feta walnut and roasted garlic dip with toasted flat bread, 98

fettuccine all'Alfredo, 193

fettuccine, egg, veal marsala with, 198

fish stew (cioppino)—a fine kettle of fish, 104

see also specific fish

five-spice beef and pepper stir-fry and rice with smoked almonds, 48

flat bread:
toasted, roasted garlic and feta walnut dip with, 98
warm, chicken tikka with charred tomato chutney and, 50
see also pita bread, pitas

floats, root beer, 27

fluffernutter brownies, 87

fondue, chocolate, 117

freezes:
champagne, 189
orange, 47

French dip roast beef sandwiches, 116

fricassee, wild mushroom, over polenta, 194–95

fries, oven steak, 201

fritters, apple, nothin' to fret about, 105

fruit(s)(ed):
and cheese board, 90
fresh, and sorbet, bar, 233
fresh, dessert cheeses, 171
salad with orange liqueur and sorbet, 41
spiced, Indian, 53
sugared stone, with cookies and cream, 85
white and wild rice, 190
see also specific fruits

garlic:
broccoli rabe with lemon and, 202–3
broccoli with Asiago and, 199
chick peas and green, 175
chili sweet-hot dressing, 233
roasted, and feta walnut dip with toasted flat bread, 98
spaghetti with zucchini and, 217
wilted spinach with oil and, 60

gemelli pasta with roasted red pepper sauce, 202

ginger, crystallized, mango sorbet with Amaretto and, 241

glaze, citrus vinegar, pan-seared salmon with green beans and, 240–41

goat cheese and herb toasts, 74

gorgonzola:
cream sauce, spinach and mushroom lasagna roll-ups with, 82–83
tenderloin steaks with, 211

Gouda, smoked, and potato pancakes, 112

granita, margarita, 207

gravy, mushroom tomato, braciole with, 59

Greek:
  grilled chicken and salad with warm pita bread for
    wrapping, 182
  meatballs in wine sauce, 156–57

green bean(s):
  and asparagus with tarragon lemon dip, 116
  pan-seared salmon with citrus vinegar glaze
    and, 240–41
  and portobello mushroom sauté, 210
  red snapper with olive salsa and, 151
  salad with red onion and tomato, 69
  Southern, 109
  in 3 bean salad, 89

greens:
  bitter, salad, 223
  garlic chick peas and, 175
  mixed, and fennel salad, 105
  spicy, with warm balsamic dressing, 243

greens, mixed baby:
  with mandarin orange and cucumber in sesame
    dressing, 49
  salmon cakes on, 133

gremolada, herb, vine-ripe tomatoes with, 237

grouper, poached, with tomato and basil, 238

Gruyère cheese, stuffed potatoes with ham, thyme
  and, 54

guacamole sauce, grilled halibut tacos with, 154

gumbo with chicken and andouille sausage, one
  great, 126–27

halibut, grilled:
  sandwiches, 40
  tacos, with guacamole sauce, 154

ham, stuffed potatoes with thyme, Gruyère and, 54

harvest turkey burgers, 31

heart-y salad: hearts of romaine, palm, and
  artichoke, 187

herb:
  and cheese chicken tenders parmigiana with
    spaghetti, 122
  and goat cheese toasts, 74
  gremolada, vine-ripe tomatoes with, 237
  polenta, eggplant caponata and, 134–35

honey:
  balsamic dressing, spinach and roasted red pepper
    salad with, 236

glazed vegetables, 63
lime chicken sandwiches, grilled, 73
mustard and red onion barbecued chicken, 86

horseradish cream dipping sauce, grilled shrimp cocktail
  with, 212

ice cream:
  bakla-squares and, 181
  crunchy, 155
  dessert, maple nut coffee, 191
  my sister Maria's easy apple and cinnamon cake
    and, 42
  Neapolitan, with cherry sauce, 61
  s'mores cups, 113
  sundae sandwiches, 33
  vanilla, see vanilla ice cream

Indian spiced fruit, 53

Israeli spice chicken, 228

jerky turkey burgers with island salsa, 24

kale, loin lamb chops with braised root vegetables and
  colcannon-creamy potatoes and, 168–69

lamb:
  boneless roast leg of, 142
  pitas with tomato, scallions, and mint yogurt
    dressing, 144

lamb chops:
  broiled, with balsamic reduction, 203
  loin, with braised root vegetables and colcannon-
    creamy kale and potatoes, 168–69
  with mint and mustard dipping sauce, 64
  Moroccan rub, 174–75

"lasagna," ravioli vegetable, 96–97

lasagna roll-ups, spinach and mushroom, with
  gorgonzola cream sauce, 82–83

leeks, too-easy chicken with, 230

lemon(s):
  broccoli rabe with garlic and, 202–3
  chive vinaigrette, romaine hearts with, 97
  coconut angel food cake, 121
  rice pilaf, 230–31
  sorbet, star anise blackberries with, 225
  tarragon dip, asparagus and green beans with, 116
  veal medallions with, on a bed of spinach, 188–89
  zest, orzo with parsley and, 242

lettuce, extra-spicy refried beans, tomatoes, and
  lime, 155

Liège waffles with berries and whipped cream, 167

lime(s):
  chili avocados, 25
  corn on the cob with chili and, 87
  dressing, watercress and mint salad with, 143
  extra-spicy refried beans, lettuce, tomatoes and, 155
  honey chicken sandwiches, grilled, 73
  sorbet, fresh oranges with, 97

limoncello dessert, 65

macaroni:
  and cheddar cheese, 106
  and meatball soup, 100–101

mahi-mahi fillets, grilled, 224

mango:
  salsa, 221
  sorbet with Amaretto and crystallized ginger, 241

maple:
  barbecue dressing, tangy, pecan-crusted chicken
    tenders and salad with, 42
  dressing, blue cheese and walnut spinach salad
    with, 201
  mustard pork chops with grilled apples, 88
  nut coffee ice cream dessert, 191

maque choux (corn and peppers), creamy, avocados
  with, 206–7

marg-alrightas, fresh strawberry, 149

margarita granita, 207

mayo, balsamic, sirloin burgers with mushrooms, Swiss
  and, 18–19

meatball(s):
  Greek, in wine sauce, 156–57
  and macaroni soup, 100–101

Mediterranean succotash: butter beans, corn, and bell
  peppers, 238

melon:
  prosciutto di Parma and, 161
  with sorbet and berries, 239

Mexican:
  chunk vegetable salad, 72
  fiesta salad, 79
  rice, 154–55

minestrone, green, 120

mint:
  chocolate parfaits, 215
  and mustard dipping sauce, lamb chops with, 64
  poached salmon with Dijon dill sauce and new
    potatoes with, 131–32
  roasted salsa with cilantro and, 38

and watercress salad with lime dressing, 143
yogurt dressing, lamb pitas with tomato, scallions
  and, 144
zucchini with parsley and, 229

Moroccan rub lamb chops, 174–75

mozzarella cheese:
  bites, fried, 36–37
  panini with prosciutto, roasted peppers and, 125

mozzarella cheese, smoked:
  grilled stuffed portobellos with tomatoes, rosemary
    and, 81
  portobello burgers with green sauce and, 20

mushroom(s):
  duxelles and paté platter with sliced baguette, 170
  egg noodles with, 165
  sausage and spinach-stuffed, 34
  sautéed, lean sirloin burgers—hold the bun—
    with, 236–37
  sirloin burgers with Swiss, balsamic mayo and, 18–19
  and spinach lasagna roll-ups with gorgonzola cream
    sauce, 82–83
  and spinach-stuffed chicken breasts, 216–17
  tomato gravy, braciole with, 59
  veal scaloppini with wine, green olives and, 196–97
  wild, see wild mushroom(s)

mustard:
  maple pork chops with grilled apples, 88
  and mint dipping sauce, lamb chops with, 64

Neapolitan ice cream with cherry sauce, 61

no-mystery: marinated beef, chicken, pork, or
  portobello mushrooms, 62

noodle(s):
  bowls, 179
  egg, see egg noodles

nuts:
  and berries parfaits, 209
  see also specific nuts

NY egg creams, 19

oil, wilted spinach with garlic and, 60

olive(s):
  green, veal scaloppini with wine, mushrooms
    and, 196–97
  rosemary crostini, 158
  salsa, red snapper with green beans and, 151
  Spanish cheese and, 153

onion(s):
  balsamic, Delmonico steaks with steak sauce
    and, 200
  peas with bacon and, 106

and potatoes, 177

soup, oh-so-good, 172

thick-cut o-rings and spicy dipping sauce, 17

onion(s), red:

green bean salad with tomato and, 69

and honey mustard barbecued chicken, 86

orange(s):

and almond salad, 240

asparagus with sesame and, 224

and brandy chicken topped with stuffed shrimp, 190–91

cherry, and cranberry compote, warm, with vanilla ice cream, 77

creamsicle liqueur dessert, 211

freezes, 47

fresh, with lime sorbet, 97

mandarin, and cucumber in sesame dressing, mixed baby greens with, 49

smoky barbecued chicken, sandwiches, 70

orange liqueur, fruit salad with sorbet and, 41

orzo:

cheesy, 63

with parsley and lemon zest, 242

with spinach and tomato, 227

oven steak fries, 201

paella for eight, 152–53

pancakes, potato and smoked Gouda, 112

pancetta, Elsa's jumbo shrimp with sage and, 68

panini with prosciutto, roasted peppers and mozzarella, 125

panzanella, tomato basil, 121

papaya salsa, in jerky turkey burgers with island salsa, 24

parfaits:

chocolate mint, 215

crème de Menthe, 203

nuts and berries, 209

parsley:

and butter egg noodles, boeuf bourguignon with, 102–3

orzo with lemon zest and, 242

and walnut pesto, penne with, 204–5

zucchini with mint and, 229

pasta:

with citrus cream sauce, 188

with parsley and walnut pesto, 204

with roasted red pepper sauce, 202

with spinach and tomato, 227

toss, chicken piccata, 94

vodka cream, you-won't-be-single-for-long, 186

see also specific pasta

pasta salads:

asparagus, 41

spinach artichoke, 21

supreme pizza, 29

tarragon, 31

paté and mushroom duxelles platter with sliced baguette, 170

peaches, ripe, port with, 197

peanut dressing, 233

pear(s):

arugula salad with blue cheese, apricot vinaigrette and, 195

Roquefort, and walnut toasts, 66

peas, sugar snap:

stuffed pork chops with cream cheese potatoes and, 114–15

tossed salad with radishes, and sweet red pepper relish dressing, 128

peas with onions and bacon, 106

pecans:

Bourbon Street candy balls with, 119

-crusted chicken tenders and salad with tangy maple barbecue dressing, 43

penne with parsley and walnut pesto, 204–5

pepper, sweet red, relish dressing, tossed salad with snap peas, radishes and, 128

peppers:

and beef stir-fry, five spice, and rice with smoked almonds, 48

bell, butter beans, and corn, 238

and corn (maque choux), creamy, avocados with, 206–7

red, chicken and chorizo burrito filling, 38–39

peppers, cherry, stuffed hot or sweet, 30

peppers, chili, see chilies

peppers, roasted red:

panini with prosciutto, mozzarella and, 125

sauce, gemelli pasta with, 202

and spinach salad with honey balsamic dressing, 236

white beans with rosemary and, 222

pesce spada rollotini (rolled swordfish), 158–59

pesto, parsley and walnut, penne with, 204–5

Philly steak sandwiches, 28

pie, quick chocolate banana cream, 109

pilaf, lemon rice, 230–31

pineapple wedges, ripe, 25

pita bread, pitas:
    grilled, village salad with, 156
    lamb, with tomato, scallions, and mint yogurt
        dressing, 144
    warm, Greek grilled chicken and salad with, for
        wrapping, 182
    see also flat bread

pizza:
    asparagus and plum tomato, 235
    with chicken, sun-dried tomatoes and
        broccoli, 32–33
    pasta salad, supreme, 29
    zucchini-roni, 234

polenta:
    herb, eggplant caponata and, 134–35
    wild mushroom fricassee over, 194–95

POPcorn, cheesy, 33

pork:
    burgers, Cajun, 22
    marinated, 62

pork chops:
    maple mustard, with grilled apples, 88
    stuffed, with cream cheese potatoes and sugar snap
        peas, 114–15

port, ripe peaches with, 197

portobello mushroom(s):
    burgers with green sauce and smoked mozzarella, 20
    and green bean sauté, 210
    grilled stuffed, with tomatoes, rosemary and smoked
        mozzarella, 81
    marinated, 62

Portuguese chicken and chorizo, 141

potato(es):
    baby, with cumin, 142
    cream cheese, stuffed pork chops with sugar snap
        peas and, 114–15
    with cumin, 51
    loin lamb chops with braised root vegetables and
        colcannon-creamy kale and, 168–69
    new, trout amandine, steamed asparagus and, 170–71
    new, with mint, poached salmon with Dijon dill
        sauce and, 131–32
    and onions, 177
    oven steak fries, 201
    roast, with rosemary, 210
    and smoked Gouda pancakes, 112
    spinach, and tomato soup, 125
    steak frites, 173

potatoes, stuffed:
    with ham, thyme, and Gruyère, 54
    super, with the works, 46

potato salads:
    deviled, 27
    mom's oil and vinegar, 89
    mom's wasabi and watercress, 68–69

pound cake with vanilla ice cream and chocolate
    sauce, 115

prosciutto di Parma:
    e melone, 161
    panini with roasted peppers, mozzarella and, 125

quesadillas, wild mushroom, with warm black bean
    salsa, 148

quick:
    chocolate banana cream pie, 109
    Italian rum cake cups, 95
    tiramisu, 199

radicchio, grilled, salad, 99

radish(es):
    red, salad, 177
    tossed salad with snap peas, sweet red pepper relish
        dressing and, 128

ragu, veal, with campanelle pasta, 110

raisins, golden, broccoli rabe with, 77

raita, banana, 51

ravioli:
    corn-meal dusted, turkey cutlets with rosemary
        and, 76–77
    vegetable "lasagne," 96–97

red bean salad, 23

red radish salad, 177

red snapper:
    Livornese, 204
    with olive salsa and green beans, 151

refried beans, 39
    extra spicy, lettuce, tomatoes, lime and, 155

rémoulade, shrimp cocktail with Rach's quick, 126

ribollita—bread soup, 162

rice:
    fragrant basmati, sweet 'n spicy chicken curry in a
        hurry with, 52
    lemon pilaf, 230–31
    Mexican, 154–55
    with smoked almonds, five-spice beef and pepper
        stir-fry and, 48

Spanish beef and, 138
special fried, 44
stuffed chilies with beef, spinach, and cheese, 139
wild and white, country captain chicken with, 118–19
wild and white, fruited, 190

Rio Grande spice rub strip steaks, 78

risotto:
best basic, 60
green, 98–99

roast beef sandwiches, French dip, 116

romaine:
hearts of palm, artichoke and, 187
hearts with lemon chive vinaigrette, 97

root beer floats, 27

Roquefort, pear, and walnut toasts, 66

rosemary:
grilled chicken and wild mushroom sauce, 163
grilled stuffed portobellos with tomatoes, smoked mozzarella and, 81
olive crostini, 158
roast potatoes with, 210
skewered vegetables, 35
turkey cutlets with, and corn-meal dusted ravioli, 76–77
white beans with roasted red peppers and, 222

rum cake cups, quick Italian, 95

sage:
Elsa's jumbo shrimp with pancetta and, 68
veal chops, 194

salad:
antipasto toss, 124
arugula, with blue cheese, pears, and apricot vinaigrette, 195
bar supreme, Thai-Vietnamese, 232–33
bitter greens, 223
blue cheese and walnut spinach, with maple dressing, 201
butter bean, see butter bean salads
fruit, with orange liqueur and sorbet, 41
green bean, with red onion and tomato, 69
and grilled chicken, Greek, with warm pita bread for wrapping, 182
grilled radicchio, 99
Mexican chunk vegetable salad, 72
Mexican fiesta, 79
mixed baby greens with mandarin orange and cucumber in sesame dressing, 49
mixed greens and fennel, 105
orange and almond, 240
pasta, see pasta salads

potato, see potato salads
red bean, 23
red radish, 177
salmon cakes on mixed baby greens, 133
sesame chicken, 44–45
Sicilian chunk vegetable, 111
slaw, see slaw salads
spicy chopped, with tortillas, 138–39
spicy greens with warm balsamic dressing, 243
spinach, see spinach salads
tabouleh, tomatoes stuffed with, 64–65
with tangy maple barbecue dressing, pecan-crusted chicken tenders and, 43
3 bean, 89
tomato basil panzanella, 121
tossed, with snap peas, radishes and sweet red pepper relish dressing, 128
two-tomato, 229
village, with grilled pita bread, 156
warm endive, 165
watercress and mint, with lime dressing, 143
whatever-your-garden-grows, 231
white bean, with thyme, 65

salmon:
cakes on mixed baby greens, 133
pan-seared, with citrus vinegar glaze and green beans, 240–41
poached, with Dijon dill sauce and new potatoes with mint, 131–32

salsa:
mango, 221
olive, red snapper with green beans and, 151
papaya, in jerky turkey burgers with island salsa, 24
roasted, with mint and cilantro, 38
warm black bean, wild mushroom quesadillas with, 148

sambucca cake with strawberries, whipped cream, and shaved bitter chocolate, 218

sandwiches:
hot Buffalo chicken, 46–47
ice cream sundae, 33
panini with prosciutto, roasted peppers and mozzarella, 125
Philly steak, 28
roast beef, French dip, 116
smoky orange barbecued chicken, 70

sandwiches, grilled
4 cheese, 101
halibut, 40
honey lime chicken, 73

sangria:
sunset, 150
white, 152

sauces:
    cherry, Neapolitan ice cream with, 61
    citrus cream, pasta with, 188
    Dijon dill, poached salmon with, and new potatoes
        with mint, 131–32
    gorgonzola cream, spinach and mushroom lasagna
        roll-ups with, 82–83
    green, portobello burgers with smoked mozzarella
        and, 20
    guacamole, grilled halibut tacos with, 154
    horseradish cream dipping, grilled shrimp cocktail
        with, 212
    mint and mustard dipping, lamb chops with, 64
    roasted red pepper, gemelli pasta with, 202
    special, for Cajun pork burgers, 22
    spicy dipping, thick-cut o-rings and, 17
    steak, Delmonico steaks with balsamic onions
        and, 200
    tartar, zesty, 40
    tomatillo, tilapia with, 206
    tomato, simple, for chicken parmigiana, 123
    wild mushroom, rosemary grilled chicken and, 163
    wine, Greek meatballs in, 156–57

sausage:
    calzones, 56
    and spinach-stuffed mushrooms, 34

scallions, lamb pitas with tomato, mint yogurt dressing
    and, 144

scaloppini, veal, with wine, mushrooms and green
    olives, 196–97

schnitzel, veal, 164

sea scallops:
    baked, and seared tournedos with artichoke hearts
        and asparagus tips, 208–9
    and shrimp skewers, pan-seared, 26
    with vermouth, 196

sesame:
    asparagus with orange and, 224
    chicken salad, 44–45
    dressing, mixed baby greens with mandarin orange
        and cucumber in, 49

shakes, black and white, 19

shallot vinaigrette, warm, grilled balsamic chicken
    cutlets over spinach salad with, 74–75

shrimp:
    Elsa's jumbo, with sage and pancetta, 68
    grilled, 157
    and scallop skewers, pan-seared, 226
    stuffed, brandy and orange chicken topped
        with, 190–91

shrimp cocktail:
    grilled, with horseradish cream dipping sauce, 212
    with Rach's quick rémoulade, 126

Sicilian chunk vegetable salad, 111

sirloin burgers:
    lean—hold the bun—with sautéed
        mushrooms, 236–37
    with mushrooms, Swiss and balsamic mayo, 18–19

skewered vegetables, rosemary, 35

slaw salads:
    fennel, 159
    red cabbage and beet, with currant dressing, 71

Sloppy Joes, super, 26

smoky orange barbecued chicken sandwiches, 70

s'mores cups, ice cream, 113

sorbet:
    and fresh fruit bar, 233
    fruit salad with orange liqueur and, 41
    lemon, star anise blackberries with, 225
    lime, fresh oranges with, 97
    mango, with Amaretto and crystallized ginger, 241
    melon with berries and, 239

soup:
    bread (ribollita), 162
    chicken and vegetable potage, 140
    green minestrone, 120
    meatball and macaroni, 100–101
    onion, oh-so-good, 172
    potato, spinach and tomato, 125

Southern green beans, 109

Southwestern stuffed peppers, 147

spaghetti:
    alla carbonara: bacon and egg "coal miner's" pasta, 84
    herb and cheese chicken tenders parmigiana
        with, 122
    with zucchini and garlic, 217

spanakopita, sorta, 180

Spanish:
    beef and rice, 138
    cheese and olives, 153

spicy:
    black bean burrito filling, 38
    chopped salad with tortillas, 138–39
    greens with warm balsamic dressing, 243

spinach:
    artichoke calzones, 55

artichoke pasta salad, 21
and mushroom lasagna roll-ups with gorgonzola cream sauce, 82–83
and mushroom-stuffed chicken breasts, 216–17
orzo with tomato and, 227
potato, and tomato soup, 125
and roasted red pepper salad with honey balsamic dressing, 236
and sausage-stuffed mushrooms, 34
stuffed chilies with beef, rice, and cheese, 139
veal medallions with lemon on a bed of, 188–89
wilted, with garlic and oil, 60

spinach salads:
artichoke pasta, 21
baby, with Swiss cheese crisps, 103
blue cheese and walnut, with maple dressing, 201
with warm shallot vinaigrette, grilled balsamic chicken cutlets over, 74–75

spring rolls, baked crab, 178

spritzer, citrus white wine, 67

star anise blackberries with lemon sorbet, 225

steaks:
au poivre and arugula-stuffed tomatoes, 213
chicken fried, with creamed pan gravy and biscuits, 108
Delmonico, with balsamic onions and steak sauce, 200
frites, 173
sandwiches, Philly, 28
strip, Rio Grande spice rub, 78
swordfish, 221
tenderloin, with gorgonzola, 211
tuna, see tuna steak(s)

stew, winter vegetable, 112

strawberry(ies):
fresh, marg-alrightas, 149
sambucca cake with whipped cream, and shaved bitter chocolate, 218

sugared stone fruits with cookies and cream, 85

sunset sangria, 150

sweet 'n spicy chicken curry in a hurry with fragrant basmati rice, 52

Swiss cheese:
crisps, baby spinach salad with, 103
sirloin burgers with mushrooms, and balsamic mayo, 18–19

swordfish:
rolled (pesce spada rollotini), 158–59
steaks, 221

tabouleh salad, tomatoes stuffed with, 64–65

tacos, grilled halibut, with guacamole sauce, 154

tarragon:
lemon dip, asparagus and green beans with, 116
pasta salad, 31

tartar sauce, zesty, 40

tenderloin steaks with gorgonzola, 211

Thai-Vietnamese salad bar supreme, 232–33

thick-cut o-rings and spicy dipping sauce, 17

30–minute Southern classic: country captain chicken with white and wild rice, 118–19

3 bean salad, 89

thyme:
stuffed potatoes with ham, Gruyère and, 54
white bean salad with, 65

tilapia with tomatillo sauce, 206

tiramisu, quick, 199

toasts:
herb and goat cheese, 74
Roquefort, pear and walnut, 66

tomatillo sauce, tilapia with, 206

tomato(es):
arugula-stuffed, steak au poivre and, 213
basil panzanella, 121
broiled, 83
bruschetta with basil and, 192
chutney, charred, chicken tikka with warm flat bread and, 50
extra-spicy refried beans, lettuce, lime and, 155
green bean salad with red onion and, 69
grilled stuffed portobellos with rosemary, smoked mozzarella and, 81
lamb pitas with scallions, mint yogurt dressing and, 144
mushroom gravy, braciole with, 59
orzo with spinach and, 227
poached grouper with basil and, 238
potato, and spinach soup, 125
stuffed with tabouleh salad, 64–65
sun-dried, pizza with chicken, broccoli and, 32–33
two-, salad, 229
vine-ripe, with herb gremolada, 237

tomato(es), plum:
and asparagus pizza, 235
broiled, individual beef Wellingtons with steamed broccoli spears and, 214–15

tomato sauce, simple, for chicken parmigiana, 123

tortillas, spicy chopped salad with, 138–39

tossed salad with snap peas, radishes, and sweet red pepper relish dressing, 128

tournedos, seared, and baked scallops with artichoke hearts and asparagus tips, 208–9

trout amandine, steamed asparagus and new potatoes, 170–71

tuna steak(s):
    au poivre, 222
    grilled Tuscan-style, 80

turkey burgers:
    harvest, 31
    jerkey, with island salsa, 24

turkey cutlets with rosemary and corn-meal dusted ravioli, 76–77

Tuscan-style grilled tuna steaks, 80

vanilla ice cream:
    pound cake with chocolate sauce and, 115
    warm cherry, orange, and cranberry compote with, 77

veal:
    chops, sage, 194
    marsala with egg fettuccini, 198
    medallions with lemon on a bed of spinach, 188–89
    ragu with campanelle pasta, 110
    scaloppini with wine, mushrooms and green olives, 196–97
    schnitzel, 164

vegetable(s):
    balsamic glazed, 63
    braised root, loin lamb chops with colcannon-creamy kale and potatoes and, 168–69
    and chicken potage, 140
    couscous, 174
    great grilled, 192
    honey glazed, 63
    rosemary skewered, 35
    salad, Mexican chunk, 72
    salad, Sicilian chunk, 111
    stew, winter, 112
    see also specific vegetables

vermouth, sea scallops with, 196

village salad with grilled pita bread, 156

vinaigrette:
    apricot, arugula salad with blue cheese, pears and, 195
    lemon chive, romaine hearts with, 97
    warm shallot, grilled balsamic chicken cutlets over spinach salad with, 74–75
    see also dressings

vodka cream pasta, 186

waffles, Liège, with berries and whipped cream, 167

walnut(s):
    and blue cheese spinach salad with maple dressing, 201
    feta and roasted garlic dip with toasted flat bread, 98
    and parsley pesto, penne with, 204–5
    Roquefort, and pear toasts, 66

wasabi and watercress potato salad, mom's, 68–69

watercress:
    and mint salad with lime dressing, 143
    and wasabi potato salad, mom's, 68–69

waterzooi de poulet, 166

whipped cream:
    chocolate cups with, 185
    Liège waffles with berries and, 167
    sambucca cake with strawberries, shaved bitter chocolate and, 218

white bean(s):
    with rosemary and roasted red pepper, 222
    salad with thyme, 65

white sangria, 152

white wine spritzer, citrus, 67

wild mushroom(s):
    fricassee over polenta, 194–95
    quesadillas with warm black bean salsa, 148
    rosemary grilled chicken and, 163

wilted spinach with garlic and oil, 60

wine:
    sauce, Greek meatballs in, 156–57
    veal scaloppini with mushrooms, green olives and, 196–97

winter vegetable stew, 112

yogurt mint dressing, lamb pitas with tomato, scallions and, 144

you-won't-be-single-for-long vodka cream pasta, 186

zucchini:
    with mint and parsley, 229
    -roni pizza, 234
    spaghetti with garlic and, 217